UNDERSTAND
Emerging
CHURCH
Theology

FROM A FORMER EMERGENT INSIDER

JEREMY BOUMA

{✝} THEOKLESIA
theology. for the church.

Published by THEOKLESIA
PO Box 1180
Grand Rapids, MI 49501
www.theoklesia.com

Title also available as an ebook for Kindle, iPad, NOOK, and Kobo eReader.

Cover Design by Derek Murphy.

ISBN: 978-0-9854703-0-2

Printed in the United States of America
10 09 08 07 06 05 04 03 02 01

About **THEOKLESIA**

We are a content curator dedicated to helping the Church rediscover the historic Christian faith for the 21st century. Jesus said that the Church is "the light of the world, a city on a hill that cannot be hidden." We provide the resources to help Her shine brightly by helping the Church connect God's Story of Rescue to our modern world, while remaining theologically rooted and biblically uncompromising.

www.theoklesia.com • info@theoklesia.com

Content

BOOK 2 • REIMAGINING THE CHRISTIAN FAITH

BOOK 3 • THE GOSPEL OF BRIAN MCLAREN

Author's Note

On February 8, 2010 I did something I thought I'd never do: I said "Goodbye, Emergent"!

(You can read more about that at http://bouma.us/emergent-story)

You see, once upon a time I was enamored by the "I-am-not-a-movement-but-a-conversation" known as the Emerging Church (In fact, at my seminary I was known as *Emergent Jeremy*!) In 2005 I stumbled upon an "emerging" author known as Brian McLaren, even attended his church for half a year. I gobbled-up his A New Kind of Christian trilogy because it's question-asking permissive narrative gave flesh to the phantom that was haunting me at the time: *What the heck is this whole Christian thing about?!*

Pastor Dan was my doppelgänger; Neo my mentor.

Nine years ago I entered a period of faith deconstruction and reconstruction the likes of which I had never experienced in my life. For the first time I was taking my faith in Jesus Christ seriously and asking a whole lot of questions along the way.

1

These questions were healthy and freeing and opened up a whole new world to explore and enjoy. I was grateful I was part of the Emerging Church conversation for several years. But as my relationship with Emergent progressed, I began to wonder why it was cool and trendy to disregard Paul; pity the fool who believed in real judgment; ignore the cross; and downplay individual participation in sin.

In short: I became uncomfortable and grew downright tired of Emerging Church theology.

I'm not exactly sure when my saucy love affair with Emergent and liberal Christianity ended. My "I don't" isn't as crystalized as my "I do."

Maybe it was when I read the writings of the heretic Pelagius and realized much of Emergent theology really does mirror his 5th century theology.

Maybe it was after the former head of Emergent Village, Tony Jones, rejected original sin, claiming that it is "neither biblically, philosophically, nor scientifically tenable."

Maybe it was when I read Fredrick Schleiermacher and realized his and modern liberalism's vapid, gospel-less faith was being repackaged and popularized to an unsuspecting, ignorant Christian community as a wholesome alternative to the historic Christian faith.

Maybe it was after I read Karl Barth and realized the natural theology pushed by popular Emergent theologians is not revitalizing the Christian faith, but killing it; it is the same kind of faith Barth so vociferously fought against in order to preserve the vintage faith.

Maybe it was after reading a leading Emerging Church voice suggest that God and grace and the Kingdom of God are not tied directly and exclusively to Jesus Christ; ultimately its not really about Jesus, but about a vanilla, generalized World-Spirit, pan-deity.

Regardless, what I came to realize is that while Emergent may believe it is believing *differently*—and consequently believe it is offering the world a different Christianity that is more believable than the current form—in reality the Emerging Church simply believes *otherly*; the form of faith this version of Christianity pushes is neither innovative nor different.

The Emerging Church is a form of Christianity *other-than* the versions that *currently* exist but mirror those that have *already* existed.

The Christian faith that the authors, leaders, and followers within Emergent believe "feels alive, sustainable, and meaningful in our day"[1] is really a form of faith from other days. They combine other forms of faith that both the Communion of Saints and Spirit of God have deemed foreign to the Holy Scriptures, Rule of Faith, and gospel of Jesus Christ.

Now this is no "heresy hunt." I am no hyper-fundamentalist who is exalting myself as a "Truth Defender," tirelessly working to expose false teachers in the church. I think this suggestion would be grossly unfair for 2 reasons:

1) I bid "au revoir" as one who had been on the inside of and involved with this conversation for half a decade. I attended Brian McLaren's church; I helped host the *Church Basement Roadshow* at my church—an innovative book tour for Tony Jones, Doug Pagitt, and Mark Scandrette; I've had several interactions with Doug Pagitt, someone I like as a person and

---

[1] Doug Pagitt, A Christianity Worth Believing (San Francisco: Jossey-Bass, 2008), 2.

3

who even introduced me to my wife and attended our wedding; and I was active in Emergent West Michigan.

In short, I am an insider who simply left the inside.

2) I approach this effort as one who has pursued academic training in biblical studies and systematic/historical theology for nearly half a decade.

I'm not playing the "education card" here, but rather offer this to give context for my leaving. When I left I was finishing a Master of Divinity and began a Master of Theology in Historical Theology. I spent way too many hours reading key primary theological sources from the Early, Reformation, and Modern Church, giving me a broad picture of the historical "movement" of church dogmatics.

In his book *The Story of Christian Theology*, Roger Olson writes, "The story of Christian theology is the story of Christian reflection on salvation." The same is true today.

I believe any theological inquiry is by nature a reflection on salvation, which means the stakes are high. Doug Pagitt, Brian McLaren, Peter Rollins, and others have commented on the nature of salvation. Which means the gospel itself is at stake.

So a few years ago I took the theology of the Emerging Church to task. The three books in this bundle represent the best fruits of that labor, and should arm you with the knowledge and understanding you need to respond like I've responded.

The first book is *Reimagining the Kingdom*. It is my Master of Theology thesis on the historical development of liberal kingdom theology from Fredrick Schleiermacher to Brian McLaren. While it is a more academic treatment of Emergent theology, it gives a solid overview of how the Emerging Church defines our problem (sin), our solution (salvation and the

4

kingdom of God), and the One who bore our solution (Jesus Christ.)

The second book, *Reimagining the Christian Faith*, is a collection of essays I wrote during my Master of Theology program. They cover some of the major teachings of key Emergent theologians, giving you an overview of their arguments and ways you can respond to their ideas.

Finally, *The Gospel of Brian McLaren* covers what the title suggests, McLaren's understanding of God's rescue in Jesus. But what he means by that rescue is radically different than what the Church has always meant. The first part of the book is taken from *Reimagining the Kingdom*, while the second is a follow up and addresses his latest book on religious pluralism.

I hope my perspective as a former Emergent insider and historical theologian will empower you to respond to the foreign theology of the Emerging Church and do what Jude urges you to do:

> contend for the faith that was once for all entrusted to God's holy people. (Jude 3)

JEREMY BOUMA. TH.M.
Summer, 2014

Reimagining

THE

Kingdom

THE GENERATIONAL DEVELOPMENT
OF LIBERAL KINGDOM THEOLOGY
FROM SCHLEIERMACHER TO MCLAREN

Foreword

I recently received an email from a car dealership that read, "We are incredibly pleased to announce the return of the $14.95 oil and filter change," but only through the end of the month. The email contained a convenient hyperlink to schedule a service appointment and avoid waiting in line.

I happily contacted the dealer, only to learn that the oil change for my car would cost twice as much. I knew this was the normal price for my oil change, so I asked whether the dealer's sale was really a special deal. The service person replied that this was their "new" price (which still sounded a lot like the old one) and that it would still be good after the end of the month. Not surprisingly, I learned that I could not schedule the promised appointment, but would have to cross my fingers and prepare to wait in line.

Wise consumers know to watch out for the bait and switch. Not every sale is actually a sale, and many "free" items end up costing you in the end. Wise Christians must be on guard too. In his classic book, *Christianity and Liberalism,* J. Gresham Machen noted that liberal Christians use terms such as "Jesus," "sin," and "salvation," but they mean something different by them. Machen concluded that "liberalism not only is a different religion from Christianity but belongs in a totally different class of religions."[2]

Jeremy Bouma explains why this is the case in his important guide, *Reimagining the Kingdom.* Liberal Christians from Schleiermacher to McLaren have spoken often of the Kingdom of God. What's not to like? Who wouldn't want the Kingdom to come to earth?

Enter *Reimagining the Kingdom,* a sort of Consumer Reports for Christians. Bouma studies how the liberal giants of the nineteenth and twentieth centuries used the term "Kingdom," and he uncovers a trend that is too consistent to be a coincidence. Just as some sales are not actually on discount, so many who speak of the Kingdom of God do not mean what Jesus meant by it. Specifically, Bouma finds that liberal Christianity offers a different King, a different Kingdom, and a different way of entering the different Kingdom.

Liberal Christianity offers the Kingdom on sale. It's cheaper to enter the liberal kingdom, for new converts do not need to believe such humbling doctrines as total depravity or Christ's penal substitutionary atonement. They do not need to accept that Jesus bore the Father's wrath to save us from the hell we deserved. It's enough to believe Jesus died to show us how special we are, and hopefully inspire us to follow his loving and trusting example.

---

2 J. Gresham Machen, *Christianity and Liberalism* (1923; repr., Grand Rapids: Eerdmans Publishing, 1994), 7.

The liberal gospel offers salvation at a steep discount, but it's no bargain. *Reimagining the Kingdom* is more than a research project. If you are one who is attracted to the liberal gospel, this consumer's guide might just save your soul.

MICHAEL E. WITTMER. PH.D.
Professor of Systematic and Historical Theology
Grand Rapids Theological Seminary

Preface

Once upon a time I was enamored with the "I-am-not-a-movement-but-a-conversation" known as the Emergent Church. I attended Brian McLaren's church while living in Washington D.C.; Doug Pagitt introduced me to my wife, and later attended our wedding; I helped host the *Church Basement Roadshow* in Grand Rapids, featuring Doug Pagitt, Tony Jones, and Mark Scandrette; I was even known as "Emergent Jeremy" at the seminary I attended. Needless to say, I was deeply embedded in all things Emergent.

My infatuation with the Emergent Church began in late 2004. That year, like many angsty young adults do in their quest to find themselves, for themselves, I entered a period of faith deconstruction and reconstruction the likes of which I had never experienced before. For the first time I was taking my faith in Jesus Christ seriously and asking a whole lot of tough, important questions.

During this deconstructive, reconstructive season, I stumbled upon a certain "emerging" author, Brian McLaren. I gobbled-up his *A New Kind of Christian* trilogy, because its question-asking, permissive narrative gave flesh to the phantom that was haunting me at the time: What on earth is this whole Christian thing about, anyway? Pastor Dan was my doppelgänger; Neo my mentor. Like many, this series launched me on an entirely new quest to reunderstand and reimagine the Christian faith outside the stuffy, stogy, stale theology that had come to define—and calcify—my evangelical world.

At the beginning, from what I remember when I entered it, the Emergent conversation really was an exploration. Such sites as emergentvillage.org and opensourcetheology.net were catalysts for bursting and burning through the cobwebs and rickety structures of conservative evangelicalism. The Emergent conversation tried to root itself in the more ancient, forgotten parts of our faith—like the Creeds—in order to moor itself while forging ahead with reimagining the Church as centered around the teachings of Jesus and the Kingdom He bore.

Theologically, it was a deconstructive tour de force with its crosshairs aimed squarely at conservative evangelicalism, and rightly so. Reconstructively (is that a word?) it helped construct a missional response to a real, genuine shift occurring within Western culture known as postmodernity. Most of the church was ill equipped to deal with the tectonic shifts our culture was undergoing, and Emergent helped navigate those shifts for church leaders as *New Tribes Missions* does for tribal missionaries in Papua New Guinea. At the time I greatly appreciated and benefited from the Emergent conversation, because it intersected with my own faith exploration at the time.

When I entered the conversation around Christmas 2004, I had been ministering on Capitol Hill since Fall 2003 for a little known entity, *The Center for Christian Statesmanship*, of a more well known entity, *Coral Ridge Ministries*, run by an even more known entity, Dr. D. James Kennedy. During this season I became increasingly uncomfortable with the theology behind this thoroughly conservative evangelical ministry, especially their theology of the gospel. The gospel Story it told was rooted in Dr. Kennedy's *Evangelism Explosion*, which started God's Story of Rescue at the end and in the middle—with heaven/hell and sin. Jesus, we were told, came to inaugurate a cosmic transaction between me and Him in order to beam me out of here "some glad morning when this life is o'r."

The theology of this Story disturbed me, so did the methods we used to sell that Story and manner in which we did ministry in our context. You see, the mission context of Capitol Hill is thoroughly postmodern and young adult: at the time there were roughly 24,000 congressional staffers (an average age of 27) who were from the brightest liberal arts institutions this country had to offer. Missionally, we sucked because we were ill-equipped to engage this young adult postmodern culture. Theologically, God's beautiful, majestic Story of Rescue was reduced to five talking points, and Jesus was reduced to a product sold like a vacuum cleaner or set of kitchen knives sans nifty accessories. After a year in ministry I began to wonder: is *this* what I've committed myself too, not only as a minister of the gospel but as a *Christian*?

Then along came the Emergent Church.

My story follows others, me thinks. Many others have endured similar frustrations before wandering into the oasis-village of Emergent, finding solace, healing, and inspiration from a band of sisters and brothers making a similar trek. There, I found what I needed at the time; I am certainly thankful for what Emergent was during those years. I absolutely appreciated the theological deconstruction and missiological reconstruction this conversation provided. At the time, this quest was a healthy and freeing journey that opened up a whole new world to explore and enjoy, particularly the world of the Kingdom of God that I had neither understood nor explored by nature of my own Christian upbringing. For this I am grateful.

In the past 5-6 years, however, it seems like the desire to missionally reconnect the Christian faith to our postmodern, post-Christian culture has faded and the desire to reconstruct Christianity anew in light of both has markedly increased. Now that the Emergent Church has established the missional response to postmodern culture, the time for theological construction has begun. For me, the development of this new era of theological construction is crystalized by four books: Peter Rollins', *How (Not) to Speak of God*;[3] Doug Pagitt's, *A Christianity Worth Believing*;[4] Samir Selmanovic's, *It's Really All About God*;[5] and Brian McLaren's, *A New Kind of Christianity*.[6] The Emergent Church movement has indeed exchanged missional engagement for theological reconstruction.[7]

As my relationship with Emergent progressed, I became deeply uncomfortable with this theological reconstructive effort. And as I have progressed in my own academic journey, I have

---

[3] Peter Rollins, *How (Not) to Speak of God* (Brewster, MA: Paraclete Press, 2006).
[4] Doug Pagitt, *A Christianity Worth Believing* (San Francisco: Jossey-Bass, 2008).
[5] Samir Selmanovic, *It's Really All About God: Reflections of a Muslim, Atheist, Jewish, Christian* (San Francisco: Jossey-Bass, 2009).
[6] Brian McLaren, *A New Kind of Christianity* (San Francisco: Jossey-Bass, 2010).
[7] You could also lump Rob Bell's *Love Wins* in with this crowd of witnesses, but Bell has disavowed the Emergent label.

become downright vexed by the theology that has bubbled-up out of the Emergent Church.

I'm not exactly sure when my saucy love affair with the Emergent Church ended. My "I don't" isn't as crystalized as my "I do."

Maybe it was when I read Pelagius' writings and realized much of Emergent theology really does mirror his 5th century theology—and 5th century heresy.

Maybe it was after the former head of Emergent Village, Tony Jones, rejected original sin, claiming that it is "neither biblically, philosophically, nor scientifically tenable."[8]

Maybe it was when I read Fredrick Schleiermacher and realized his and modern liberalism's vapid, gospel-less faith are being repackaged and popularized to an unsuspecting, ignorant Christian community as a wholesome alternative to what has been.

Maybe it was after I read Karl Barth and realized the natural theology pushed by popular Emergent theologians is not revitalizing the Christian faith, but killing it; it is the same kind of faith Barth so vociferously fought against in order to preserve historic, orthodox Christianity.

Maybe it was after reading a leading Emergent Church voice suggest that God and grace and the Kingdom of God are not tied directly and exclusively to Jesus Christ; ultimately its not really about Jesus, but about a vanilla, generalized World-Spirit god (lower-case "g").[9]

---

[8] Tony Jones, "Original Sin: A Depraved Idea," *BeliefNet*, January 26, 2009, http://blog.beliefnet.com/tonyjones/2009/01/original-sin-a-depraved-idea.html.
[9] See Samir Selmanovic, *It's Really All About God: Reflections of a Muslim, Atheist, Jewish, Christian* (San Francisco: Jossey-Bass, 2009).

My growing discomfort and vexation at Emergent theology culminated with a move I thought I would never make: in a widely tweeted and trafficked blog post I wrote two years ago I said "Goodbye" to the Emergent Church.[10]

I had to.

As I progressed in my studies as a pastor and theologian, I came to realize that while Emergent may think it is believing differently—and consequently think it is offering the world a different Christianity that is more believable than the current form—in reality they simply believe *otherly*; the form of Christianity that Emergent pushes is neither innovative nor different: it is a form of Christianity other-than the versions that *currently* exist, but mirror those that have *already* existed.

As I wrote back in February 2010, "The Christian faith that the authors, leaders, and followers within Emergent believe 'feels alive, sustainable, and meaningful in *our* day'[11] is really forms of faith from *other* days. They combine other forms of faith that both the Communion of Saints and Spirit of God have deemed foreign to the Holy Scriptures, Rule of Faith, and gospel of Jesus Christ throughout the history of Christ's Bride, the Church." Particularly, the Emergent Church is simply repackaged historic, theological Protestant liberalism for present evangelicalism.

I've shared some of my story here to make it clear that I am not writing as a nit-picky outsider, but as one who was on the inside of and deeply involved with the Emergent Church conversation for over half a decade. Personally, I understand the type of disillusionment and dissatisfaction often engendered by

---

[10] Jeremy Bouma, "Goodbye Emergent: Why I'm Taking the Theology of the Emerging Church to Task," at www.novuslumen.net. February 10, 2010.
[11] Doug Pagitt, *A Christianity Worth Believing* (San Francisco: Jossey-Bass, 2008), 2.

mainstream evangelicalism, while also understanding the pull toward the supposed "new kind of Christianity" offered by Emergent as an antidote. I understand something else, too: the theological problems with such an antidote.

Over the last three years, I have dedicated much of my academic pursuits, through pursuing the Master of Theology in Historical Theology, to better understanding the theological roots of the Emergent Church in order to better understand how it is affecting the Church generally and evangelicalism particularly. That academic pursuit has culminated in this work, my ThM thesis. It explores a trend within evangelicalism that owes its genesis to the Emergent Church: an increased interest in the Kingdom of God and use of *Kingdom* language to define itself.

Recapturing the Kingdom is a good thing, as it is central to the teachings of Jesus Himself. How some evangelicals are talking about the grammar of the Kingdom—the problem for which the Kingdom solves; the One who bore the Kingdom; and the nature of the Kingdom's solution—is becoming increasingly problematic, however. Though some theologians have noted similarities between the *Kingdom* grammar of Protestant liberalism and Emergent, the significance of these similarities have note been fully explored. Until now.

This book traces the contours of liberal *Kingdom* grammar through four generations of liberalism—from Schleiermacher to Ritschl, Rauschenbusch, and Tillich—that precedes the Emergent Church's appropriation of that grammar for the 21st century American Church, particularly by famed Emergent founder and author Brian McLaren.

I hope this tracing effort will help mainstream evangelicals better understand the contours of Protestant liberal theology in order to better understand how some are reimagining the Kingdom, which is really an effort at reimagining the gospel of Jesus Christ itself.

JEREMY BOUMA. TH.M.
Grand Rapids, MI • May 4, 2012
(Commencement Day)

1

Introduction

In recent years evangelical Christians have rediscovered the biblical emphasis on the Kingdom of God. They have written books, such as *The King Jesus Gospel*,[12] *The Secret Message of Jesus*,[13] and *The Next Christians*,[14] which remind evangelicals that the Kingdom of God lies at the heart of Jesus' mission. They lead mission trips which seek to do more than merely lead sinners to Jesus; they also want to bring the Kingdom of God to earth. In many ways this rediscovery of the Kingdom is right and beneficial, for its advent is the overarching plot line of the Bible. However, as this book will show, its current use often comes with deleterious baggage as many of its most popular proponents uncritically borrow its grammar from unorthodox historical sources.

---

[12] Scot McKnight, *The King Jesus Gospel: The Original Good News Revisited* (Grand Rapids: Zondervan, 2011).
[13] Brian McLaren, *The Secret Message of Jesus* (Nashville: W Publishing Group, 2006).
[14] Gabe Lyons, *The Next Christians: The Good News About the End of Christian America* (New York: Doubleday, 2010).

The Kingdom of God has not always played such a prominent role in Christian theology, however. Augustine represents the typical manner in which the early church defined the Kingdom of God, equating it with the Church itself. While equating God's Kingdom-rule with the Church largely continued with medieval theological discourse, Christian princes sought to promote an imperial-political view of the Kingdom in order to control their Feudal lands. In the Reformation, Luther individualized the concept for the purpose of emphasizing the Christian's spiritual citizenship over against a citizenship of a secular kingdom. He also represented the Reformation tendency in general to view the Kingdom in entirely eschatological, even apocalyptic, terms that pointed toward heaven in the future. Eventually, the Kingdom played little role in Protestant theology, especially evangelical theology, reflecting the general trajectory of the historic Church that seems to have had little interest in Jesus' central teaching. That is until the nineteenth century.

In the late eighteenth century and early nineteenth century, historical, cultural, and intellectual forces coalesced to foster an environment that gave renewed interest in the Kingdom, giving it a place of theological prominence. The person most credited with such renewal is the German theologian Friedrich Schleiermacher. The Kingdom of God formed the basis of his teachings, governing his system of doctrine and ethics to such an extent that it rose to prominence within theology in a way it had not before. Schleiermacher's voice echoed throughout much of nineteenth century Protestant thought through the likes of Bauer, Herrmann, and Harnack, finding a strong advocate in the theology of Albrecht Ritschl. But while Ritschl praised Schleiermacher for employing the Kingdom of God as the *telos* of Christianity, he believed Schleiermacher did not go far enough in grasping its significance. Ritschl believed Schleiermacher made an important contribution to Christian theology by restoring the Kingdom to a place of importance, but he thought his *Kingdom* grammar was deficient. Building on the original work of Schleiermacher, Ritschl brought this grammar to bear on his entire theological enterprise, making *Kingdom of God* its controlling doctrine. Ritschl's Kingdom-centric theology kindled a new generation of twentieth century liberal theologians, particularly Rauschenbusch and Tillich, who envisioned the Kingdom itself as humanity's salvation.

Now, like the nineteenth century, there has been a resurgence in the use of *Kingdom* language at the start of the twenty-first century, particularly within mainstream evangelicalism. In prior generations, *Kingdom* had not been part of the normal evangelical ecclesial repertoire. Instead, evangelicalism had primarily centered upon the language of *gospel*, which translated into salvation from sins through a conversion experience, personal piety, and moral living. Rarely had *Kingdom* language been employed within evangelicalism. Even when *Kingdom* was utilized, its primary usage was usually future oriented, centering on the return of Jesus Christ and reign on earth at the expense of its present activity. This definition of *Kingdom*, however, changed with the advent of what has become known as the Emergent Church movement, originally a progressive evangelical movement that sought to re-imagine traditional Christianity in light of postmodernity. In fact, the Kingdom of God is central to the Emergent Church's protest against Traditionalism.

As Jim Belcher explains, "The emerging protest argues that the traditional church has focused too much attention on *how* an individual becomes saved and not enough on how he or she *lives* as a Christian...The critics say the good news is more than forgiveness from sins and a ticket to heaven; it is the appearance of the kingdom of God."[15] This argument, that not enough attention has been paid to Jesus' teaching on the Kingdom of God, has formed the beachhead of protest against Traditionalism, particularly mainstream evangelicalism, and is the central identifying doctrine of this movement. As two prominent Emergent researchers note, the Kingdom of God offers a "reference point for emerging churches" as they deconstruct Traditionalism and reconstruct church in a postmodern context.[16] The Kingdom-way Jesus founded through His life provides a model for emerging churches and actually is their gospel; for them, the Kingdom saves. No thinker within this movement has sought to redirect the focus of twenty-first century evangelicalism more than Brian McLaren, who helped found the national organization Emergent, is the author of several books that have set out to re-imagine the Christian faith,[17] and was christened as one of the top twenty-five most

---

[15] Jim Belcher, *Deep Church: A Third Way Beyond Emerging and Traditional* (Downers Grove: IVP Books, 2009), 41.

[16] Eddie Gibbs and Ryan K. Bolger. *Emerging Churches: Creating Christian Community in Postmodern Culture* (Grand Rapids: BakerAcademic, 2005), 46. This book provided one of the most exhaustive examinations of the Emerging Church movement. It especially provides an important look at the Emerging Church's *Kingdom* grammar in p. 47-64.

[17] See *A New Kind of Christian* (San Francisco: Jossey-Bass, 2001); *The Story We Find Ourselves In* (San Francisco: Jossey-Bass, 2003); *The Last Word and The Word After That* (San Francisco: Jossey-Bass, 2005); *A Generous Orthodoxy* (Grand Rapids: Zondervan, 2004); *The Secret Message of Jesus* (Nashville: W Publishing Group, 2006); *Everything Must Change* (Nashville: Thomas Nelson, 2006); and *A New Kind of Christianity* (New York: HarperOne, 2010).

influential evangelicals in America. [18] He is a fitting contemporary theological dialogue partner, then, in our effort to understand the nature of the *Kingdom* grammar that has surfaced in the twenty-first century, as it did in the nineteenth.

Over the past decade, Emergent generally and McLaren specifically have sought to reclaim what McLaren calls the secret, essential message of Jesus, which he says has been unintentionally misunderstood and intentionally distorted, missed and disregarded.[19] According to McLaren and the rest of the Emergent Church, this message is the Kingdom of God. While many have lauded McLaren's efforts to recapture Jesus' secret Kingdom-message, others argue that his and Emergent's use and description of *Kingdom* is deficient. Belcher writes, "I worry about what is missing in the description [of the Kingdom of God]. It is curious to me that nowhere does he mention or link the kingdom of God to the doctrines of atonement, justification, union with Christ or our need to be forgiven."[20] Likewise, Scot McKnight believes what McLaren says about the Kingdom is not enough:

> [They] believe that penal substitution theories have not led to a kingdom vision. What I have been pondering and writing about for a decade now is how to construct an 'emerging' gospel that remains faithful to the fulness of the biblical texts about the Atonement, and lands squarely on the word kingdom. Girard said

---

[18] "25 Most Influential Evangelicals In America," *Time Magazine*, February 7, 2005.
[19] McLaren, *The Secret Message of Jesus*, 3.
[20] Belcher, *Deep Church*, 118.

> something important about the Cross; so does McLaren. But they aren't enough. 21

The reason contemporary articulations of *Kingdom* by the Emergent Church are not enough is because those articulations are simply appropriations of liberal *Kingdom* grammar.

Rather than offering the Church a new kind of Christianity that somehow recaptures a long-lost concept central to Jesus and the Church, the Emergent Church's use of the Kingdom of God as instantiated in the writings of McLaren is fully entrenched in the Protestant liberal theological tradition, a link several people have already noted. In his book, *Don't Stop Believing*, Michael Wittmer argues that a "postmodern turn toward liberalism is penetrating the evangelical church." He goes on to say that "an increasing number of postmodern Christians are practicing a liberal method: accommodating the gospel to contemporary culture and expressing greater concern for Christian ethics than its traditional doctrines,"[22] including the Kingdom of God.[23]

In reviewing one of McLaren's latest books, *A New Kind of Christianity*, McKnight notes how this prominent Emergent Church voice "has fallen for an old school of thought," rehashing the ideas of prominent classic Protestant liberals like Adolf Von Harnack and modern ones like Harvey Cox.[24] McKnight has registered such a concern in regards to McLaren's

---

[21] Scot McKnight, "McLaren Emerging," *Christianity Today Online*, September 26, 2008, www.christianitytoday.com/ct/2008/september/38.59.html.
[22] Michael E. Wittmer, *Don't Stop Believing: Why Living Like Jesus is Not Enough* (Grand Rapids: Zondervan, 2008), 18.
[23] See Wittmer, *Don't Stop Believing*, 110-115.
[24] Scot McKnight, "Review: Brian McLaren's 'A New Kind of Christianity," *Christianity Today Online*, February 26, 2010, http://www.christianitytoday.com/ct/2010/march/3.59.html.

Kingdom definition, as well.[25] Furthermore, Belcher voices worry over the Emergent Church's potential pitfall of correlating the Christian faith to culture, which he notes Liberal theology has done for years.[26] Likewise, Belcher worries about what is missing in McLaren's description of the Kingdom, noting that his definition of the Kingdom reduces the gospel and arguing that if his gospel is nothing more than recycled theological liberalism it must be rejected.[27] While these scholars have noted a connection between Protestant liberalism and the Emergent Church, this book will fully explore and demonstrate such a connection.

More precisely, this book will argue that the *Kingdom* grammar of the Emergent Church movement is continuous with four previous generations of Protestant liberalism, including how it defines the Kingdom of God, who is in, how one gets in, and how it solves for our human problem. In order to understand liberalism's impact on contemporary evangelical *Kingdom* grammar, this examination will trace the generational development of liberal *Kingdom* grammar from Friedrich Schleiermacher to Albrecht Ritschl, Walter Rauschenbusch, and Paul Tillich, concluding that Emergent's *Kingdom* grammar is more or less repackaged liberal grammar. By examining the most prominent Protestant liberals, I will demonstrate a direct link between them and show how they are contributing to the comeback of evangelical *Kingdom* grammar, as evidenced in Emergent's *Kingdom* grammar.

---

[25] McKnight, "McLaren Emerging," www.christianitytoday.com/ct/2008/september/38.59.html.
[26] Belcher, *Deep Church*, 118.
[27] Belcher, *Deep Church*, 116.

While each of these theologians adds his own unique contribution to liberalism's use of *Kingdom,* there are several features common to this grammar. This grammar teaches that sin is social and environmental, rather than an inherited nature and guilt; Jesus is the moral, rather than metaphysical, Son of God; in founding the Kingdom of God, it was necessary that Jesus lived but the grammar gives no compelling reason that His death was necessary; the Kingdom of God is concerned with humanity's progress; the Kingdom comes into the here-and-now through the power of loving human action; it is inclusive, in that every act counts as Kingdom acts; it is universalistic, in that everyone will be saved; the Kingdom centers on the words, deeds, and suffering of Jesus—His inspiring personality provides humanity the proper example of the universal human ideal; and ultimately, the Kingdom is concerned with bringing the universal human ideal to bear on human existence, empowering individuals and society to reach their fullest human potential and live their best life now.

Understand, however, that in tracing the generational continuity and development of *Kingdom* grammar, this examination does not mean to suggest that each of these theologians is somehow mixed in together to produce one unified *Kingdom* porridge. Not at all. Each theologian provides a unique contribution to liberal *Kingdom* grammar by nature of his historical context and theological development. Yet, they are remarkably similar in their definitions of our human problem, the One who bore that problem's solution, and the nature of that solution itself, the Kingdom of God. In so tracing, we will see how such grammar is impacting contemporary evangelicalism, particularly through its progressive Emergent form.

Roger Olson has said that the story of Christian theology is the story of Christian reflection on the nature of salvation, which is why this examination is important. In it, we will see that the theological reflection offered by progressive evangelicals on the nature of salvation is repetitive and cyclical. While the Emergent Church claims to be helping evangelicalism rediscover authentic Christianity by rediscovering the Kingdom, it is merely repackaging liberalism for a new day. Like liberal *Kingdom* grammar, the Emergent Church ultimately urges people to place their faith in the *way* of Jesus—i.e. the Kingdom of God—rather than the *person* and *work* of Jesus. This is a significant departure from authentic, historic Christianity. Therefore, it is imperative that evangelicals understand the contours of liberal *Kingdom* grammar in order to understand how such grammar is affecting how some evangelicals are reflecting upon the nature of salvation, and consequently how they understand, show, and tell the gospel itself.

2

Schleiermacher's Grammar

Friedrich Schleiermacher is universally recognized as the father of modern theology. Particularly, Protestant liberalism effectively begins with Schleiermacher as he introduced the theological method and content that would come to define it. Even more pertinent to our cause, it was Schleiermacher who restored the concept of the Kingdom of God to a place of importance after it played little role in Protestant theology.[28] The restoration, and subsequent definition, of that concept would have great bearing upon the development of Protestant theology in an Enlightenment and post-Enlightenment world. As the most influential theologian since John Calvin,[29] Schleiermacher inaugurated a new theological epoch, the influence of which has

---

[28] Derek R. Nelson, "Schleiermacher and Ritschl on Individual and Social Sin," *Journal of the History of Modern Theology* 16n2 (2009): 144.
[29] Richard R. Niebuhr, *Schleiermacher on Christ and Religion* (New York: Scribner, 1964), 6.

lasted for nearly two hundred years. For Schleiermacher the Kingdom of God is the universal realm in which the universal human ideal is active by nature of Jesus' loving example working in and through humanity, which solves for our human problem. Our problem is a conscious absence of relating to the universal human ideal in individual human existence. Thus, we needed a new way of existing, which we find when we follow the influence of Christ's loving example and perpetuate His loving activity. Understanding how Schleiermacher defined the Kingdom and how it solves for our human problem will help us trace this grammar's development through three successive generations of liberal theologians, while also understanding the impact of that grammar today.

SCHLEIERMACHER'S HISTORICAL CONTEXT

Schleiermacher was born into the world of the Enlightenment, the period of European thought and culture that consumed roughly the entire eighteenth century.[30] It was a period known as the "Age of Reason" in which the cultural ethos was defined by a revolt against authoritarianism and gave rise to individual autonomy and reason; the individual rational man was the primary arbiter of truth and action. This reason was not the reason of classical rationalism, but the empirical, experimental reason of Bacon and Locke, which required that the "facts of experience" be examined through the use of a

---

[30] Keith W. Clements, *Friedrich Schleiermacher, Pioneer of Modern Theology* (London: Collins, 1987), 8.

universal, immutable force called Reason.[31] Furthermore, the Enlightenment method led to an ethos of optimistic progress, in which the idealized hope for a this-world transformation became the *telos* (i.e end goal) of modern human living.[32] As Keith W. Clements explains, "the innate and universal endowments of human thought were adjudged to be capable of providing man with whatever knowledge of nature, morality, and religion was necessary for his welfare." [33] Through this seismic epistemological shift, orthodox Christian theology in Europe was pushed toward the periphery of intellectual and social life, because the credibility and necessity for such "supernaturally inspired doctrines" were confronted by "rational, anti-dogmatic modes of thought." [34] This particular contour of the Enlightenment—the exile of orthodox Christianity—(partly) grounds us in understanding Schleiermacher's theology.

Understanding the Enlightenment context only partly grounds us in Schleiermacher's historical context, however, because alongside this historical phenomenon lay another significant movement that impacted his theology and method: the Romantic movement. Romanticism was a reactionary movement within modernity itself that was both akin to and distinguished from the spirit of the Enlightenment. Rather than a repudiation of the Enlightenment's Age of Reason, the Romantics of the nineteenth century hoped to enlarge the vision of the eighteenth century by cherishing both experience and

---

[31] James C. Livingston, *Modern Christian Thought: From Enlightenment to Vatican II* (New York: Macmillan Publishing Co., 1971), 4.
[32] Livingston, *Modern Christian Thought*, 7.
[33] Clements, *Friedrich Schleiermacher*, 9.
[34] Clements, *Friedrich Schleiermacher*, 9.

tradition, emotion and reason, religion and science. As Clements explains, "Romanticism was above all a journey into the inner feelings and passions which constituted the soul and which were to be regarded, ultimately, as a microcosm of the infinite life with which they were in continuity."[35] Thus, contrary to a Cartesian dualism in which Man and Nature are undeniably separate, they are fundamentally akin and variations of the one Infinite Whole; "the sense of Nature's organic unity" is experienced, felt and intuited as an "aesthetic wholeness."[36] Furthermore, they commonly felt that behind Nature a Spirit or Vital Force was at work and immanent in all things, which sharply contrasted with the Deistic "watchmaker God" that was impassively transcendent over creation.[37] It was in this tension between Enlightenment rationality and Romantic passion that Schleiermacher was born, raised, educated, and worked toward recasting the Christian faith for his day. In so working, he pioneered an approach to God that was centrally rooted in universal human experience, as born out of his Romantic context.

In light of modernity, Schleiermacher sought to provide a basis for which the modern man—the so-called "cultured despisers" of his time—could believe in God. In so doing, he wrested issues of faith out of the hands of both science and morality and placed them in a separate category called "piety" or religious affection. [38] According to Schleiermacher, science concerns knowledge, morality concerns activity, but piety and

---

[35] Clements, *Friedrich Schleiermacher*, 12.
[36] Livingston, *Modern Christian Thought*, 82.
[37] Livingston, *Modern Christian Thought*, 82-83.
[38] Schleiermacher, *On Religion*, 35.

religion concerns *feeling*. Specifically, religion and piety is described as "the feeling of absolute dependence;"[39] this feeling or experience is the essence of religion[40] and a universal element of life itself.[41] Schleiermacher termed this feeling the *God-consciousness*, which can take on varying forms (i.e. other religions).[42] This feeling is not categorized as *emotion*, however, but instead is a *state of mind*; it is "the immediate consciousness of the universal existence of all finite things, in and through the Infinite, and of all temporal things through the Eternal."[43] In other words, piety and religious affection is the contemplation and self-awareness of our connection with the whole Universe, our relation with God. In fact, he says "to feel oneself absolutely dependent and to be conscious of being in relation with God are one and the same thing."[44] Understanding what Schleiermacher means by the idea *God* and its correlating historical context is important to grasping his *Kingdom* grammar.

Schleiermacher describes God as an idea, which "signifies for us simply that which is the co-determinant in this feeling and to which we trace our being in such a state."[45] This 'idea' is the object to which our state of awareness of and connection to something outside ourselves is directed. In a series of meditations, he names this object "the Deity," which is a "poetic

---

[39] Schleiermacher, *Christian Faith*, 45.
[40] Schleiermacher, *On Religion*, 106.
[41] Schleiermacher, *Christian Faith*, 133.
[42] Schleiermacher, *Christian Faith*, 26, 47. For Schleiermacher, this religious *feeling* plus religious *content* equals so-called *intuition*. Our intuition varies by nature of the varying religious content. Our religious feeling, however, is common among all religions because every person has such a feeling of absolute dependence and connection to God. See *On Religion*, 42-51; 278-280.
[43] Schleiermacher, *On Religion*, 36.
[44] Schleiermacher, *Christian Faith*, 17.
[45] Schleiermacher, *Christian Faith*, 17.

symbol of what humanity should be."[46] This is an important definition, as this God-Idea seems to function as a symbol for the highest universal human ideal, which sets the stage for his theological enterprise. Throughout his works, Schleiermacher uses several words that are synonymous for God and this God-Idea: Universe, Deity, Infinite, Eternal, Whole, World-Spirit, and Highest Being. These terms are consistent with the way in which romantic spirituality described God, particularly Neoplatonic romanticism.[47] Schleiermacher's God is conceived in classic romantic spirituality: God is "the Deity," "the eternal and holy Being that lies beyond the world" who is "the Universe that made you," the "One in All and All in One."[48] While some may insist this language simply reflects his romantic historical context, it is important to realize that Schleiermacher uses these words in place of the historic Christian language of God, because Schleiermacher has replaced the historic definition for God itself with an introspective contemplation of one's "own true being."[49] Schleiermacher envisions grasping this universal human ideal (i.e. God) as my human purpose because it is the very purpose of piety itself: "My only purpose is ever to become more fully what I am,"[50] because God is merely a symbol of what humanity ought be.[51] I know "what I am," the ideal universal human ideal, by finding myself through my "inner life."[52] I grasp "God" not

---

[46] Friedrich Schleiermacher, *Schleiermacher's Soliloquies: An English Translation of the Monologen with a Critical Introduction and Appendix.* (transl. Horace Leland Friess; Chicago: The Open Court Publishing Company, 1926), 24.
[47] See John W. Cooper, *Panentheism: The Other God of the Philosophers* (Grand Rapids: BakerAcademic, 2006), 80-82.
[48] Schleiermacher, *On Religion*, 1, 2, 7.
[49] Schleiermacher, *Soliloquies*, 25.
[50] Schleiermacher, *Soliloquies*, 71.
[51] Schleiermacher, *Soliloquies*, 24.
[52] Schleiermacher, *Soliloquies*, 20.

through an external principle (i.e. revelation), but in myself. Hence, religious faith is reformulated as individual human experience. As we will see shortly, this human religious experience through the Kingdom of God is what ultimately solves for our human problem of the absence of the universal human ideal. It is to this problem we now turn.

THE PROBLEM WHICH THE KINGDOM SOLVES

Schleiermacher believed that the Christian faith is "essentially distinguished from other such [monotheistic faiths] by the fact that in it everything is related to the redemption accomplished by Jesus of Nazareth." [53] According to Schleiermacher, the term *redemption* itself is "a passage from a bad condition, which is represented as a state of captivity or constraint, into a better condition."[54] This passage from a bad condition to a better one is directly connected to the context established earlier, for both relate to the theological construct of *God-consciousness*: "We may give to [the evil/bad condition] the name *God-lessness*, or better, *God-forgetfulness*...this condition is nothing but a kind of imprisonment or constraint of the feeling of absolute dependence."[55] *God-forgetfulness* is an "inability to do what our God-consciousness requires us to strive after."[56] Again, in Schleiermacher's words, it is "an obstruction or arrest

---

[53] Schleiermacher, *Christian Faith*, 52.
[54] Schleiermacher, *Christian Faith*, 54. Translation "bad condition" altered from "evil condition" by Walter E. Wyman, "Sin and Redemption," in *The Cambridge Companion to Friedrich Schleiermacher* (Ed. Jaqueline Mariña; Cambridge: Cambridge University Press, 2005), 129.
[55] Schleiermacher, *Christian Faith*, 54, 55.
[56] Schleiermacher, *Christian Faith*, 366.

of the vitality of the higher self-consciousness [i.e. God-consciousness], so that there comes to be little or no union of it with the various determinations of the sensible self-consciousness, and this little or no religious life."[57]

According to Schleiermacher, everyone has the so-called God-consciousness, a feeling of absolute dependence and connection to the universal human ideal (i.e. God). Our problem is we forget that universal human ideal and our life isn't determined by it. Our problem, then, isn't that we have rebelled against God and His ways. Our problem is an inability to "join the thought of God with every thought of any importance that occurs to us;" our human condition is one in which we do not consciously relate to God in everyday existence.[58] As previously argued, the idea of God seems to be taken as the universal human ideal, the image of which is missing from human existence. In his words, "the image of the Infinite in every part of finite nature has gone extinct."[59] We still possess a God-consciousness, but it is missing from our existence. This reinterpretation of sin as the absence of the universal human ideal from actual human experience is further understood through Schleiermacher's understanding of the "flesh" and "spirit," two Pauline concepts Schleiermacher refashioned into a "positive antagonism of the flesh against the spirit."[60] Whereas Paul used the *flesh–spirit* antithesis in eschatological terms to describe the new tension between humanity's relationship to the

---

[57] Schleiermacher, *Christian Faith*, 54.
[58] Friedrich Schleiermacher, "Selected Sermons of Schleiermacher" (Transl. Mark Wilson; London: Hodder and Stoughton, 1890), 38.
[59] Schleiermacher, *Christian Faith*, 241.
[60] Schleiermacher, *Christian Faith*, 271.

world versus God in Christ,[61] Schleiermacher defines both in anthropological terms to describe humanity's lower existence vis-a-vis his higher existence.

For Schleiermacher, everything that arrests the free development of the God-consciousness is considered sin, which he explains through his *flesh–spirit* dichotomy. *Flesh* is conceived as "the totality of the so-called lower powers of the soul,"[62] while the *spirit* is a term that refers to man's "inner side, as a self-active being in whom God-consciousness is possible."[63] Elsewhere Schleiermacher pits the "sensuous animal life" over against a "higher level" and "higher being," in which man it is humanity's goal to attain the essence of the universal human ideal by turning away from the former in order to grasp the latter.[64] It appears that Schleiermacher equates these terms with the *finite* and the *Infinite*, the reality of existence and ideality of human essence. Perhaps Schleiermacher's "spiritualizing" of humanity's goal was a way to counter the earthiness of Enlightenment empiricism that focused on brute facts in order to overcome existence. I quote Schleiermacher at length to explain man's plight:

> Man is born with the religious capacity...If only his sense for the profoundest depth of his own nature is not crushed out, if only all fellowship between himself and the Primal Source is not quite shut off, religion would, after its own fashion, infallibly be developed...I

---

[61] For a more complete description of this antithesis to compare against Schleiermacher's, see James D. G. Dunn, *The Theology of Paul the Apostle* (Grand Rapids: Eerdmans Publishing, 1998) 477-482.

[62] Schleiermacher, *Christian Faith*, 271.

[63] Schleiermacher, *Christian Faith*, 238.

[64] Schleiermacher, *Soliloquies*, 30, 31.

> see how all things unite to bind man to the finite...that
> the Infinite may as far as possible vanish from their
> eyes. 65

He further says we have consciousness of sin whenever "the God-Consciousness...determines our self-consciousness as pain," which Wyman rightly interprets as experiencing "a sense of incompleteness, mental discomfort, of things somehow out of joint, of the world lacking religious meaning."[66] In other words, we sense a disconnect between our existence and the universal ideal, between the so-called "sensible-consciousness"[67] (flesh) that conditions his existence and the God-consciousness (spirit) that conditions the essence of humanity. According to Schleiermacher, this disconnection is traced to the beginning of man's development itself.

Unlike the historic Christian faith that roots man's sinful condition in the Augustinian concept of *original sin*, Schleiermacher dismisses the idea of a pre-Fall idyllic state. As he says, "we have no reason for explaining universal sinfulness as due to an alteration in human nature brought about [by the first human pair] by the first sin."[68] He does not want to say human

---

[65] Schleiermacher, *On Religion*, 124-125. (emph. mine)

[66] Wyman, "Sin and Redemption," 133.

[67] The *sensible-consciousness* constitutes "the whole field of experience in the widest sense of the word and...all determinations of self-consciousness which develop from our relations to nature and to man." (CF, 19) It is the normal sphere of consciousness that man experiences in relation to his worldly existence. It is a *lower consciousness* set over against the *higher consciousness* man experiences in relation to "God." In the only example Schleiermacher gives in this discussion, he states there can be "a sorrow of the lower and a joy of the higher self-consciousness, as for example whenever with a feeling of suffering there is combined a trust in God." (CF, 24) Thus, existence is given meaning when there is an awareness of and relationship to God, the ideal. The inhibition of this awareness (i.e. God-consciousness) is what constitutes the "bad condition."

[68] Schleiermacher, *Christian Faith*, 291.

nature in anyway was changed, but instead "human nature was the same before the first sin as it appears subsequently alike in them and their posterity."[69] In fact, he suggests that Adam must have already been apart from God before his first sin, leading him to reject the traditional formulation of human nature (i.e. original sin) in favor of a new one: "persons corrupt themselves and one another."[70] He says this is "an adequate description of all the sin that ever appears amongst man" because it keeps nature out of the matter and places the genesis of sin outside ourselves. Instead of placing the shift toward sin in human *nature*, Schleiermacher places the shift toward sin in human *history*: sinfulness operates in individuals "through the sin and sinfulness of others...it is transmitted by the voluntary actions of every individual to others and implanted within them."[71] As he famously said: "in each the work of all, and indeed all the work of each."[72] There is a universal sinfulness, because of a "corporate consciousness" of sin; a solidarity exists in humanity across time and space in which the total existence of those sharing a common life combine to form an "aggregate power of the flesh" that is opposed to the spirit.[73] Individuals exist in families and clans and communities in which the God-consciousness is already deficient and obstructed, manifesting and perpetuating that history in their own existence.

Note the underlying Pelagianism inherent in Schleiermacher's reformulation of the human condition: bad

---

[69] Schleiermacher, *Christian Faith*, 296.
[70] Schleiermacher, *Christian Faith*, 298.
[71] Schleiermacher, *Christian Faith*, 287.
[72] Schleiermacher, *Christian Faith*, 288.
[73] Schleiermacher, *Christian Faith*, 288.

examples from the community form bad habits in the individual, which perpetuate the bad condition discussed earlier that suppresses the universal human ideal (i.e. God-consciousness) in existence. The result, according to Schleiermacher, is that "throughout the entire range of sinful humanity there is not a single perfectly good action, that is, one that purely expresses the power of the God-consciousness; nor is there one perfectly pure moment, that is, one in which something does not exist in secret antagonism to the God-consciousness."[74] And this leads to our definition of sin itself.

Schleiermacher writes, "what gives a moment the character of sin is the self-centered activity of the flesh...for all activities of the flesh are good when subservient to the spirit and all are evil when severed from it." Here sin is located in human consciousness, as perpetuated by the human community, which results in actual sin—which Fries notes is "the sinful condition and action of the individual giving expression to the sin of the race."[75] These self-centered activities add to the "force of habit and thus the vitiation of the God-consciousness," which "spreads and establishes itself by communication to others."[76] This vitiation, or impairment, of the God-consciousness—our connection to and relationship with the universal human ideal— *is* sin, and this impairment is "inherited" from one person to the next through bad examples and the habit wrought through following those bad examples, resulting in social and moral evils that fail to realize the universal human ideal. Therefore, the

---

[74] Schleiermacher, *Christian Faith*, 305.
[75] Paul Roy Fries, "Religion and the Hope for a Truly Human Existence" (PhD diss., Utrecht University, 1979), 61.
[76] Schleiermacher, *Christian Faith*, 313.

individual is guilty for having participated in the human incapacity for the human ideal and perpetuating faulty human existence, resulting in "a complete incapacity for the good, which can be removed only by the influence of Redemption."[77] Humanity needed a redeemer, then, to do something with that faulty human existence and help us "remember" our God-consciousness, to remember the universal human ideal. We found such a Redeemer in Jesus, who stopped the perpetuation of God-forgetfulness by destroying 'originating' original sin through His loving life example, while completing humanity through that life.

THE BEARER OF THE KINGDOM: THE PERSON & WORK OF JESUS

According to Schleiermacher, Christianity is the most developed form of religion, because of the person who exhibited the highest human ideal: Jesus of Nazareth.[78] Schleiermacher describes Jesus as having "an absolutely powerful God-consciousness," in Him was a "constant potency of God-consciousness, which was a veritable existence of God in him."[79] In Christ we see God active—which is equated with the existence of God;[80] all His activities proceeded from "the being of God in Him"[81] —which seems to be the universal human ideal working

---

[77] Schleiermacher, *Christian Faith*, 282.
[78] Schleiermacher, *Christian Faith*, 38.
[79] Schleiermacher, *Christian Faith*, 387.
[80] Schleiermacher, *Christian Faith*, 387.
[81] Schleiermacher, *Christian Faith*, 426.

in and through His life. This principle—the being of God—is timeless and eternal, but expressed itself temporally in Jesus' human life.[82] Thus, His life was determined by the universal human ideal that revealed itself in human existence, because He possessed the God-consciousness in its fullness. This doesn't mean Jesus was God Himself. Instead it means Jesus somehow grasped, in word and deed, the highest human spirit. It would help to quote Schleiermacher at length in order to understand how he conceived of Jesus' divinity:

> if it is only through Him that the human God-consciousness became an existence of God in human nature, and only through the rational nature that the totality of the finite powers can become an existence of God in the world, that in truth He alone mediates all existence of God in the world and all revelation of God through the world, in so far as He bears within Himself the whole new creation which contains and develops the potency of the God-consciousness. 83

Notice that as the "revelation of God" Jesus possessed the new creation, which is the fully potent God-consciousness, the universal human ideal realized in human existence. Consequently, Jesus is considered the completion and perfection of humanity by nature of His potent God-consciousness.

As Schleiermacher plainly puts it, Jesus is "the One in whom the human creation is perfected…" As the Second Adam Jesus is "altogether like all those who are descended from the first, only that from the outset He has an absolutely potent God-

---

[82] Schleiermacher, *Christian Faith*, 426.
[83] Schleiermacher, *Christian Faith*, 388.

consciousness....His whole activity stands under the law of historical development, and that activity is brought to perfection through the gradual expansion, from the point at which He appears, over the whole."[84] Schleiermacher maintained that at the beginning of His life, Jesus had a "new implanting of the God-consciousness," which Schleiermacher regarded as the completed creation of human nature itself. It is this universal human ideal—the being of God and God-consciousness—that Jesus sought to impart to His followers through His earthly life. The imparting of His God-consciousness comes about through a strengthening of that state of awareness and an assumption of the believer into the power of His own God-consciousness.[85] In Schleiermacher's words, Jesus' whole redemptive mission was "to raise men to fellowship with God and to rule spiritually," to grasp the feeling of dependence and relation to the universal human ideal. This was His redeeming activity, accomplished by founding a new fellowship, a new corporate life: the Kingdom of God.

Schleiermacher frames our problem's solution and Jesus' work in terms of a *state of blessedness* that is rooted in the corporate life of the Kingdom. He writes, "We are conscious that all approximations to the state of blessedness which occurs in the Christian life as being grounded in a new divinely-effected corporate life, which works in opposition to the corporate life of sin and the misery which develops in it."[86] This blessedness of Christ signifies none other than the completion, or perfection, of humanity: "the appearance of Christ and the institution of this

---

[84] Schleiermacher, *Christian Faith*, 367.
[85] Schleiermacher, *Christian Faith*, 425.
[86] Schleiermacher, *Christian Faith*, 358.

new corporate life [i.e. Kingdom of God] would have to be regarded as the completion, only now accomplished of the creation of humanity."[87] In the first stage of human existence, humanity was "under the law of earthly existence," existing in the "sensuous animal life" and sensuous self-consciousness, while the "higher life" and God-consciousness only gradually came later; the God-consciousness that began in the first stage was "inadequate and impotent."[88] In this second stage, however, the God-consciousness "broke forth in perfection in Christ, from whom it continually extends its authority, and proves its power to bring peace and blessedness to men,"[89] which is the ever expanding Kingdom of God instantiated in the ever-expanding loving activity of humanity. This human activity is the crux of Jesus' redemptive work; Jesus "redeems" humanity when they follow His loving example and perpetuate His loving activity.

Schleiermacher believed the essence of the work of Jesus is "that the God-consciousness already present in human nature, though feeble and repressed, becomes stimulated and made dominant by the entrance of the living influence of Christ..."[90] The redemptive work of Christ is essentially His *living*, rather than his dying. Though Schleiermacher does not deny the importance of the cross, it is important insofar as it is an extension and climax of Jesus' life; the cross is simply the greatest act of love, the greatest in a long series of loving actions that have reverberated throughout history. Redemption takes place, then, when "The Redeemer assumes believers into the

---

[87] Schleiermacher, *Christian Faith*, 366.
[88] Schleiermacher, *Christian Faith*, 368.
[89] Schleiermacher, *Christian Faith*, 368.
[90] Schleiermacher, *Christian Faith*, 476.

power of His God-consciousness, and this is his redemptive activity."[91] This assumption takes place when the individual takes upon himself the influence of Christ by following His example of love and perpetuates His life of love. As Schleiermacher writes, "the total effective influence of Christ is only the continuation of the creative divine activity out of which the Person of Christ arose. For this, too, was directed towards human nature as a whole, in which that being of God was to exist, but in such a way that its effects are mediated through the life of Christ..."[92] So the universal human ideal (i.e. being of God) was to exist in human nature as a whole, and the effect of it is mediated to humanity through Christ's life-example and influence, so that "the former personality may be slain and human nature...be formed into persons in totality of that higher life."[93] In other words, the goal of redemption is that the sensuous-conscious of real human existence might be replaced with the God-consciousness of the ideal human essence, which occurs in the corporate life of the Kingdom, the true nature of Jesus' redemptive work.

It is through the corporate life of the Kingdom of God that "fallen" human existence is resolved and humanity itself is redeemed. The redemptive work of Jesus is the life He lived, perpetuated in the Kingdom He founded. This redemption is effected in humanity when the sinless perfection of Jesus is "communicated" to it.[94] Jesus' sinless perfection is, of course, His perfect, potent God-consciousness, an absolutely pure

---

[91] Schleiermacher, *Christian Faith*, 425.
[92] Schleiermacher, *Christian Faith*, 427.
[93] Schleiermacher, *Christian Faith*, 428.
[94] Schleiermacher, *Christian Faith*, 361.

connection to that which is the universal human ideal. And it is this awareness of the universal human ideal that He (somehow) communicates to His followers, even to all people. Schleiermacher explains that Jesus' God-consciousness is communicated to humanity through belief in Him, which is also belief that the universal human ideal has made its way into real human experience: "to believe that Jesus was the Christ, and to believe that the Kingdom of God (that is the new corporate life which was to be created by God) has come, are the same thing. Consequently, all developing blessedness has its grounding in this corporate life."[95] Thus, redemption comes by way of the community that Jesus founded, which takes its influence from Jesus' example and represents the universal human ideal spreading throughout human existence and transforming human history. Note that *this* is the saving work of Christ, this founding of a Kingdom and influential example of love perpetuated by this Kingdom-fellowship is how Jesus "saves" humanity.

This is a significant departure from historic Christian orthodoxy, which orients the saving work of Christ around His death on the Cross, rather than simply His life of love. Schleiermacher did not understand Jesus' death as the moment where God objectively dealt with the penalty of sin, but instead viewed the cross event as an example of self-denying love exhibited in suffering at the hands of the state. He doesn't eliminate the cross, but he does redefine it. Jesus' death is a *modeling* death, not an *atoning* death. In what will become a consistent theological pattern over the next several generations

---

[95] Schleiermacher, *Christian Faith*, 360.

of liberalism, the life of Jesus is more significant than the death of Jesus, where even His death is simply the culmination of His life. As Schleiermacher argues, "For in His suffering unto death, occasioned by His steadfastness, there is manifested to us an absolutely self-denying love."[96] He goes on to say, "in this there is represented to us with perfect vividness the way in which God was in Him to reconcile the world to Himself," mainly through His self-sacrificing love, which was the culmination of cruciform *living*.

While emphasizing the cruciformity of Jesus' life is a good thing, even with regards to salvation, that cruciform life saves insofar as it provides a prototype for living the universal human ideal. It is this cruciformity—both the living and dying examples of love—that we are to share in order to overcome the sin of the world: "Those who are assumed into the fellowship of Christ's life are called to share the fellowship of His suffering, until the time when sin has been completely overcome and through suffering satisfaction has been made in the corporate life of humanity."[97] This is the nature and purpose of the Kingdom: it is a corporation, fellowship, community from among the human race in history who, under Christ's influence, are living out His loving example, in order to transform society in to the image of the universal human ideal. As an "example" and the human "ideal,"[98] Christ's influential life functions as the mechanism by which that transformation is possible; the Kingdom is the community that perpetuates and spreads that influential life through human history, in order that "Thy will be done on earth

---

[96] Schleiermacher, *Christian Faith*, 458.
[97] Schleiermacher, *Christian Faith*, 461.
[98] Schleiermacher, *Christian Faith*, 462.

as in heaven." Through the Kingdom of God, then, humanity finds salvation.

THE SALVATION OF THE KINGDOM

Though Schleiermacher is credited with reintroducing the concept and language of the Kingdom of God into the Church's vernacular, he defines it in a new, different way for his modern context. Schleiermacher uses various terms to represent the Kingdom of God: it is a new corporate life founded by Jesus;[99] it is fellowship with Christ, as such fellowship is always fellowship with his Kingdom mission;[100] it is a special divine activity in the world;[101] the Kingdom is the Church itself;[102] it is the sphere of Christ's redeeming activity;[103] in its most basic sense the Kingdom of God is the realm in which the God-consciousness is active;[104] ultimately, it is the union of Divine essence with human nature, the reunion of ideal human essence with real human existence.[105] The founding of the Kingdom, then, is the principal work of Christ and the way in which He solves our human problem.

The Kingdom of God is the vehicle through which human nature is transformed and redeemed; the community of Jesus mediates His influence and the redeeming activity of the Kingdom throughout human history in order to change it. That

---

[99] Schleiermacher, *Christian Faith*, 444.
[100] Schleiermacher, *Christian Faith*, 517.
[101] Schleiermacher, *Christian Faith*, 552.
[102] Schleiermacher, *Christian Faith*, 528.
[103] Schleiermacher, *Christian Faith*, 530.
[104] Schleiermacher, *Christian Faith*, 43.
[105] Schleiermacher, *Christian Faith*, 738, 739.

influence is, of course, Jesus' powerful, potent God-consciousness that manifested itself in His powerful, potent loving model of the universal human ideal. That loving life example was perpetuated through founding the Kingdom and calling people to its redeeming mission. As Schleiermacher states, "We are conscious of all approximations to the state of blessedness which occur in the Christian life as being grounded in a new divinely-effected corporate life, which works in opposition to the corporate life of sin and the misery which develops in it."[106] Salvation, or the "state of blessedness" is rooted in the new corporate life of the Kingdom of God. Such salvation happens when our lives correspond to the Kingdom-life established by Jesus, when our life is seized by the living example of Jesus. As Schleiermacher explains, "Assumption into living fellowship with Christ is his justification;" conversion is regarded as a changed form of living. [107]

This assumption and conversion does not happen all at once, but rather intermittently: "the true life of Christ in us announces itself at first only in weak and intermittent impulses, and then gradually a unified activity emerges. The only marks we can point to are steady progress in sanctification taken in its full meaning, and active participation in the extension of Christ's Kingdom."[108] The "life of Christ" of which Schleiermacher speaks is not the actual presence of the resurrected Christ living in us, but the example of Jesus' life as perpetuated in the Kingdom of God and its activity. Schleiermacher writes, "the life of Christ in us is nothing but activity in behalf of the Kingdom of

---

[106] Schleiermacher, *Christian Faith*, 358.
[107] Schleiermacher, *Christian Faith*, 478.
[108] Schleiermacher, *Christian Faith*, 516.

God which embraces men all together in the grasp of love flowing from Him; that is it is the power of the Christian common spirit."[109] This "Christian common spirit" is nothing more than the personal influence of Christ—His "Divine Essence," His God-consciousness—living on through the Church outward to humanity. And this perpetuated personal influence of Christ, the life of Christ living in us through the loving activity of the Kingdom of God, is the actual salvific work of Jesus' redemption.[110] The salvation of humanity, then, is bound up with our extension of the Kingdom of God through acts of love by loving both God and neighbor. Here, there is a social link between the God-consciousness and love, and Kingdom salvation.

In order to understand how the Kingdom saves humanity through acts of love, it is important to note the social connection between this love and *God-consciousness*. Schleiermacher was interested in helping people reconnect to the universal ideal, which seems to be symbolized by *God*. Some have noted a panentheistic (even pantheistic) dimension to Schleiermacher's understanding of God.[111] Several times Schleiermacher invokes Spinoza's moniker "the One in All, and All in One."[112] Though he does distinguish between God and the world,[113] it is clear the All and the One cannot be separated: "The Absolute Causality to which the feeling of absolute dependence points back can only be described in such a way that, on the one hand, it is

---

[109] Schleiermacher, *Christian Faith*, 576-577.
[110] Schleiermacher, *Christian Faith*, 577.
[111] Cooper, *Panentheism*, 88.
[112] Schleiermacher, *On Religion*, 7.
[113] Schleiermacher, *Christian Faith*, 39: "God and the world will remain distinct at least as regards to function."

distinguished from the content of the natural order and thus contrasted with it, and, on the other hand, equated with it in comprehension." [114] John Cooper translates Schleiermacher's motto as evidence of his panentheism: "There is no God without the world, just as there is no world without God."[115] Thus, God and humanity are intimately wrapped up in Schleiermacher's *God-consciousness* language. In fact, he uses the language of *Whole* when discussing humanity's relationship to God, where individuals compose the Whole: "Every form, every creature, every occurrence is an action of the Universe upon us, and religion is just the acceptance of each separate thing as part of the Whole, of each limited thing as an exhibition of the Infinite."[116] In light of this panentheistic connection between humanity and God, note the social link in Schleiermacher's *God-consciousness*: When I love God, I love the Whole; when I love the Whole I love my neighbor. Thus, love of neighbor actually *is* love of God. When one loves their neighbor, they are loving and affirming the universal human ideal, and consequently living the life of the Kingdom and perpetuating its activity.

Schleiermacher maintains that the true nature of the activity of the Kingdom is love: "love to men and love to Christ and love to God."[117] This love is the love of Christ's life-example living in us and our community of faith; the activity of the Kingdom is

[114] Schleiermacher, *Christian Faith*, 200.
[115] Cooper, *Panentheism*, 84.
[116] Schleiermacher, *On Religion*, 279. In commenting on the self-existence of every individual he wrote: "What is it merely as act, as movement? Is it not the coming into being of something for itself, and at the same time in the Whole? It is an endeavor to return into the Whole, and to exist for oneself at the same time...Your whole life is such an existence for self in the Whole." Schleiermacher, *On Religion*, 42-43.
[117] Schleiermacher, *Christian Faith*, 521.

"Christ's love working in and through us."[118] Therefore, the activity of the Kingdom of God involves living out the loving example of Christ through acts of love, which is an affirmation of the universal human ideal. This activity of the Kingdom is the activity of the Redeemer (i.e. Jesus Christ) Himself, because "the original activity of the Redeemer," Schleiermacher writes, is "that by means which he assumes us into this fellowship of His activity and His life."[119] By definition, then, the activity of love that we perform is an extension of the activity of Jesus Christ, because His activity of Redemption is our activity of love. As Schleiermacher goes on to say, "It is scarcely thinkable that a man should be received into unity of life with Christ without very soon actively proving himself an instrument of his redeeming activity."[120] Assumption into the life of Christ and His community means assuming His redeeming activity by being taken up into Christ's vocation of love. Christ's own vocation is bound up with His will for the Kingdom of God and transformation of human history through loving good works. For Schleiermacher, any loving work is good because it reflects the loving vocation of Christ, and every good work necessarily lies within the sphere of the Kingdom of God.[121] Therefore, whatever activity that reflects the loving life-example of Christ is activity that is part of the Kingdom of God. Schleiermacher has everybody in view here, because Christ's love works in and through every good work that comports with the will of the

---

[118] Schleiermacher, *Christian Faith*, 521.
[119] Schleiermacher, *Christian Faith*, 165.
[120] Schleiermacher, *Christian Faith*, 516.
[121] Schleiermacher, *Christian Faith*, 522.

Kingdom. [122] In the end, everybody's loving activity will be considered Kingdom activity because all people will eventually become members of it, which cashes out as universalism.

While Schleiermacher did equate the Church with the Kingdom and those who have faith in Christ as members of it, his reformulation of election and divine foreknowledge ultimately includes everyone as members of the Kingdom. Schleiermacher insists that those currently outside the fellowship of Christ—meaning those who do not consciously or willfully identify with Him—will go on to become members of the Church, because as they advance in Kingdom-acts of love, this "leaves no doubt as to their justification." [123] He assumes that "all belonging to the human race are eventually taken up into living fellowship with Christ, because of what he called "a single divine fore-ordination." While the majority of humanity is not yet regarded as chosen and elected in Christ, the person whose fore-ordination has not yet been fulfilled during this life is held in reserve in death in an "intermediate state," where he will eventually be "taken up into living fellowship with Christ." [124] Schleiermacher put it even more plainly when he argued, "There is a single divine fore-ordination, according to which the totality of the new creation is called into being out of the general mass of the human race," to which he then added "the totality of the new creation is equal to the general mass," so that the redeeming

---

[122] Schleiermacher, *Christian Faith*, 521.

[123] Schleiermacher, *Christian Faith*, 547, 549

[124] Schleiermacher, *Christian Faith*, 549. Though Schleiermacher is vague in his description of the afterlife—he is unclear what he means by "taken up into living fellowship with Christ"—it seems as though Schleiermacher held a sort of post-mortem universal salvation, in which even after death everyone will experience salvation. Even then, however, it isn't clear that Schleiermacher even held a view of an actual everlasting life of heaven post-death.

power of Christ saves from common ruin the totality of the new creation contained in the human race.[125] Thus, the redeeming activity of Christ (i.e. the Kingdom of God) is universal, not simply in opportunity but in outcome, so that the Kingdom of God is formed out of "the whole actual inward manifold of the human race in space and time."[126] All who belong to the human race are eventually taken up into living fellowship with Christ in the Kingdom and experience the essence of the universal human ideal that is divine love, by nature of the historical transformation of society through the advancement of the Kingdom. Schleiermacher's solution to the human problem is truly a universal salvation.

CONCLUSION

In the end, Schleiermacher conceives of the human problem relating to our failure as individuals, and collectively as humans, to live up to our greatest human potential, an ideal common spirit of brotherly love. This impairment of the universal human ideal is a historical phenomenon that demands a historical solution. This solution came in the historical person of Jesus of Nazareth, who had a potent connection to the universal human ideal and established a community of people who would carry forth His inspiring example of love through the Kingdom of God. The Kingdom is the movement of love-inspired action to help humanity grow beyond their sensuous-consciousness to live fully within their God-consciousness, to bring about the

---

[125] Schleiermacher, *Christian Faith*, 550, 551.
[126] Schleiermacher, *Christian Faith*, 555.

universal human ideal in human existence. When one loves his neighbor, he loves God because He is in All and All are in Him; love of brother is an affirmation of the universal human ideal. As one progresses through this historical theological comparison, one will notice how subsequent generations of German liberals continued Schleiermacher's *Kingdom* grammar and problem/solution formulation, even though they revised and extended his arguments along the way. Chief among those revisers and extenders was Schleiermacher's successor, Albrecht Ritschl.

3

Ritschl's Grammar

Though Schleiermacher is credited with founding modern Protestant theology and fathering Protestant liberalism, Albrecht Ritschl became virtually synonymous with liberalism, founding a school and influencing a generation of theologians.[127] With the publication of the English translation of his magnum opus, *The Christian Doctrine of Justification and Reconciliation*, in 1900, Ritschl's influence grew in width and depth beyond the dominance he had already achieved in German theological discourse.[128] This influence would extend through Harnack, Rauschenbusch, and Tillich; one even finds vestiges of his school in the contemporary Emergent Church through thinkers such as McLaren. It is no wonder that Ritschl has been called the "most important Protestant theologian of the last [19th] century after Schleiermacher."[129] Ritschl's influence upon several generations

---

[127] Grenz and Olson, *20th Century Theology*, 53.
[128] Livingston, *Modern Christian Thought*, 247.
[129] David L. Mueller, *An Introduction to the Theology of Albrecht Ritschl* (Philadelphia: Westminster Press, 1969), 15.

of theologians has come primarily through his revision and extension of Schleiermacher's *Kingdom* grammar. For Ritschl, humanity's problem is individual selfishness, a collective social consciousness that compels us to do evil, and a rejection of the universal human ideal. As the founder of the higher common good and universal ideal of the Kingdom of God, Jesus conquered bad human existence by founding, living, and teaching this Kingdom of love, which is the source of our salvation.

RITSCHL'S HISTORICAL CONTEXT

Ritschl was born a generation after Schleiermacher, yet he still experienced the cultural and ecclesiastical effects of the Enlightenment. Early in his academic development Ritschl was influenced by C. F. Bauer and the German idealism of G. W. F. Hegel, though Ritschl later rejected both the radical left wing Hegelianism of Feurerbach and the orthodox speculative Hegelianism of the right.[130] He was, however, heavily influenced by two 18th and 19th century thinkers: Kant and Schleiermacher.

Unlike Schleiermacher, who attempted to overcome the Enlightenment by way of Romanticism, Karl Barth explains that Ritschl "energetically seized upon the theoretical and practical philosophy of the Enlightenment in its perfected form. That is, he went back to Kant."[131] Grenz and Olson maintain that

---

[130] Mueller, *Introduction to the Theology of Albrecht Ritschl*, 17.
[131] Karl Barth, *Protestant Thought: From Rousseau to Ritschl* (New York: Harper and Brothers, 1959), 391.

Ritschl's theological method was harmonious and consistent with Kant's philosophy: "Ritschl followed Kant in trying to expunge metaphysics from theology and in bringing religion into the closest possible connection with ethics."[132] Germane to this examination is the interesting note that Ritschl drew upon Kant's vision of the Kingdom as an ethical community where everyone is ruled by the highest moral virtue. As Derek Nelson explains, "Kant's vision of the Kingdom of God presented an ethical community wherein all people were perfectly ruled by virtue and the power of their consciences."[133] Rather than rooting ethics in the knowledge of God, Kant rooted ethics in the knowledge of the universal human ideal. For Kant, it is impossible to know God and His way and to have a moral faith rooted in the knowledge of God as defined by religious faith. Therefore, all that remains is to know and serve your neighbor through simple moral virtue that's rooted in the common moral good. Nelson goes on to explain that "Kant positively links this notion [of the common moral good] to the development of a 'moral faith' from the then regnant so-called 'ecclesiastical faith.' If this were to happen, according to Kant, then we could say that 'the Kingdom of God has come unto us.'"[134] And Kant's notion of this "kingdom of ends" impacted Ritschl's own *Kingdom* grammar and concept of sin by provoking him to root both in Kant's idea of the highest common good. Furthermore, in adopting Kant's moral vision of the Kingdom, Ritschl also adopted Kant's theory of knowledge that suited the requirements

---

[132] Grenz and Olson, *20th Century Theology*, 55.
[133] Nelson, "Schleiermacher and Ritschl on Individual and Social Sin," 145.
[134] Nelson, "Schleiermacher and Ritschl on Individual and Social Sin,", 145.

of his own theological system and epistemic proof for God's existence. James Orr explains:

> That our knowledge is only of phenomena; that God is theoretically incognoscible; that our conviction of His existence rests on a practical, not on a theoretical judgment...The Kantian 'moral' proof for the existence of God Ritschl accepts as alone valid; and with it he adopts the Kantian deduction of the Kingdom of God, or association of men through laws of virtue, and the idea of a final end of the world thence resulting. 135

Whereas Schleiermacher sought to move beyond the impasses created by the Enlightenment by pursuing an alternative route through Romanticism, Ritschl was attracted to Kant's ethics and certain forms of Neo-Kantianism.[136] Beyond Kant, however, undoubtedly the most significant impact upon Ritschl's theology was Schleiermacher.

Ritschl's feelings toward Schleiermacher ranged from attraction to repulsion. Orr explains that what "chiefly repelled Ritschl to Schleiermacher was the element of 'mysticism' in his theology; that which attracted him was, above all, his teleological view of Christianity, and the place given to the idea of 'fellowship' in religion." [137] This "teleological view" in Schleiermacher's *Kingdom* grammar refers to the end goal toward which Christianity is oriented and the end toward which humanity is called to move. While he appreciated how Schleiermacher restored the Kingdom-concept to its rightful,

---

[135] James Orr, *The Ritschlian Theology and the Evangelical Faith* (London: Houghton and Stoughton, 1897), 5-6.
[136] Mueller, *Introduction to the Theology of Albrecht Ritschl*, 17.
[137] Orr, *The Ritschlian Theology*, 42.

central place in Christian theology, Ritschl did not believe Schleiermacher went far enough in making it part of his ethic; Ritschl sought to make the Kingdom both a religious *and* ethical concept.[138] We have already seen that for Schleiermacher, the Kingdom was primarily an individual religious feeling of absolute dependence and relationship with God, the universal ideal. As Claude Welch explains, "Schleiermacher first identified the teleological character of the kingdom as decisive for Christianity. For this we should be grateful. Yet the significance of this discovery of the ethical had not been fully exploited. That was the task Ritschl set for himself."[139] While Ritschl displays fealty to Schleiermacher when he notes that the Christian redemptive end is presupposed by Schleiermacher's religious "dependence on God," he also transcends Schleiermacher's "general form of religious experience as distinct from a moral relationship" by arguing that the Christian life is both "perfectly religious and perfectly ethical." [140] Schleiermacher established the foundation for such religious and ethical redemption by emphasizing the individual's loving feeling for God and neighbor through loving the Whole: in loving God I love the Whole, in loving the Whole I love my neighbor. Ritschl built on this foundation by emphasizing one's ethical posture before all humanity with his *Kingdom* grammar, the first part of which we now turn in order to understand the problem for which the Kingdom solves.

---

[138] Nelson, "Schleiermacher and Ritschl on Individual and Social Sin," 145.
[139] Claude Welch, *Protestant Thought in the Nineteenth Century* (2 vols.: Eugene, OR: Wipf & Stock Publishers, 2003) 2:18.
[140] Albrecht Ritschl, *The Christian Doctrine of Justification and Reconciliation: The Positive Development of the Doctrine.* Edited by H.R. Mackintosh and A.B. Macaulay (Edinburgh: T & T Clark, 1902.), 13.

THE PROBLEM WHICH THE KINGDOM SOLVES

Significant to Ritschl's understanding of the human problem is his rejection of the historic doctrine of original sin. Ritschl relegated original sin to the sphere of "doctrine," merely an intellectual idea which does not conform to experience.[141] As with Schleiermacher, Ritschl rejected the notion that our original parents historically fell from an original righteousness.[142] Ritschl challenged the doctrine of original sin that developed in the early church by insisting that it simply does not reflect the New Testament: "Neither Jesus nor any of the New Testament writers either indicate or presuppose that sin is universal merely through natural generation." [143] Likewise, he disputed as unbiblical the Reformed assertion that humans are incapable of doing good because of their inherent sinfulness.[144] Furthermore, Ritschl argued that original sin is neither derived from the natural endowment of man [145] nor inherited from previous generations. [146] Instead, Ritschl argued that sin is acquired through human history and development.

He asserted that the generations from our first human parents became trapped in an avalanche of crises that engulfed humanity in ethically dysfunctional systems and destructive stories, resulting in a "selfish bias." According to Ritschl, humanity is now caught in a "whole web of sinful actions and reactions, which presuppose and yet again increases the selfish

---

[141] Ritschl, *Justification and Reconciliation*, 328.
[142] Ritschl, *Justification and Reconciliation*, 331.
[143] Ritschl, *Instruction in the Christian Religion*, 203.n27.
[144] Ritschl, *Instruction in the Christian Religion*, 206-207.n4.
[145] Ritschl, *Instruction in the Christian Religion*, 204.
[146] Ritschl, *Justification and Reconciliation*, 348.

bias in every man."[147] Humans were originally created with the capacity to freely choose the highest or the "perfect common good."[148] From the beginning humans possessed an internal goodness, and out of that goodness they were to act in accordance with the highest common good, which the Kingdom of God now reflects. However, our problem is that we are caught in webs of ethically dysfunctional systems and destructive stories that have escalated throughout human history. Our problem is not a natural, internal one—in that I am born a rebel against God and the object of His righteous wrath, in need of a rescuer—but an environmental, external one: I follow the bad ethical examples around me and do ethically bad things, and need someone to show me how to live my best life now. Accordingly, *I* am not the problem; *life* and my environment is the problem, and I respond with more bad actions. Thus, Ritschl has a Pelagian view of original sin and human nature.

Ritschl defines sin in several ways: In content, sin is selfishness; in form, it is enmity toward God, a mistrust and indifference toward Him; in origin, it arises out of ignorance, bad examples, and habit.[149] Ritschl's definitions gain steam when he interprets sin through the lens of the Kingdom of God. Taking his cues from Schleiermacher, Ritschl posits a *kingdom of sin*[150] set over against the Kingdom of God in which all humanity shares in its guilt: "All these grades of habitual sin we include in

---

[147] Ritschl, *Justification and Reconciliation*, 350.
[148] Ritschl, *Instruction in the Christian Religion*, 202.
[149] Ritschl, *Justification and Reconciliation*, 334-336.
[150] In *Justification and Reconciliation*, 339, Ritschl acknowledges the merit of Schleiermacher's *common sin* equation, though believed he wrongly subsumed it under the traditional heading of original sin. Instead, Ritschl substituted the idea of the *kingdom of sin* in place of original sin.

the vast complexity of sinful action when we form the idea of the *kingdom of sin*...we can only regard ourselves as sharing its guilt when we not only attribute to ourselves our own sinful action as such, but at the same time calculate how they produce sin in others also..."[151] The subject of sin is not simply individuals who do selfish acts that run contrary to the highest common good (i.e. the Kingdom of the God), but instead "is *humanity as the sum of all individuals*, in so far as the selfish action of each person...is directed in any degree whatsoever towards the opposite of the good, and leads to the association of individuals in common evil."[152] Thus, I and my sin nature are not the problem; humanity and the environment it creates is the problem.

For Ritschl, the *kingdom of sin* is an alternative hypothesis to original sin that explains the human condition.[153] While the doctrine of original sin views Adam's sin as a nature-altering act, Ritschl views Adam's sin as an *environment*-altering act. In Adam, there is a universal loss of connection, dependence, reverence, and trust in God, because every generation has actively participated in the transgression of freely mistrusting God and rejecting the perfect moral good, the universal human ideal. These collective acts have resulted in the *kingdom of sin* or "web of sin," which is set over against the Kingdom of God. This kingdom or universal sinfulness is the collective human sinfulness that acts as a collective consciousness out of which individuals act. Ritschl describes this kingdom and universality as "united action" which leads to a reinforcement of sin in every

---

[151] Ritschl, *Justification and Reconciliation*, 338.
[152] Ritschl, *Justification and Reconciliation*, 335.
[153] Ritschl, *Justification and Reconciliation*, 344.

generation: "United sin, this opposite of the kingdom of God, rests upon all as a power which at least limits the freedom of the individual to do good."[154] The sin that swirls around us compels us to sin, resulting in a sinful bias that individuals acquire because of bad examples. Ritschl explains, "The sinful bias...is not described by [Paul] as inherited, and can with perfect reason be understood as something acquired. In the individual [the sinful bias] comes to be the principle of the will's direction."[155] This individual bias contributes to the larger whole of "wickedness and untruth" in what Ritschl terms a "web of sinful action." It is the collective contribution of individual actions and reactions and also "increases the selfish bias in every man." [156]

Ritschl believed our human problem is what we do and not who we are by nature—we do not sin because we're sinners; we are a sinner because we sin in concert with humanity and its web of sin. The web of sin that surrounds us creates a bias within us toward selfishness and compels us to sin; we are oppressed on the outside not affected on the inside. Therefore, our solution must address this evil web of systems, the person who came to bring us that solution had to do something with that web. We didn't need a savior to stand in our place of punishment; we needed someone to launch a better system, a better Kingdom. As Barth explains Ritschl's position, solving our human problem means "the realized ideal of human life."[157] Jesus was such a person who provided such a solution by living such an ideal human life.

---

[154] Ritschl, *Instruction in the Christian Religion*, 206.
[155] Ritschl, *Justification and Reconciliation*, 346, 347.
[156] Ritschl, *Justification and Reconciliation*, 350.
[157] Barth, *Protestant Thought*, 393.

THE BEARER OF THE KINGDOM: THE PERSON & WORK OF JESUS

Like other generations of liberal theologians, Ritschl's understanding of Jesus plays a significant role in Ritschl's *Kingdom* grammar. How Ritschl understands and interprets the person of Jesus has great bearing on how he understands His work, and thus the solution found in the Kingdom of God to humanity's problem. Whereas Schleiermacher tended to make Jesus out to be simply a religious figure who solved our religious problem—mainly, our God-forgetfulness—Ritschl emphasized both the religious and ethical aspects of the "Founder of Christianity." For Ritschl, "Jesus, the Founder of the perfect moral and spiritual religion, belongs to a higher order than all other men;" "His unique worth lies in the manner in which He mastered His spiritual powers through a self-consciousness which transcends that of all other men..."[158] As a uniquely higher man, He was "conscious of a new and hitherto unknown relation to God."[159] Here we see great continuity with Schleiermacher's own understanding of Jesus, who he said had a potent God-consciousness, a perfect feeling of absolute connection with and relation to God (i.e. the universal human ideal). Similarly, Ritschl does not describe Jesus as being God himself; Jesus is only a unique *man* belonging to a higher order of humanity. In regard to this relationship with God, Jesus is described as having a *"strength of a fellowship or unity with God* such as no one

---

[158] Ritschl, *Justification and Reconciliation*, 2, 332.
[159] Ritschl, *Justification and Reconciliation*, 386.

before Him had ever known."[160] Ritschl did not suggest Jesus is ontologically one with God, but that He simply has a unique relationship with Him as demonstrated in His ethical life.

Like Schleiermacher, Ritschl does not indicate that Jesus Himself is God, only that He shows us the Divine and has a connection with the Divine. Christ's ethical actions are what connect Him to God and give Jesus what Ritschl termed the Godhead attribute. As Ritschl explains, "Christ's Godhead is understood as the power which Christ has put forth for our redemption...[the Godhead attribute] of Christ is to be found in the service He provided, the benefit He bestows, the saving work He accomplishes...it is an attribute revealed to us in His saving influence upon ourselves."[161] In other words, Jesus of Nazareth is God because of what He *does,* not because of *who He is.* Jesus is not ontologically God, but only ethically so: He only shares in the Divine because of His ethical services and actions, rather than being God Himself. For Ritschl Jesus is the *moral* rather than the *metaphysical* Son of God.

As Ritschl makes clear, it is in the ethical activity of Jesus that we find God present. While Ritschl does say "[Jesus] is equal to God," it is clear from his writings that this equality is ethical, rather than ontological. He is equal with God because of His moral activity.[162] This activity is primarily the fulfillment of His vocation as the founder of the Kingdom. "Vocation" is another concept for which Ritschl is indebted to Schleiermacher. As Ritschl says, Jesus is the "personal vehicle of the Divine self-end;" He is "that Being in the world Whose self-end God makes

---

[160] Ritschl, *Justification and Reconciliation*, 333. (emphasis mine.)
[161] Ritschl, *Justification and Reconciliation*, 395, 396-397, 398.
[162] Ritschl, *Justification and Reconciliation*, 483.

effective and manifest after the original manner His own eternal self-end, Whose whole activity, therefore, in discharge of His vocation, forms the material of that complete revelation of God which is present in Him, in Whom, in short, the Word of God is a human person."[163] Jesus reveals God through His vocation as the founder of the Kingdom of God, as a "teacher" and "liver" of the "universal ethical kingdom of God," which is the "supreme end of God Himself in the world."[164] Jesus' ethical teachings and kingdom vocation, then, constitute Him as participating in the Divine "Godhead." Understanding the person of Jesus in His vocation as the Founder of the Kingdom provides the needed theological context for understanding the work of Jesus, what He did in that vocation.

Because the realization of the universal human ideal is the manner in which our human problem is solved, the nature of Jesus' work must be refashioned and re-understood. Rather than conceiving that reconciling, solving work happening at Jesus' death on the cross, Ritschl believed that work centered upon His life, a life that simply climaxed at the cross. Insofar as Jesus' work is re-understood as centering around His Kingdom-vocation, so too is the cross itself. This re-understanding is different than historic Christianity that views the cross as the event at which Jesus Christ went to sacrifice Himself for our sins in our place as a vicarious substitute. Ritschl maintained this view is patently unbiblical and instead is a principle of Hellenic religion.[165] As with Schleiermacher before him, Ritschl rejected the traditional substitutionary view of the cross that provides the

---

[163] Ritschl, *Justification and Reconciliation*, 451.
[164] Ritschl, *Justification and Reconciliation*, 451.
[165] Ritschl, *Justification and Reconciliation*, 478.

solution to our human problem of sin: "The view that Christ, by the vicarious endurance of the punishment deserved by sinful men, propitiated the justice or wrath of God, and thus made possible the grace of God, is not found on any clear and distinct passage in the New Testament."[166] Ritschl did not believe the solution to man's problem of alienation comes through the substitution of Christ on the cross. Instead, he argued that the significance of Jesus' work on the cross was simply a continuation or climax of His life. For him the cross served as an example to the rest of the world: "It is not mere fate of dying that determines the value of Christ's death as a sacrifice; what renders this issue of his life significant for others is His willing acceptance of the death inflicted on Him by His adversaries as a dispensation of God, and the highest proof of faithfulness to His vocation."[167] In other words, as with Schleiermacher, Jesus is important not because He *died*—as a substitutionary sacrifice for the sins of the world—but because He *lived*; salvation comes through the *life* of Christ in executing His vocation as founder of the Kingdom.

The significance of the work of Jesus is "'related to the moral organization of humanity through love-prompted action,"[168] the Kingdom of God. His vocation was founding, living, and teaching the love-prompted actions of the Kingdom, providing the means by which humanity can triumph over and transcend the ethically bad systems of the world. Through this vocation He provided the paradigmatic example of self-sacrifice, discipline, and attainment of virtue for others to follow, which crescendoed

---

[166] Ritschl, *Instruction in the Christian Religion*, 220.n3.
[167] Ritschl, *Justification and Reconciliation*, 477, 479
[168] Ritschl, *Justification and Reconciliation*, 13.

at the cross. The cross was an extension of Jesus' life in that His sufferings served as a means of testing His faithfulness to His Kingdom vocation, while also confirming and explaining it.[169] For Ritschl, the work of Christ did not center on the cross, but on founding, living, and teaching the Kingdom; the cross was the culmination of that vocation in that this highest ethical common good was tested and displayed for all the world to see and follow. In this testing and display, humans find their moral example to aid their moral failure and their solution to their problem of selfishness and dominion over bad existence, which is the Kingdom of God, the true nature of Christ's work.

Ritschl explicitly argues that the Kingdom of God "offers the solution to the question...implied in all religions: namely, how man, recognizing himself as a part of the world, and at the same time as being capable of a spiritual personality, can attain that dominion over the world, as opposed to limitation by it, which this capability gives him the right to claim." [170] Mirroring Schleiermacher's own view of the human predicament Ritschl wondered how humanity could attain dominion over and conquer the limitations of human existence? Humanity's limited human existence is conquered through attaining the universal human ideal found in the Kingdom of God, which is the end toward which all of humanity is to move because it is the supreme end of God Himself. [171] Attaining the ethical ideal of the Kingdom is possible through the justification and reconciliation Christ provides, which are really one in the same.

---

[169] Ritschl, *Justification and Reconciliation*, 480.
[170] Ritschl, *Instruction in the Christian Religion*, 179.
[171] Ritschl, *Justification and Reconciliation*, 451.

While others often separate justification and the Kingdom of God, claiming that "justification and reconciliation concern men as sinners, while the Kingdom of God concerns them as reconciled," Ritschl insisted this dichotomy is "not quite exact."[172] Instead, "the conception of the Kingdom of God and justification are homogeneous," for they are one and the same idea.[173] The aim of justification and reconciliation is "lordship over the world" in order to transcend the systems and stories of human existence through "dominion over the world and participation in the Kingdom of God."[174] As Ritschl defines reconciliation: "[it] is not merely the ground of deliverance from the guilt of sin...it is also the ground of deliverance from the world, and the ground of spiritual and moral lordship over the world."[175] Rather than deliverance from the *condition* of sin, we receive deliverance from the *effects* of sin. This conclusion seems to be established through Ritschl's claims that justification leads to eternal life now, "which is present in our experiences of freedom or lordship over the world, and in the independence of self-feeling both from the restrictions and from the impulses due to natural causes or particular sections of society."[176] Rather than the person of Jesus and His work on the cross, the Kingdom itself is the mode of salvation. Jesus saves only insofar as He brings in the Kingdom, rather than His own meritorious work on the cross. Thus, it could be said that the *Kingdom*, rather than *Jesus*, is what saves.

---

[172] Ritschl, *Justification and Reconciliation*, 31.
[173] Ritschl, *Justification and Reconciliation*, 33.
[174] Ritschl, *Justification and Reconciliation*, 609, 628.
[175] Ritschl, *Justification and Reconciliation*, 357.
[176] Ritschl, *Justification and Reconciliation*, 534-534.

THE SALVATION OF THE KINGDOM

Ritschl described the Kingdom of God in various ways: "The kingdom of God is the divinely vouched-for highest good of the community;"[177] it is the community of people who "are knit together in union with everyone who can show the marks of a neighbor," who do good in the Christian sense, which is the "uninterrupted reciprocation of action springing from the motive of love;"[178] finally, "it is that union of men in which all good are appropriated in their proper subordination to the highest good."[179] As Ritschl plainly put it, the Kingdom of God is the product of "love-inspired action" and "the righteous conduct in which the members of the Christian community share in the bringing in of the kingdom of God [which] has its universal law and its personal motive in love to God and to one's neighbor."[180] The Kingdom is not the eschatological reign of God per se that will restore the world from the consequences of sin, but rather the "moral society of nations" and ultimately "the organization of humanity through action inspired by love."[181] In Ritschl's *Kingdom* grammar, then, one finds community, love-motivated action, and good defined by the "highest good." This latter characteristic—the highest good—is of particular interest because it further defines the Kingdom as the "ethical ideal." The Kingdom forms "the ethical ideal for whose attainment the members of the community bind themselves together through

---

[177] Ritschl, *Instruction in the Christian Religion*, 174.
[178] Ritschl, *Justification and Reconciliation*, 334.
[179] Ritschl, *Justification and Reconciliation*, 451.
[180] Ritschl, *Instruction in the Christian Religion*, 178, 174.
[181] Ritschl, *Justification and Reconciliation*, 10, 12.

their definite reciprocal action." [182] The members of the community are viewed as everyone who takes upon himself the ethical ideal found in the Kingdom.

In order to understand who is part of the Kingdom, one must understand that Ritschl distinguished between two separate communities that are drawn together by Jesus: the Church and the Kingdom. Contrary to Schleiermacher, Ritschl insisted that the Church is not the Kingdom, and spends a great deal of time explaining how Augustine and the Reformers were "erroneous" and ultimately "lost sight of the idea of the Kingdom of God." [183] As was previously addressed in the introduction chapter, Augustine equated the Kingdom of God with the Catholic Church and the Reformers generally viewed the Kingdom as the spiritual realm of God's worshippers and will over against that of the State. Instead of these conceptions, Ritschl insisted the Church—or more specifically "a legally constituted" church, as in a local congregation—is a *religious* idea, whereas the Kingdom is an *ethical* idea that's entirely distinct from the Church. As he argues, a Church is a "fellowship of Christians for the purpose of religious worship" and "its members unite in the same religious worship and create for this purpose a legal constitution."[184] The Kingdom, however, is a fellowship that "acts reciprocally from love, and thus calls into existence that fellowship of moral disposition and moral blessing which extends to the limits of the human race." This community "gives themselves to the interchange of action prompted by

---

[182] Ritschl, *Instruction in the Christian Religion*, 174-175.
[183] Ritschl, *Justification and Reconciliation*, 286.
[184] Ritschl, *Justification and Reconciliation*, 289, 290.

love."[185] Here Ritschl makes an important distinction between the *religious* and *ethical* fellowships of Jesus: the visible, religious fellowship of Christ is simply those who are part of the Christian religion, whereas the invisible, ethical fellowship is those who do moral acts prompted by love. This former category is related to the latter, yet is specific to those who confess the Christian religion; the latter category is far more general and includes everybody who performs acts of brotherly neighbor-love. Whereas Schleiermacher equated the Kingdom with the Church, Ritschl subsumes the Church underneath the Kingdom; the Church is a subset of the Kingdom, which inevitably universalizes the Kingdom to include every loving act by everybody.

Conceiving of the fellowship of Christ in these two manners means that anyone who does acts of love is part of the Kingdom, whether they specifically believe in Jesus (or even know of Him) or not. By Ritschl's definition, doing acts of love means one believes in Christ insofar as one believes in the "ruling *idea* of Jesus"[186] by living out His example of love. As Ritschl writes, "The presence of the Kingdom...is always invisible and a matter of religious faith," but still the Kingdom "exists in the world as the present product of action motivated by love."[187] Read in light of the above distinction between Church and Kingdom, it is important to note that the Kingdom is not simply present when

---

[185] Ritschl, *Justification and Reconciliation*, 289, 290.
[186] Ritschl, *Justification and Reconciliation*, 284. Ritschl presents a sharp distinction between *moral* followers of Christ and *devotional* followers of Christ, relegating the former to the conception of the Kingdom of God who follow Jesus by nature of their moral actions and the latter to the conception of the worshipping community of the Church who follow Jesus by their devotional actions (i.e. prayer, Sunday worship, baptism, etc...).
[187] Ritschl, *Instruction in the Christian Religion*, 179.

the *Church* performs acts of love; any act of love from *anyone* counts as the presence of the Kingdom. Whereas Schleiermacher identified the Kingdom with the Church—though he still envisioned the whole human race would eventually be part of this new corporate life—Ritschl widened the scope of Kingdom activity beyond its previously narrow identification with the Church to include everyone from every culture and society that participates in the "highest good." Widening the margins of the Kingdom makes sense as Ritschl envisions the Kingdom to be the final end of everyone.

Ritschl makes it clear that the Kingdom of God is "the final end of all," which he defines as "the moral organization of humanity through love-prompted action."[188] It is the final end of all, the end goal for which we all live, because it is the final end of God Himself.[189] The Kingdom rises above the mundane (i.e. life existence) and is "supernatural, in so far as it is higher than the ethical forms of society," because it is the "product of love-inspired action" and is "the highest good of those who are united in it."[190] This love-inspired action flows directly from God, who is Himself love. Ritschl explains:

> The Christian idea of the Kingdom of God, which has been proved the correlate of the conception of God as love, denotes the association of mankind—an association both extensively and intensively the most comprehensive possible—through the reciprocal moral action of its members, action which transcends all merely natural and particular considerations. 191

---

[188] Ritschl, *Justification and Reconciliation*, 13.
[189] Ritschl, *Instruction in the Christian Religion*, 211.
[190] Ritschl, *Instruction in the Christian Religion*, 178.
[191] Ritschl, *Justification and Reconciliation*, 284.

In order to get into the Kingdom, then, one only has to direct his impulses and activity toward living out the love of God, which is instantiated in the inspiring example of Jesus. *Kingdom* is the catch-all language for describing every activity from every person that conforms to the universal human ideal originally modeled by Jesus Christ. By performing the Kingdom in following the loving example of Jesus, one finds salvation and is counted among the members of that Kingdom, making it clear that the Kingdom saves, and saves everybody.

CONCLUSION

Like Schleiermacher, Ritschl raised the profile on the Kingdom by placing it at the center of his theology. Whereas Schleiermacher's emphasis was religious, Ritschl's was both religious and ethical. In fact, the term *Kingdom* served as the interpretive lens for his theological method. Our human problem is the *kingdom of sin*, which creates a selfish bias in individuals who form bad habits from following bad examples. For Ritschl, sin isn't part of the human nature, but is developmental and historical, in that every generation perpetuates and reinforces a collective sinful bias. Thus, our problem is an external, environmental problem in need of an environmental solution, rather than an internal one requiring a change to our sinful nature; the evil systems that compel people to do evil actions need an alternative ethical system that directs people toward the universal human ideal. That solution is found in the Kingdom of God, which is founded by Jesus Christ.

Rather than dying for our sins in order to transform our human nature, Jesus showed us and lived out the universal ethical ideal of the Kingdom. Salvation is found when a person aligns his life with Jesus' teachings and Kingdom, and participates in His own vocation of love-inspired activity. Such an alignment and participation is what transforms humanity's existence, which stands opposed to the highest ethical ideal. Thus, the Kingdom saves, rather than Jesus Himself. Ritschl's foundation catalyzed an entire theological movement, bent on re-formulating the gospel itself. Chief among this movement was Walter Rauschenbusch, architect of the so-called Social Gospel. To him we now turn.

4

Rauschenbusch's Grammar

If Schleiermacher focused almost entirely on the religious aspect of the Kingdom and Ritschl emphasized both its religious and ethical nature, Rauschenbusch stressed almost exclusively the ethical. And whereas Schleiermacher and Ritschl emphasized the individual in relation to the universal human ideal, Rauschenbusch's unique contribution to liberal *Kingdom* grammar was his emphasis on the social: "The kingdom of God is the true human *society*," [192] not simply the true human individual. This socializing of *Kingdom* grammar led Rauschenbusch to envision the gospel socially, as well—hence the so-called *social gospel*. Cornel West described Rauschenbusch as "the most influential and important religious

---

[192] Walter Rauschenbusch, *Christianity and the Social Crisis in the 21st Century*. (ed. Paul Rauschenbusch; New York: HaperOne, 2007), 58. (emph. mine)

public intellectual in early-twentieth-century America,"[193] an influence that has continued even today. Therefore, understanding his *Kingdom* grammar and how it solves the human problem of social evil and personal selfishness through the power of Christ's life will help us understand how that grammar is defined even today.

RAUSCHENBUSCH'S HISTORICAL CONTEXT

Rauschenbusch was born into a German Baptist family, falling under the influence of his professor father and his theologically conservative pietism.[194] He eventually accepted a pastorate position at Second German Baptist Church in Hell's Kitchen, one of the most impoverished slums of New York City. [195] It was in this context of mass poverty and systemic injustice that Rauschenbusch began his turn toward a social understanding of the gospel, and especially the Kingdom of God. As Gary Dorrien puts it, "His searing encounter with urban poverty, especially the funerals that he performed for children, drove him to political activism and a social-progressive understanding of Christianity."[196] It is this "social-progressive understanding of Christianity" that would result in the so-called *social gospel* and formulation of his *Kingdom* grammar in social terms.

---

[193] Cornel West, "Can These Dry Bones Live?" in *Christianity and the Social Crisis in the 21st Century*. (ed. Paul Rauschenbusch; New York: HaperOne, 2007), 231.
[194] Livingston, *Modern Christian Thought*, 262.
[195] Livingston, *Modern Christian Thought*, 262.
[196] Gary Dorrien, "Kingdom Coming: Rauschenbusch's Christianity and the Social Crisis." *Christian Century* 124 no 24 (2007): 27.

Whereas Schleiermacher and Ritschl attempted to connect the Christian faith to a post-Enlightenment culture skeptical of the faith's reasonableness, Rauschenbusch sought to connect the Christian faith to a post-Industrial culture skeptical of the faith's ethical viability. He wrote during a time when the modern city was hemorrhaging from the effects of economic inequity and insecurity, poor working conditions, alcoholism, immigration tensions, and other moral blights associated with modern industrial life. In response, Rauschenbusch did for American Christianity what Schleiermacher did for the European faith: He resurrected the language of the *Kingdom* from the neglect of Christian history in order to solve the "social crisis" of his day. Rather than applying the Kingdom religiously, as Schleiermacher had by emphasizing the individual's religious affections toward God, Rauschenbusch applied it ethically. This ethical emphasis most acutely arose during the time he spent studying in Germany where he came under the influence of Ritschlianism.[197]

While Rauschenbusch was theologically eclectic—drawing upon the theologies of Schleiermacher, German Idealism, and evolutionary doctrine—his major theological themes have a strong Ritschlian ring to them. Ritschl and his school dominated the European theological scene when Rauschenbusch was studying sociology and New Testament in Germany in 1891, leading some to conclude a special Ritschlian influence upon his theological outlook. [198] A generation prior, Ritschl had emphasized the ethical nature of the Kingdom and Jesus as

---

[197] Grenz and Olson, *Twentieth Century Theology*, 61.
[198] Max L. Stackhouse, introduction to *The Righteousness of the Kingdom*, by Walter Rauschenbusch (ed. Max L. Stackhouse. New York: Abingdon Press, 1968), 18.

founder of a new corporate life that centered around the highest human good. This corporate life, centering around the influential words and deeds of Jesus Himself, solved the systemic "kingdom of sin" that defines our human problem. Many of these themes found their way into Rauschenbusch's theology, especially Ritschl's preoccupation with a social-progressive understanding of the gospel and emphasis on the ethical Kingdom. Though he later parted with Ritschl's "ellipses" understanding of Christianity—while Ritschl maintained Christianity had two centers, eternal life for the individual and the Kingdom for humanity, Rauschenbusch came to believe Jesus had one center of thought, the Kingdom of God—[199] Rauschenbusch's major theological themes are extraordinarily similar to Ritschlian liberalism. As Livingston points out, "Like the Ritschlians, he was disinterested in metaphysics and dogma as the initiator of the divine community—the Kingdom of God. He saw man as caught in the struggle between his spiritual and natural impulses and conceived salvation in ethical and social terms." [200] Rauschenbusch combined these Ritschlian themes with two other important forces in American thought: evolution and socialism.

Consistent with a Darwinian scientific perspective of the world, Rauschenbusch appealed in several of his works to the progressive, evolutionary development of humanity. He speaks of an "infinite slowness and imperfection of historical progress." He goes on to argue that for the first time in religious history humanity can direct religious energies "by scientific knowledge,"

---

[199] Dorrien, "Kingdom Coming," 27.
[200] Livingston, *Modern Christian Thought*, 263.

knowledge that takes into account "the modern comprehension of the organic development of human society."[201] Elsewhere, Rauschenbusch makes an overtly positive assessment of evolutionary thought in relation to social change: "Evolution teaches the possibility of change for the better, not the certainty of it....The assumption that, on the whole, evolution is moving forward and upward rests partly on sight, but even more on faith."[202] This positive assessment of evolution plays a significant role in the backdrop to Rauschenbusch's *Kingdom* grammar, as does his curious assessment of socialism and communism.

Of socialism, Rauschenbusch writes, "how quickly [will] Christian thought realize that individualism is coming to be an inadequate and antiquated form of social organization which must give place to a higher form of communistic organization," adding "communism will afford a far nobler social basis for the spiritual temple of Christianity."[203] Elsewhere he writes positively that socialism itself is the answer to the social crisis facing modern industrial life, arguing that this socialistic "solution" should be "hailed with joy by every patriot and Christian."[204] Rauschenbusch even goes so far as to wed socialism and the Christian principle of brotherly association, which the Kingdom of God represents, as a necessary ally of the working class.[205] Understanding this socialism aspect to his historical context is important considering the words *social* and *solidaric* are key to Rauschenbusch's conception of Christianity. Socialism especially

---

[201] Rauschenbusch, *Christianity and the Social Crisis*, 164, 171, 72.
[202] Rauschenbusch, *Righteousness and the Kingdom*, 280.
[203] Rauschenbusch, *Christianity and the Social Crisis*, 320.
[204] Rauschenbusch, *Christianity and the Social Crisis*, 328.
[205] Rauschenbusch, *Christianity and the Social Crisis*, 328-329.

undergirds his understanding of the person and work of Jesus, the heart of whom was the message of the Kingdom, a message of social redemption and human progress.

THE PROBLEM WHICH THE KINGDOM SOLVES

If Rauschenbusch read traditional theological categories through a social lens, particularly the person and work of Jesus, then we should expect to find the human problem to be defined in much the same way. Rauschenbusch asserts that sin is essentially selfishness, emphasizing that it possesses ethical and social dimensions.[206] He insists that conceiving sin as selfishness "furnishes an excellent theological basis for a social conception of sin and salvation."[207] This definition works in his system because Rauschenbusch believes humanity is the object against which we sin, rather than God. He states that we sin against "our higher self, against the good of men, and against the universal good."[208] Perhaps a better way of putting it is that we sin against the universal human ideal, against the way things ought to be in human relations. While traditional theology views the human problem as "a sort of solitary duel of the will between him and God," Rauschenbusch curiously maintains that "in actual life such titanic rebellion against the Almighty is rare...We do not rebel; we dodge and evade." Instead of humanity being an enemy of God through willful sin, "The really grinding and

---

[206] Walter Rauschenbusch, *A Theology for the Social Gospel* (Nashville: Abingdon Press, 1945), 47.
[207] Rauschenbusch, *A Theology for the Social Gospel*, 47. (emph. mine)
[208] Rauschenbusch, *A Theology for the Social Gospel*, 47.

destructive enemy of man is man."[209] In place of a theo-centric definition of sin, Rauschenbusch asserts a social, human-centric definition of sin. Sin is social because sin is selfishness. And the way we fall into selfishness is through bad examples, difficult social circumstances, and habit.

According to Rauschenbusch, we are conditioned to sin for a variety of social reasons: we are "ignorant," thus we need to be educated upward; people are placed in socially "difficult situations" that overwhelmingly tempt them beyond their capacity to resist; "evil habits of boyhood" draw us into sin, which originate "by the examples and social suasion of boys just one stage older."[210] This description of sin is obviously Pelagian, as it roots the cause of sin in ignorance, bad examples, and habit. Like Schleiermacher and Ritschl, Rauschenbusch does not conceive of our human problem in terms consistent with the historic understanding of original sin; sin is not part of our nature given to us by Adam, it is part of our nature because of our social conditioning. In classic Pelagian form he writes, "One generation corrupts the next...sin is lodged in social customs and institutions and is absorbed by the individual from his social group."[211] Our social class, profession, neighborhood, and nation compel us to sin by overtaking our moral judgments and valuations.[212] We are united in our social condition because of our sin environment, not our sin nature. And because our sin is social, so too is our guilt.

---

[209] Rauschenbusch, *Christianity and the Social Crisis*, 178. (emph. mine)
[210] Rauschenbusch, *A Theology for the Social Gospel*, 60, 61, 71
[211] Rauschenbusch, *A Theology for the Social Gospel*, 60.
[212] Rauschenbusch, *A Theology for the Social Gospel*, 61.

As we become more enlightened, Rauschenbusch insists we "can not help feeling a growing sense of responsibility and guilt for the common sins under which humanity is bound and to which we all contribute." [213] Rather than being individually responsible and guilty before God as a rebellious sinner against Him and His laws, we are collectively guilty because the "human spirit" as a collective whole gives itself to evil and interferes with efforts to better society.[214] As he explains, "the sin of all is in each of us," [215] which is remarkably similar to Schleiermacher's own description that "in each the work of all and in all the work of each."[216] We are united in our sin socially; we sin because others sin and are collectively guilty because of it. This sense of social solidarity stems from Rauschenbusch's concept of the Kingdom of Evil, a concept that mirrors Ritschl's kingdom of sin.

For Rauschenbusch the doctrine of the Kingdom of Evil is an important organizing concept for his understanding of sin because every human life is tightly interwoven. He writes, "The evils of one generation are caused by the wrongs of the generation that preceded, and will in turn condition the sufferings and temptations of those who come after." [217] Rauschenbusch goes on to say that "Our theological conception of sin is but fragmentary unless we see all men in their natural groups bound together in a solidarity of all times and all places, bearing the yoke of evil and suffering."[218] Rauschenbusch is careful to point out that while the concept of the Kingdom of

---

[213] Rauschenbusch, *A Theology for the Social Gospel*, 91.
[214] Rauschenbusch, *Righteousness and the Kingdom*, 282.
[215] Rauschenbusch, *A Theology for the Social Gospel*, 91.
[216] Schleiermacher, *The Christian Faith*, 288.
[217] Rauschenbusch, *A Theology for the Social Gospel*, 79.
[218] Rauschenbusch, *A Theology for the Social Gospel*, 81.

Evil is not new, his modern conception is historical and social rather than spiritual; his concept has nothing to do with a realm of Satan and demonic spirits, but social solidarity and the historic realities of sin. [219] The agents of this theological reunderstanding are what Rauschenbusch calls "supra-personal forces." These forces are the institutions and systems of society that combine to exert their power and influence over individuals, compelling them to sin. The power of these forces results in the social sins that frustrate the Kingdom of God, resulting in social misery. At the time of Rauschenbusch, our social misery and human problem was the result of the industrial revolution and its resulting effects on land and people, work and wages, health and nutrition, family, and democracy.[220] Perhaps today such social misery is the result of the information revolution and social fragmentation that has accompanied it. Because of this social misery, Rauschenbusch says humanity is "haunted by the horrible emptiness of his life and feels that existence is a meaningless riddle and delusion."[221] Thus, we are in need of a solution that provides a new system and way of collectively being human, one where existence is as it ought.

THE BEARER OF THE KINGDOM: THE PERSON & WORK OF JESUS

Rauschenbusch insists that "the better we know Jesus, the more social do his thoughts and aims become." [222] For

---

[219] Rauschenbusch, *A Theology for the Social Gospel*, 87. Also, see 81-86.
[220] Rauschenbusch, *Christianity and the Social Crisis*, 182. See 184-230.
[221] Rauschenbusch, *Christianity and the Social Crisis*, 41.
[222] Rauschenbusch, *Christianity and the Social Crisis*, 41.

Rauschenbusch, Jesus was more than simply a moral teacher: He learned the greatest and deepest secret of them all: "how to live a religious life," which helps solve for the emptiness of man's life and feeling that "existence is a meaningless riddle and delusion." [223] According to Rauschenbusch, Jesus "saw the evil in the life of men and their suffering" and He wanted people "to live a right life in common."[224] This right life in common is foundational to Jesus' person and work, which centers around the "creation and progress of social redemption," the revolutionary force of the Kingdom.

Like Schleiermacher and Ritschl before him, Rauschenbusch's Jesus is the founder of the Kingdom of God. He described this founding in these ways: Jesus Christ was the "initiatory power" of the Kingdom—Jesus' life set the Kingdom into motion;[225] He is the one who set in motion the historical forces of Kingdom redemption in order to overthrow the Kingdom of Evil;[226] in founding the Kingdom, Jesus "labored to set up the true standard of goodness," through His teachings and his living;[227] and finally, the Kingdom itself constitutes the fundamental purpose of Jesus's person and life. [228] Jesus' initiation, labor, and purpose was wholly oriented toward bringing systemic social change through His inspiring teachings and loving example.

Central to Rauschenbusch's Jesus is the understanding that He "lived in the hope of a great transformation of the national,

---

[223] Rauschenbusch, *Christianity and the Social Crisis*, 41.
[224] Rauschenbusch, *Christianity and the Social Crisis*, 41.
[225] Rauschenbusch, *Righteousness and the Kingdom*, 118.
[226] Rauschenbusch, *A Theology for the Social Gospel*, 147.
[227] Rauschenbusch, *Righteousness and the Kingdom*, 118.
[228] Rauschenbusch, *Christianity and the Social Crisis*, 123.

social, and religious life about him. He shared the substance of that hope with his people, but by his profounder insight and his loftier faith he elevated and transformed the common hope." [229] Accordingly, Rauschenbusch argued that Jesus emphasized the transformation of "single centers of influence and of social nuclei," meaning He envisioned human social progress through transforming social systems. [230] Jesus' scope was universal, emphasizing a "human hope" over against the previous "Jewish hope" of his people; and the future gaze of that hope turned to "faith in present realities and beginnings, and found its task here and now." [231] This hope for here-and-now transformation resulted in a new type of humanity which was the beginnings of a new social organism and social transformation. As he framed it, "The personality which [Jesus] achieved was a new type in humanity...it became the primal cell of a new social organism." [232] Furthermore, Jesus' life created an entirely new epoch in the social evolution of humanity by introducing a new type of living, and consequently new social standards by which humans were called to live.[233] Jesus could create such an epoch and introduce a new type of living because of who He was in His unique relationship with God.

Rauschenbusch described this "unique relationship" thusly: "He is the real revelation of God;" "Jesus experienced God in a new way;" "All His mind was set on God and one with Him."[234] We see the influence of Schleiermacher on Rauschenbusch's

---

[229] Rauschenbusch, *Christianity and the Social Crisis*, 53.
[230] Rauschenbusch, *Christianity and the Social Crisis*, 53.
[231] Rauschenbusch, *Christianity and the Social Crisis*, 53.
[232] Rauschenbusch, *A Theology for the Social Gospel*, 152.
[233] Rauschenbusch, *A Theology for the Social Gospel*, 152.
[234] Rauschenbusch, *A Theology for the Social Gospel*, 152, 155.

understanding of Jesus' deity when he describes Jesus as having an "intuition of God" and "consciousness of God," who is "a perfectly religious personality, a spiritual life completely filled by the realization of a God who is love." [235] Furthermore, Rauschenbusch approvingly quotes Johann Fichte's description of Jesus, who wrote that "The consciousness of the absolute unity of the human and the divine life is the profoundest of insights possible to man. Before Jesus it did not exist...Jesus evidently had this insight"[236] Rauschenbusch's belief that Jesus had a unique God-relationship seems to differ from Nicaea's conception, in that it isn't clear that He believed that Jesus Himself is God. Instead, Jesus the man had a profound connection with and consciousness of the "divine life." Jesus possessed the divine (i.e. God) within himself by nature of His words and deeds. Rauschenbusch even states that he is not particularly interested in the "metaphysical problems involved in trinitarian and christological doctrines;"[237] He is not interested in how Jesus is God. Instead, Rauschenbusch's interest was in how the "divine *life* of Christ" gained control of human society.

Elsewhere, speaking in trinitarian terms, Rauschenbusch argued that the *idea* of the glorified Christ and the Holy Spirit are "nearly identical," stating "Christ and the Spirit are not two distinct forces."[238] He seems to suggest no trinitarian distinction at all between Father, Son, Spirit. In fact, Rauschenbusch suggests the Spirit of God that acted upon the early Christians was simply the inspirational words and deeds of Jesus. Speaking

---

[235] Rauschenbusch, *A Theology for the Social Gospel*, 154-155.
[236] Rauschenbusch, *A Theology for the Social Gospel*, 152.
[237] Rauschenbusch, *A Theology for the Social Gospel*, 148.
[238] Rauschenbusch, *The Righteousness of the Kingdom* , 148.

about the early Christians who had a sense of being acted upon by the Spirit of God, Rauschenbusch wrote, "do they ever conceive of [the Spirit of God] as anything but the Christ whose words they have heard and whose person they have loved as they have seen him in the gospels? Do they not feel the personal nearness and guidance and love of their Friend and Master?"[239] Instead of the two forces—Christ and Spirit—acting upon the disciples, Rauschenbusch collapsed them into the "twofold influence of the *one force*, the Logos of God."[240]

Note that the "force" of Christ and the Holy Spirit are not personal. Rather, he defined the *Logos of God* impersonally as the enduring influence of His historic appearance in human history (i.e. the life of Jesus) and the perpetual influence of Himself upon humanity (i.e. the influence of Jesus). Like Ritschl, Rauschenbusch seems to hold that Jesus is not the metaphysical but the moral Son of God. He bluntly states that questions about Christ's divinity are not about nature, but *character*: "We shall come closer to the secret of Jesus if we think less of the physical process of conception and more of the *spiritual* process of desire, choice, affirmation, and self-surrender within his own will and personality."[241] He goes on to accuse "theology" of defining Jesus' divinity in terms of *nature* rather than *character*.[242] Instead, Rauschenbusch seems to insist Jesus' divinity does not consist in an ontological fact, but as the universal human ideal of love He lived.

---

[239] Rauschenbusch, *The Righteousness of the Kingdom*, 148-149.
[240] Rauschenbusch, *The Righteousness of the Kingdom*, 149. (emph. mine)
[241] Rauschenbusch, *A Theology for the Social Gospel*, 150. (emph. mine)
[242] Rauschenbusch, *A Theology for the Social Gospel*, 150.

Ultimately, Jesus came to show humanity that their normal human existence—"the ordinary life of selfishness and hate and anxiety and chafing ambition and covetousness"—was no life at all, and instead humanity "must enter into a new world of love and solidarity and inward contentment."[243] For Rauschenbusch, then, the secret to Jesus was the new life of love He lived and brotherhood He showed that confronted and transcended the normal ways of living out human existence. Over and against this normal life of humanity, "Jesus set love into the center of the spiritual universe, and all life is illuminated from that centre. This is the highest idealistic faith ever conceived, and the greatest addition ever made to the spiritual possessions of mankind."[244] Jesus brought humanity the universal human ideal of love, which he insists solves for our human problem of selfishness. The true nature of the work of Jesus, then, was establishing the Kingdom with His life and the love and service He modeled, rather than saving humanity through His sacrificial death on the cross.

It seems clear that for Rauschenbusch, the power of Christ to solve our human problem came not through His work on the cross or even chiefly in His teachings. Rather the chief power of Christ is His personality, His enduring example.[245] Even where he comments on the social gospel and atonement, Rauschenbusch holds a solidaric interpretation of Jesus' death rather than a vicarious, substitutionary interpretation.[246] In describing the nature and impact of Jesus' death on the cross,

---

[243] Rauschenbusch, *Christianity and the Social Crisis in the 21st Century* , 42.
[244] Rauschenbusch, *A Theology for the Social Gospel*, 154.
[245] Rauschenbusch, *Righteousness and the Kingdom*, 122.
[246] Rauschenbusch, *A Theology for the Social Gospel*, 258.

Rauschenbusch insisted that Jesus bore six so-called "social sins"[247] that have impacted the whole race and everyone in it. The reader should note, however, that by using the term "bore," Rauschenbusch does not mean vicariously as a substitutionary sacrifice. Instead, he argues that Jesus bore them "by direct experience." He goes on to say, "In so far as the personal sins of men have contributed to the existence of these public sins, he came into collision with the totality of evil in mankind. it requires no legal fiction of imputation to explain that 'he was wounded for our transgressions, he was bruised for our iniquities.' Solidarity explains it."[248] Jesus' atoning death on the cross, then, is defined by his direct experience of the forces of the Kingdom of Evil and their impact on His own life, an experience that was an extension of His life.

Rauschenbusch makes clear that "the death of Christ was an integral part of his life."[249] In fact, he argues that theology makes a "fundamental mistake" when it treats the atoning death of Christ as something separate and distinct from the life of Jesus.[250] Instead, Jesus' death was "wholly of one piece with his life. He gathered all the radiance of his character and purpose in a focus-point of blazing light, and there he died."[251] Notice that

---

[247] These six sins include: 1) religious bigotry, "the most persistent force that pushed Jesus to death;" 2) the combination of bribery and political power, in which Jesus was a threat to the ruling class both politically and monetarily; 3) corruption of justice, where Jesus was a victim of the court; 4) the mob spirit and mob action, which is the "social spirit gone mad" and which Jesus bore by experience; 5) militarism, in which Jesus "fell into the hands of the war system" from the time of His arrest in Gethsemane to His crucifixion at Golgotha; and 6) class contempt, which is the contempt for the lower class by the upper class and which Jesus bore "when he was nailed to the tree." Rauschenbusch, *A Theology for the Social Gospel*, 248-257.
[248] Rauschenbusch, *A Theology for the Social Gospel*, 248.
[249] Rauschenbusch, *A Theology for the Social Gospel*, 260.
[250] Rauschenbusch, *A Theology for the Social Gospel*, 260.
[251] Rauschenbusch, *A Theology for the Social Gospel*, 260.

Jesus' character and vocation is squarely in view. At the cross Jesus' higher life, the universal human ideal that He modeled to humanity, was clearly and brightly seen; at the cross Jesus' life-purpose and Kingdom vocation culminated in the most visible and truest picture of love and service. Thus, Rauschenbusch argued that the "spiritual and redemptive value of his death" was not in suffering as a substitute but "in the willingness with which he took himself this highest and hardest part of his life-work."[252] Because Jesus' death and life were one continuous tapestry of love and service, the benefit that Jesus' followers receive from His death is identical to what they receive from His life: His "higher impulse" and model of love and service, manifested as the Kingdom of God.

Rauschenbusch maintains the "higher impulse" of Christ was implanted in His followers, and over time it has blossomed so that we are finally comprehending the "real meaning and spirit of Christ," which was His higher social life for humanity, the Kingdom of God.[253] Christ wanted His life to be in His disciples, so that they would find the chief good of their lives in him: "His thoughts became their thoughts. His sympathies and antipathies were theirs."[254] By taking upon themselves the life example of Christ through adopting His thoughts and ways, the early followers of Jesus found salvation. The same is true for us today. Jesus' life and example, rather than His death and resurrection, are what solve our human problem.

Through humanity generally, Jesus' personality—His life and example—has endured throughout history as a force that is

---

[252] Rauschenbusch, *A Theology for the Social Gospel*, 261.
[253] Rauschenbusch, *Christianity and the Social Crisis*, 115.
[254] Rauschenbusch, *Righteousness and the Kingdom*, 150.

progressively transforming society from what it is to what it ought to be. As Rauschenbusch says, "whenever [Jesus'] personality gains influence over a human soul, the result will be that that soul will go forth to live a revolutionary life."[255] Jesus' powerful example has abiding power because "his true character is forever bursting forth and impelling new men to revolutionary effort;" His life continues to inspire people throughout generations to bring social change and live their best life now.[256] Therefore, we can say that the Kingdom, rather than the atoning death of Jesus, is the mode by which humanity is saved. Jesus saves insofar as He brings in the Kingdom. Thus, as with the other liberals, the Kingdom itself is what saves us.

THE SALVATION OF THE KINGDOM

Like Schleiermacher and Ritschl before him, Rauschenbusch sought to help the Church "once more preach the Kingdom of God as the central and all-embracing doctrine,"[257] which he agreed had been neglected for most of the life of the Church. Rauschenbusch believed that the grammar of the Kingdom of God should be given a central place, because "without [the doctrine of the Kingdom of God] the idea of redeeming the social order will be but an annex to the orthodox conception of the scheme of salvation."[258] The "scheme of salvation" to which Rauschenbusch refers is the type of personal salvation common to modern evangelicalism. As he argued, the Kingdom of God

---

[255] Rauschenbusch, *Righteousness and the Kingdom*, 128-129.
[256] Rauschenbusch, *Righteousness and the Kingdom*, 129.
[257] Rauschenbusch, *Righteousness and the Kingdom*, 130.
[258] Rauschenbusch, *A Theology for the Social Gospel*, 131.

"is not a matter of saving human atoms, but of saving social organisms. It is not a matter of getting individuals to heaven, but of transforming the life on earth into the harmony of heaven." [259] Instead of an individualized hope, the Kingdom is a social hope "involving the whole social life of man." [260] Like Ritschl, Rauschenbusch's Kingdom grammar is inherently social rather than individual.

Rauschenbusch defines the social-ness of the Kingdom of God in several ways: it is the "true human society, it is a fellowship of justice, equity, and love;"[261] it means "normal and wholesome human relations;" [262] and the Kingdom is "the better humanity."[263] The Kingdom is inherently social and the highest expression of humanity. It is fundamentally defined as the progressive development of humanity from the-way-it-is to the-way-it-ought-to-be. Human progress and social hope sits at the center of Rauschenbusch's Kingdom grammar. He also described the Kingdom as a "historical force" that seeks to save the human social order within history: "The Kingdom of God is not a concept or an ideal merely, but a historical force. It is a vital and organizing energy now at work in humanity. Its capacity to save the social order depends on its pervasive presence within the social organism."[264] From where does this historical saving force come that advances and saves humanity? The history transforming force of the Kingdom comes from the

---

[259] Rauschenbusch, *Christianity and the Social Crisis*, 54.
[260] Rauschenbusch, *Christianity and the Social Crisis*, 54.
[261] Rauschenbusch, *Christianity and the Social Crisis*, 62.
[262] Rauschenbusch, *Christianity and the Social Crisis*, 62.
[263] Rauschenbusch, *Christianity and the Social Crisis*, 168.
[264] Rauschenbusch, *A Theology for the Social Gospel*, 165. (emph. mine)

historical person and continuing inspiring "presence" of Jesus Christ.

As Rauschenbusch insists, we needed someone to come along and show us a better existence, to inspire us with a better way of living the universal human ideal. That person was Jesus, and he came to solve our human problem of selfishness and bad human existence by founding the Kingdom and calling disciples to it as a great revolutionary movement "pledged to change the world-as-it-is into the world-as-it-ought-to-be."[265] Here we see Rauschenbusch's continuity with the liberal tradition of Schleiermacher and Ritschl that preceded him: our salvation comes by way of a transformation of human existence (world-as-it-is) into the human ideal (world-as-it-ought-to-be). Note the generational continuity: our human solution is found in the universal human ideal over against the problem of human existence, which, in reality, means our solution is found in ourselves.

He states plainly that human "ethical and religious forces can really do something to check and prevent the transmission of sin along social channels."[266] Rauschenbusch contrasts this social view of sin with a "biological transmission," where checking and preventing the transmission of sin is "beyond our control."[267] This Pelagian understanding of our human solution makes sense because Rauschenbusch has a Pelagian view of human nature. According to him, we on our own have the power to stem the tide of sin; human social forces can prevent social sin. Humans have the capacity within themselves to advance or retard

---

[265] Rauschenbusch, *Christianity and the Social Crisis*, 123.
[266] Rauschenbusch, *A Theology for the Social Gospel*, 68.
[267] Rauschenbusch, *A Theology for the Social Gospel*, 68.

humanity. Consequently, out of our own gumption and ingenuity we humans can and should build the Kingdom to solve our social crises, because such human progress actually "depends largely on us."[268] We have the power to change the world if we would only use it: we have "the power to win stubborn hearts, the power to uncover social lies, the power to make injustice blush and skulk away, the power to shame immodesty into hiding places."[269] Curiously, Rauschenbusch neglected the role of the Holy Spirit, relegating the power of human transformation in the force of Jesus' moral example and human gumption and ingenuity. Where he did talk about the Holy Spirit, Rauschenbusch spoke of Him merely as a "religious doctrine" and "energetic religious consciousness."[270] In omitting the Holy Spirit, humanity is all that's left to work toward bringing about the life transformation that results in social change. Instead of the Holy Spirit, the Kingdom's presence on earth depends upon humanity. We have the power to create social change because we have the power of Jesus' enduring example, which inspires us to live as we ought by living and loving as He did.

In the words of Rauschenbusch, "His life is what counted," a life that was wholly purposed on establishing the Kingdom of God, which is the "historical current of salvation" that extends from Him through history to save humanity.[271] Jesus saves because His inspiring life-example lives on in the Kingdom, which was His revolutionary movement to progress the human

---

[268] Rauschenbusch, *Righteousness and the Kingdom*, 107.
[269] Rauschenbusch, *Righteousness and the Kingdom*, 108.
[270] See Rauschenbusch, *A Theology for the Social Gospel*, 188-196.
[271] Rauschenbusch, *A Theology for the Social Gospel*, 165. (emph. mine)

social order. Jesus was able to catalyze social change because He alone "fully married the real and the ideal, the life here and the life beyond, the inward perfection and its steady reconstruction of the outward perfection."[272] Because Jesus' life successfully combined real human existence with the essence of the human ideal, He brought the force of the Kingdom to bear on human social order, resulting in universal social salvation.

Rauschenbusch believed that the Kingdom embraces all realms of society, not just the Church; the Church isn't the only place the Kingdom is present. This position is consistent with Ritschl who himself broke from Schleiermacher's conflation of the Kingdom with the Church. Rauschenbusch argued, "The Kingdom of God is not confined within the limits of the Church and its activities. It embraces the whole of human life…The Kingdom of God is in all these [social institutions] and realizes itself through them all."[273] Whether the family, industry, or State, the Kingdom of God is working to transform these social orders, Christian or not. He goes on to say that "Every approximation to [the Kingdom of God] is worthwhile. Every step toward personal purity and peace…carries its own exceeding great reward."[274] It seems that for Rauschenbusch, every human activity that aligns itself with the defining characteristics of the Kingdom counts as Kingdom activity. Every single life can join in with advancing human progress by simply accepting the Kingdom as their own task: "Every human life is so placed that it can share with God in the creation of the Kingdom, or can resist and retard its progress. The Kingdom is for each of us the supreme task and

---

[272] Rauschenbusch, *Righteousness and the Kingdom*, 130.
[273] Rauschenbusch, *A Theology for the Social Gospel*, 145.
[274] Rauschenbusch, *Christianity and the Social Crisis*, 338. (emph. mine)

the supreme gift of God." He goes on to say that if we accept the Kingdom task, then we receive the gift of the Kingdom, which is "the joy and peace of the Kingdom as our divine fatherland and habitation."[275] Again, Rauschenbusch seems to suggest that everyone experiences the gift of God's solution to our human problem by doing Kingdom acts.

There is a decidedly universal ring to Rauschenbusch's work, as he envisioned that the Kingdom extended to all of humanity. He suggested that it was guaranteed that "Christ would limit his work not by the bounds of nationality but by the bounds of humanity."[276] Thus, every step forward, "every increase in mercy, every obedience to justice, every added brightness of truth would be an extension of the reign of God in humanity, an incoming of the Kingdom of God."[277] Again, Rauschenbusch seems to suggest that every act counts as Kingdom activity, whether the person knows it or not. Rauschenbusch uses several examples to illustrate how the whole life, abilities, and interests of every person can be enlisted as Kingdom work: the life of the farmer who toils for the daily bread of humanity; the engineer who builds bridges over chasms and holds back "the seething river from the cottages of his brother" with dams; carpenters, masons and plumbers who build safe, dry, sunny houses "in which little children will not be strangled to death by poison germs;" even just lawyers and merciful doctors are included in his Kingdom Hall of Fame.[278] Each of these people illustrate how the Kingdom of God embraces every simple, useful everyday act of humanity.

---

[275] Rauschenbusch, *A Theology for the Social Gospel*, 141.
[276] Rauschenbusch, *Righteousness and the Kingdom*, 83.
[277] Rauschenbusch, *Righteousness and the Kingdom*, 88.
[278] Rauschenbusch, *Righteousness and the Kingdom*, 112.

And everyone "who fulfills the conditions of the Kingdom" are promised the salvation of Christ.[279] What are those conditions, what defines the "usefulness" of a particular activity? As with Schleiermacher and Ritschl, Rauschenbusch says useful Kingdom activity is loving activity. As long as we love we do Kingdom work; love is the Kingdom-condition.

Rauschenbusch argued that "the Kingdom of God implies a progressive reign of love in human affairs;"[280] it is the "fellowship of humanity acting under the impulse of love."[281] Because Jesus Christ Himself made love the defining characteristic of God and highest law of human activity, "the reign of God would be the reign of love."[282] And the highest expression of love is "the free surrender of what is truly our own, life, property, and rights."[283] Love is by nature self-sacrifice and the Kingdom of God is a "cooperative labor" in which we actively love others by serving their needs with our abilities.[284] Self-sacrificing service and love is at the center of the Kingdom of God because it was the way of Jesus Himself. As Rauschenbusch writes, "Jesus desired to found a society resting on love, service, and equity." He goes on to say that "when Jesus prepared men for the nobler social order of the kingdom of God, he tried to energize the faculty and habits of love and to stimulate the dormant faculty of devotion to the common good."[285] In the end this new love-defined society is exactly what defines Rauschenbusch's Kingdom grammar. And

---

[279] Rauschenbusch, *Righteousness and the Kingdom*, 97.
[280] Rauschenbusch, *A Theology for the Social Gospel*, 142.
[281] Rauschenbusch, *A Theology for the Social Gospel*, 155.
[282] Rauschenbusch, *A Theology for the Social Gospel*, 54.
[283] Rauschenbusch, *A Theology for the Social Gospel*, 143.
[284] Rauschenbusch, *A Theology for the Social Gospel*, 55.
[285] Rauschenbusch, *Christianity and the Social Crisis*, 57, 56.

this love-acting fellowship frames his solution: The Kingdom is what saves us.

CONCLUSION

Put plainly, Rauschenbusch insisted that "a man is saved according as he enters or does not enter the Kingdom."[286] The dividing lines that once existed between Jew and Greek are now along those who "open their heart to the new life" of the Kingdom and "those who are closed to it."[287] Thus, salvation is found by entering into the universal human ideal initiated by Jesus through His teachings and inspiring example of love, which all people can participate in by nature of their Kingdom-oriented activity. It will help to quote Rauschenbusch to provide a final examination of his Kingdom grammar:

> The fundamental contribution of every man is the change of his own personality. We must repent of the sins of existing society, cast off the spell of the lies of protecting our social wrongs, have faith in a higher social order, and realize in ourselves a new type of Christian manhood which seeks to overcome the evil in the present world, not by withdrawing from the world, but by revolutionizing it. 288

There are several items to note in this quotation which aptly summarizes Rauschenbusch's theological positions regarding the Kingdom of God as the solution to the human problem.

---

[286] Rauschenbusch, *Righteousness and the Kingdom*, 99.
[287] Rauschenbusch, *Christianity and the Social Crisis*, 51.
[288] Rauschenbusch, *Christianity and the Social Crisis*, 331.

Notice that Rauschenbusch has "every man" in view, which is seemingly consistent with a universalistic view of Kingdom-participation; everyone is (or has the potential to be) Kingdom-oriented, because every action of love counts as Kingdom activity. Furthermore, the problem for which "every man" must solve is the "sins of existing society" and "social wrongs." And every person has the inner capacity to "change" themselves and "realize" a new type of human existence. They apparently don't need the Holy Spirit to awaken their faith and transform their lives. Instead, individuals themselves are charged with the task of solving their own problem, which comes by "having faith in a higher social order," the universal human ideal or the Kingdom of God. Rather than calling on people to have faith in the finished work of Jesus Christ on the cross and His bodily resurrection, Rauschenbusch instead calls people to have faith in *the new way of living*, the higher way of Kingdom living. Ultimately, the object in which we are to place our faith isn't in Jesus Christ, but in the Kingdom of God, which is the consistent liberal appeal for people to have faith in their own self-potential by nature of humanity's potential. Such an appeal was strengthened and renewed one generation later with the *Kingdom* grammar of Paul Tillich.

5

Tillich's Grammar

Both Grenz and Olson maintain that Paul Tillich's contribution to 20th-century theology "is comparable to Barth's in terms of overall influence and impact," giving him the title "apostle to the intellectuals."[289] In fact, Tillich graced the cover of TIME magazine on March 16, 1959, where he was recognized for the significance of his theological and philosophical achievements. Already while Tillich was still alive, some argued that his *Systematic Theology* "could go down in history alongside the systems of Aquinas and Hegel...it will stand in the history of philosophical-theologies as one of the distinct systems and another bold attempt to wed the two sciences."[290] Furthermore, the staying power and lasting impact of Tillich has shown itself recently in apparent appropriations of his material.[291] Thus, it is

---

[289] Grenz and Olson, *Twentieth-Century Theology*, 114.

[290] R. Allan Killen, *The Ontological Theology of Paul Tillich* (Kampen, J. H. Kok, 1956.), 9.

[291] In his newest book, *Love Wins: A Book About Heaven, Hell, and the Fate of Every Person Who Ever Lived* (New York: HarperOne, 2011), Rob Bell seems to appropriate several of Tillich's existential theological concepts—including God, the person of Jesus

appropriate to examine this theological heavyweight's understanding of the Kingdom of God in order to trace the generational theological development of *Kingdom* grammar from liberalism to evangelicalism. Tillich's unique contribution to the liberal development of *Kingdom* grammar lay in his emphasis on the historical nature of the Kingdom, insisting that the Kingdom of God is the symbolic expression of both the immanent and transcendent sides of history, functioning as the answer to the problem of the meaning of human history. For Tillich, the Kingdom of God is both in and above history.

TILLICH'S HISTORICAL CONTEXT

Tillich was a German Lutheran who studied at several major universities, including Halle and Berlin, while pursuing a career in ministry. World War I interrupted his theological and ministerial pursuits where he served as a chaplain to the German Army, an experience that profoundly changed him. As Grenz and Olson explain, "His encounters with mass death and destruction became a turning point in his personal life and faith. He suffered two nervous breakdowns and underwent a severe crisis of faith and doubt that transformed his view of God."[292] It took the war to make Tillich aware of the real social conditions of Germany, particularly the conditions of the lower classes and the antagonism that existed between the Bourgeois and labor masses. [293] This social and theological transformation was

---

the Christ, Cross, Resurrection, and the Afterlife—in order to argue for a universal salvation.

[292] Grenz and Olson, *Twentieth-Century Theology*, 115.

[293] Killen, *The Ontological Theology of Paul Tillich*, 32.

solidified in his post-WWII experience in America. It was then that he joined many neo-liberals in their sober recognition of the tragic dimensions of human existence and history, a recognition that was lacking in eras before both World Wars. These historical experiences would help give rise to Tillich's theological method and system when combined with a potent philosophical one: existentialism.

In part, the re-emergence of existentialism represents a response to the irrational events of the two World Wars that form part of our historical context. The historic optimism birthed out of the Enlightenment and Industrial Revolution gave way to a realism not felt for generations. In the wake of such human tragedies as war, poverty, and urban stresses, theologians gravitated toward existentialism in order to provide a theological response to tragic twentieth-century existence. Grenz and Olson comment that Tillich "provides perhaps the most lucid example of a neo-liberal who chose existentialism as theology's conversation partner."[294]

Several characteristics of existentialism provide the backdrop to Tillich's own theology and *Kingdom* grammar: existentialism emphasizes the situation into which a person has been thrown, one's "being-in-the-world;" anxiety qualifies man's existence because he realizes that he is not at home in the world and the world is without meaning; such anxiety gives way to authentic living in order to break from ordinary everyday existence; everyday we are confronted with the alienness and meaninglessness of the world, giving us a sickening feeling of danger and insecurity; such confrontations force us to face our

---

[294] Grenz and Olson, *Twentieth-Century Theology*, 114.

fragility and alienness in the world; ultimately, our existence ends in death, the fact of which should cause us to give our lives a significance and purpose in the here and now before we are robbed of the gift of life.[295]

Tillich himself admits to standing within the existentialist movement, correlating the structure of his theology with man's existential questions and concerns. As Livingston writes, "the existentialist stance dominates Tillich's theological method and system." [296] Tillich was strongly impacted by two particular existentialists: Kierkegaard and Heidegger. In fact, Tillich's *The Courage to Be* is his existentialist attempt to solve for Kierkegaard's problems of anxiety, guilt, and despair with an ontology of Being and Non-Being.[297] And while Tillich initially found it hard to accept existentialism, it slowly took root in his mind largely as the result of Heidegger's influence.[298] Some even go so far as to say that had it not been for Heidegger's *Being in Time*, Tillich's ontology would not have developed as it did.[299] Likewise, Andrew O'Neill refers to Tillich's own self-proclaimed passion for "post-Idealist existential responses to Neo-Kantianism evident in Kierkegaard and Heidegger." [300] Particularly, existentialism dominates Tillich's *Kingdom* grammar, affecting his definitions of sin, Jesus' person and work, the Kingdom itself, and even God.

---

[295] Livingston, *Modern Christian Thought*, 348-350.
[296] Livingston, *Modern Christian Thought*, 356.
[297] Killen, *The Ontological Theology of Paul Tillich*, 52.
[298] Killen, *The Ontological Theology of Paul Tillich*, 35, 52.
[299] Wilhelm and Marion Pauck, *Paul Tillich: His Life and Thought* (New York: Harper & Row Publishers, 1989), 98.
[300] Andrew O'Neill, *Tillich: A Guide for the Perplexed* (London: T & T Clark, 2008), 29.

THE PROBLEM WHICH THE KINGDOM SOLVES

As with three generations of liberals before him, understanding how Tillich defined our human problem is vital to understanding how he defined the Kingdom. Tillich's treatment of our human problem is different than how the Church has understood it in the past, but consistent with the view of Schleiermacher, Ritschl, and Rauschenbusch. As Killen argues, "He bases his view of sin upon a consideration of the conditions which he finds in existence rather than upon the view of sin given in the Bible."[301] It is important to note at the outset that Tillich's view of sin and the human condition is predicated upon his view of God. What Tillich means by *God* has great bearing on our discussion of Tillich's *Kingdom* grammar, as it plays into his understanding of the problem for which the Kingdom solves. The vague term *Ground of Being* is how Tillich describes our sense of God, doing so in the context of estrangement.

In one sense, we are estranged from the "Ground of our being" because we are estranged from "the origin and aim of our life," estranged from the point of existence.[302] Elsewhere, Tillich indicates this terms stands for God himself: "The name of this infinite and inexhaustible depth and ground of all being is *God*. That depth is what the word *God* means."[303] Tillich does not seem to assume the existence of an actual Being alongside and above others in the traditional sense. Instead, God is understood

---

[301] Allan, *The Ontological Theology of Paul Tillich*, 185.
[302] Paul Tillich, *The Shaking of the Foundations* (New York: Charles Scribner's Sons, 1948), 155.
[303] Tillich, *Shaking of the Foundations*, 57.

as *being-itself* or as the *ground of being*. Consistently, Tillich refers to God as an *idea*, an existential idea in which God is the foundation of existence and meaning. "God" is the word that signifies that which is meaningful and gives meaning to existence. As Tillich says, "The word 'God' points to ultimate reality."[304] Note that God is merely a symbol for that which is ultimately meaningful in existence, which means we are merely estranged from the *symbol* rather than the *being* of God.

Rather than believing humanity is separated from an ontological *Being* called God, the Father almighty, maker of all things visible and invisible in the vein of Nicaea, Tillich suggested we are separated from the *aim of our life* and *center of all meaning*. As Tillich argued, "if [God] has no meaning for you, translate it, and speak of the depth of your life, of the source of your being, of your ultimate concern, of what you take seriously."[305] For Tillich, that which gives meaning to and is of ultimate concern in life, actually *is* God. We are separated and estranged from that which is meaningful in life that which is of ultimate existential concern, which leads to anxiety, despair, and death.[306] Because Tillich believed God was a symbol for that which is of ultimate meaning, Tillich views the human problem as *separation* and *estrangement* from that meaning, which leads to the conditions of meaninglessness, anxiety, and death. As Tillich said, our problem is one of historical existence: "Man's historical existence is threatened,"[307] threatened by each of these

---

[304] Tillich, *Systematic Theology*, 2:94.
[305] Tillich, *Shaking of the Foundations*, 57.
[306] Tillich, *Shaking of the Foundations*, 97.
[307] Tillich, "Victory in Defeat: The Meaning of History in Light of Christian Prophetism," Interpretation 6 (1952): 18.

conditions. Therefore, our solution must do something with our historical existence by solving our estrangement from the universal ideal.

Tillich's early definition of sin in *The Shaking of the Foundations* provides a glimpse into the formation of his doctrine of sin: "Have the men of our time still a feeling of the meaning of sin? Do they, and do we, still realize that sin does not mean an immoral act, that 'sin' should never be used in the plural, and that not our sins, but rather our sin is the great, all-pervading problem of our life?"[308] Early on, Tillich rejected the notion that sin is an act or a collection of acts, instead interpreting it as a *condition*, a *state* of man's existence. As we will see, this view is not the same as the historic Christian view of original sin. As Tillich argued, there is no "bondage of the will," no original, hereditary sin.[309] Tillich clarified his position by reinterpreting sin entirely: "I should like to suggest another word to you, not as a substitute for the word 'sin,' but as a useful clue in the interpretation of the word 'sin': 'separation'...*sin is separation*. To be in the state of sin is to be in the state of separation."[310] For Tillich, *separation* is key to understanding the human problem. Humanity is separated from that which is of ultimate meaning and the aim of life, which creates the existential conditions of anxiety, meaninglessness, despair, and death. A decade later, Tillich revised and extended this definition to mean *estrangement:* our basic human condition is a "state of estrangement of man and his world from God;"[311]

---

[308] Tillich, *Shaking of the Foundations,* 154.
[309] Tillich, *Systematic Theology,* 2:39-41.
[310] Tillich, *Shaking of the Foundations,* 154. (Italc. his); *Systematic Theology,* 2:46.
[311] Tillich, *Systematic Theology,* 2:27.

"estrangement points to the basic characteristic of man's predicament."[312]

Tillich did not believe that an original state of Edenic perfection existed. Instead, an original perfection of humanity is rooted in what Tillich called our "state of essential being" and a state of so-called "dreaming innocence,"[313] both symbols and a *state of mind* that signify the way humanity ought to be in created goodness in their essential nature. Accordingly, the traditional notion of "the Fall" is merely a symbol for our "transition from essential to existential being."[314] This transition (i.e. Fall) from essentiality—the ideal of how man *ought to be* in his goodness—to existential estrangement—the reality of *how man is* in his meaningless condition and separation from the aim of life—is simply part of human development and growth.[315] In other words, while humanity is innately good, throughout humanity's evolutionary development they have always been estranged from ethical actions that pave the way for that which is of ultimate meaning in life. Thus, man has never been or acted the way he ought. For this reason, like Schleiermacher, Ritschl, and Rauschenbusch before him, Tillich reinterpreted original sin, viewing it not in hereditary terms but in existential terms. As Tillich argued, "The transition from essence to existence is not an *event* in time and space but the transhistorical *quality* of all events in time and space."[316] The importance of the idea of the Fall is not that it *happened*, but that it *happens*. Adam is merely a

---

[312] Tillich, *Systematic Theology*, 2:39, 44, 45.
[313] Tillich, *Systematic Theology*, 2:33.
[314] Tillich, *Systematic Theology*, 2:30.
[315] Tillich, *Systematic Theology*, 2:33.
[316] Tillich, *Systematic Theology*, 2:40. (emph. mine)

symbol for essential man—how he ought to be, what is the ideal—and symbolizes the transition from essence to existence; original sin is simply the "universal destiny of estrangement" that plagues all people.[317] Thus, Tillich insisted that original sin is much more a universal fact and state than a nature out of which individuals act; in their own existence, individuals actualize the universal state of human existence.[318] Because we are separated from the ultimate meaning of existence (i.e. God), we experience a number of negative "consequences" that wreak havoc on our self-existence.

In his existential condition, man is in a state of despair, the pain of which stems from the conflict between what he potentially is (essence) and what he actually is (existence), resulting in self-estrangement.[319] The consequences of this self-estrangement is the loss of meaning and a despairing existence, which ultimately results in death: "Estranged from the ultimate power of being, man is determined by his finitude. He is given over to his natural fate. He came from nothing, and he returns to nothing. He is under the dominion of death and is driven by the anxiety of having to die."[320] Though sin is not the cause of death, it is its sting; self-estrangement from that which is of ultimate meaning is the pain of death, which is much more symbolic than literal: "Death has become powerful—that is to say that the End, the finite, and the limitations and decay of our being have become visible..."[321] According to Tillich, we are not separated

---

[317] Tillich, *Systematic Theology*, 2:56.
[318] Tillich, *Systematic Theology*, 2:56.
[319] Tillich, *Systematic Theology*, 2:75.
[320] Tillich, *Systematic Theology*, 2:66.
[321] Tillich, *New Being*, 170, 171.

from our Creator through collective and personal rebellion, but separated from that which is of ultimate meaning in life, resulting in meaningless, fearful, tragic, miserable existence, culminating in death. Our solution, therefore, must be one that conquers our self-estrangement and brings in love, which Tillich explained is stronger than the conditions of existence.[322] For that, we needed a bearer of a solution of love and new existence who shared in our existential condition, yet triumphed over it. We found such a bearer in the existence of Jesus, who brought us the Kingdom by showing us a new, better existence, one we can participate in by following His teachings and deeds.

THE BEARER OF THE KINGDOM: THE PERSON & WORK OF JESUS

Central to any *Kingdom* grammar is how it defines the person and work of Jesus. There is a consistent pattern among liberal theologians in their definition of Jesus that subsequently shifts their *Kingdom* grammar. Tillich views the historical conceptions of the nature of Jesus (as the) Christ as wholly inadequate to understanding the person of Jesus.[323] Whereas the historic Christian faith frames Christology as two natures (i.e. God and human), Tillich argued, "The assertion that Jesus as the Christ is the personal unity of a divine and human nature must be replaced by the assertion that in Jesus as the Christ the eternal

---

[322] Tillich, *New Being*, 172.

[323] As he says, ""The doctrine of the two natures in the Christ raises the right questions but uses wrong conceptual tools. The basic inadequacy lies in the term 'nature.' When applied to man, it is ambiguous; when applied to God, it is wrong. This explains the inescapable definitive failure of the councils, e.g. of Nicaea and Chalcedon."; Tillich, *Systematic Theology*, 2:142.

unity of God and man has become a historical reality."[324] Instead, Jesus is "divine" because the essence of the universal human ideal (i.e. God) became a historical reality in His life. Consistent with the other liberal theologians, Jesus is the moral Son of God, not the metaphysical one.

In describing Jesus' divinity, Tillich used language similar to Schleiermacher, Ritschl and Rauschenbusch to emphasize His loving life and character. Some typical examples include: "In the picture of Jesus...is the picture of a man in whom God was manifest in a unique way;"[325] "They look at a life which never lost the communication with the divine ground of all life, and they look at a life which never lost the union of love with all beings;"[326] Jesus is "one man in whom God was present without limit...;"[327] "In the face of Jesus the Christ, God 'makes his face shine upon us."[328] Tillich goes on to say that the Gospels give us a picture of Jesus' existence that never broke with the universal human ideal, despite His participation in "the ambiguities of human life;" through His words, deeds, and sufferings we see the expression of this universal human ideal.[329] Thus for Tillich, the words and deeds, the teachings and life of Jesus equate Him with the divine. Jesus is divine because He maintained a unity with the essence of ultimate meaning, which in the end cashes out as love (i.e. God).[330] In Jesus, ultimate existence is present because

---

[324] Tillich, *Systematic Theology*, 2:148.
[325] Tillich, *Systematic Theology*, 2:146.
[326] Tillich, *New Being*, 74.
[327] Tillich, *New Being*, 178-179.
[328] Tillich, *New Being*, 100.
[329] Tillich, *Systematic Theology*, 1:135-136.
[330] In *The New Being*, 26, Tillich seems to suggest God and love are not two realities but one, where the statement "God is love" is taken to mean God is *equated* with love, rather than *characterized* by it. As Tillich later wrote, "It is a rare gift to meet a human being in whom love—and *this means God*—is so overwhelmingly manifest...For God is

"God" is present and unveiled in the picture of Jesus; the universal human ideal of loving activity was present in Jesus' existence. In His existence we find the essence of our salvation, the New Being, which is the Kingdom of God.

In *The New Being*, Tillich defines the central message of Christianity as the message of a new existence, the New Being that appeared with Jesus who brought a new state of things.[331] The New Being is contrasted with the old being, the old state of things under existential estrangement, and finds its historical expression in the symbol *Kingdom of God*. The New Being—a term synonymous with the Kingdom of God—is a reality "in which the self-estrangement of our existence is overcome, a reality of reconciliation and reunion, of creativity, meaning, and hope."[332] Tillich makes plain that Jesus the man, as the Christ, is the bearer of this new way of existing, of the Kingdom of God. Jesus' existence and life on earth made Him the Christ, the bearer of the New Being, because He possessed the characteristics and qualities of the one who has overcome estrangement and separation from that which is of ultimate meaning in life, mainly love. [333] As with Schleiermacher, Ritschl, and Rauschenbusch before him, Tillich believed our solution is found in Jesus' *life*, not His death, though Tillich did believe the cross mattered.

---

love. And in every moment of genuine love we are dwelling in God and God in us;" Tillich, *New Being*, 29. For Tillich, God is an experience of that which is ultimately meaningful and essential to good existence, which is love. In other words, God actually *is* Love.

[331] Tillich, *New Being*, 15.

[332] Tillich, *Systematic Theology*, 1:49.

[333] Tillich, *Systematic Theology*, 2:121.

For Tillich, the "Cross of Christ" was an extension of His life and is where Jesus' "subjection to existence is expressed."[334] Tillich was not so much concerned with a single event in history in which Jesus was nailed to and hung from a cross. For him, the *story* of the cross of Jesus is what counts: "The story of the Cross of Jesus as the Christ does not report an isolated event in his life, but that event toward which the story of his life is directed and in which the others receive their meaning."[335] The cross, then, merely symbolizes the whole of Christ's cruciform life, the meaning of which is that He subjected himself to the ultimate negativities of existence, which He did not allow to separate Him from that which is of ultimate meaning in life.[336] Tillich insisted it was through the negation at the cross by the old existence that the new reality of the Kingdom was born here and now, which is what ultimately "saves" humanity. The New Being is the new reality that enables personal conquest over separation from ultimate meaning because of our existence. It is a saving "power" that triumphs over existence. The saving work of Jesus, then, is to be conceived of as the healing and saving power of the New Being right now in history that came through Jesus' life and culminated in His death.[337] The New Being is central to Tillich's *Kingdom* grammar, providing the solution to our human problem, which is found wherever essence overcomes existence, wherever love is actualized in existence through human progress.

---

[334] Tillich, *Systematic Theology*, 2:153.
[335] Tillich, *Systematic Theology*, 2:158.
[336] Tillich, *Systematic Theology*, 2:158.
[337] Tillich, *Systematic Theology*, 2:167.

Though Jesus is considered the bearer of the New Being because He brought the Kingdom, Tillich seems to suggest He isn't necessarily the exclusive saving power of the New Being: "he is the ultimate *criterion* of every healing and saving power...in him the healing quality is complete and unlimited. Therefore *wherever* there is saving power in mankind, it must be judged by the saving power of Jesus as the Christ."[338] In other words, while Jesus is the *standard* for salvation—in that He bore and represented the new reality of existential conquest with the Kingdom in His life and death—He is not the exclusive entry point into it. Instead, He stands as a model for *anything* that brings hope, healing, reconciliation, and love. Where there is healing, there is the New Being and the Kingdom in history; where there is love, there is the Kingdom of God. Love powerfully solves our problem, because it creates what Tillich calls the *unambiguous life*, the new existence of the Kingdom. Tillich often frames our human problem—existential estrangement—using the term *ambiguity*. Ambiguity is the gap between the essential and the existential, between the intended created goodness and estrangement from that goodness. The quest for the New Being, then, is a "quest for the unambiguous life...All creatures long for an unambiguous fulfillment of their essential possibilities." [339] In other words, humans want to reconcile *how they are* with *how they ought to be*, to reconcile reality with ideality. The unambiguous life is rooted in the reality of the Kingdom, the true nature of Jesus' work that provides the answer to meaningless historical existence. Tillich

---

[338] Tillich, *Systematic Theology*, 2:168. (emph. mine)
[339] Tillich, *Systematic Theology*, 3:107.

envisioned the personal and historic saving effects of the manifestation of the New Being of the Kingdom threefold: participation, acceptance, and transformation. These three characteristics reflect the classical theological categories for Jesus' saving work: Regeneration, Justification, and Sanctification.

First, Tillich emphasized that "the saving power of the New Being in Jesus as the Christ is dependent on man's participation in it." [340] Jesus brought the new eon of the Kingdom and individuals are called to enter that new reality, participating in it and being reborn in that participation. [341] For Tillich, participation in the New Being comes through faith, which he defined as *"the courage to say yes to one's own life and life in general, in spite of the driving forces of fate, in spite of the insecurities of daily existence, in spite of the catastrophes of existence and the breakdown of meaning;"*[342] it is the *"reception of the message that one is accepted."*[343] Acceptance of one's acceptance, then, is the entry-point into the new reality of the Kingdom and solution to our problem of meaningless, anxious existence. After this self-acceptance through regeneration comes the central event of salvation: Justification. For Tillich, Justification is the act of "making man that which he essentially is from which he is estranged," which he argues is in no way dependent on man himself, but instead is God's acceptance of humanity despite themselves. [344] In reality, however, the

---

[340] Tillich, *Systematic Theology*, 2:176.
[341] Tillich, *Systematic Theology*, 2:177.
[342] Tillich, *New Being*, 53. (emph. mine)
[343] Tillich, *Systematic Theology*, 3:130; 2:85. (emph. mine)
[344] Tillich, *Systematic Theology*, 2:178.

reconciliation of which justification provides is not to a being *God*. Instead, we are reconciled to *existence* because we cease to be hostile toward ourselves, a hostility that manifests itself in self-rejection, disgust, and self-hatred.[345] Ultimately, then, we are called to be reconciled to *ourselves* in our existential condition. Tillich says this very thing when he remarkably equates reconciliation to God with reconciliation to ourselves.[346]

That Tillich framed reconciliation as self-centered rather than God-centered makes sense considering he believes the questions of the past—How do I become liberated from the Law? (Paul); How do I find a merciful God? (Luther)—are replaced by a new one: How do I find meaning in a meaningless world?[347] Finding myself, making sense of my life, and exploring self-meaning leads to salvation. According to Tillich, a person is justified "because they are accepted with respect to the ultimate meaning of their lives."[348] Is this not simply double-speak for a person accepting the meaning of their own lives, or perhaps accepting how they ought to live (i.e. their essentiality) as a way of creating meaning for themselves in their meaningless existence? Tillich himself said that a person experiences this mark of the Kingdom when "one accepts one's self as something which is eternally important, eternally loved, eternally accepted. The disgust at one's self, the hatred of one's self has disappeared."[349] Deep reconciliation to and acceptance of one's own self-existence, then, is the heart of Tillich's *Kingdom*

---

[345] Tillich, *New Being*, 21.
[346] Tillich, *New Being*, 21.
[347] Tillich, *Systematic Theology*, 3:227.
[348] Tillich, *Systematic Theology*, 3:228.
[349] Tillich, *New Being*, 22.

grammar. Reconciliation to God was not Tillich's concern; he was concerned with self-reconciliation to one's self-existence.

Finally, after participating in the New Being of the Kingdom and accepting that they are accepted, humanity experiences salvation as transformation by the New Being of the Kingdom. Tillich defined this transformation as, "the process in which the power of the New Being transforms personality and community, inside and outside the church." [350] Sanctification is the progressive conquest of the ambiguities of the personal life, a closing of the gap between essential goodness and existential estrangement, between how man ought to be and how he is, between ideality and reality.[351] Tillich conceived this process of transformation as a completely human endeavor. Humanity has the power within itself—by consequence of Jesus' participation and overcoming of existential estrangement and his example of love by living the universal human ideal—to close the gap and make the transition from essence to existence, from *life-as-it-is* to *life-as-it-ought-to-be*.

While the effects of Jesus' saving Kingdom-work are historical in scope, it is clear they apply to individuals universally, too. As Tillich stated, "Only if salvation is understood as the healing and saving power through the New Being in all history is the problem put on another level. In some degree *all men participate* in the healing power of the New Being.[352]" As he wrote elsewhere, "No longer is the universe subject to the law of death out of birth. It is subject to a higher law, to the law of life out of death by the death of him who

---

[350] Tillich, *Systematic Theology*, 2:179-180.
[351] Tillich, *Systematic Theology*, 2:180.
[352] Tillich, *Systematic Theology*, 2:167. (emph. mine)

represented eternal life." In His suffering and death Jesus as the Christ represented the height of ultimate meaning, which means that "nature has received another meaning; history is transformed and you and I are no more what we were."[353] *All individuals* right now participate in the inner/trans-historical reality of the New Being found in the symbol of the Kingdom of God, because the ultimate solution to our human problem is the Kingdom; the *Kingdom* is what saves us.

THE SALVATION OF THE KINGDOM

For Tillich, the Kingdom of God "is the answer to the ambiguities of man's historical existence, but because of the multidimensional unity of life, the symbol includes the answer to the ambiguity under the historical dimension in all realms of life...[It] embraces the destiny of the life of the universe..." In the symbol *Kingdom of God*, historical existence is conquered in an ultimate transformation and fulfillment of history.[354] The Kingdom of God stands as the historical symbol for the ultimate meaning and aim of all life universal through the appearance of the new eon. This new eon is the reunion of *essence* and *existence* experienced within human life and history.[355] Jesus of Nazareth as the Christ was the one who brought in the new eon and with it the end of history. As Tillich argued, "In Jesus as the Christ the kingdom of God is present...Jesus is the Christ, that is, he who

---

[353] Tillich, *New Being*, 178-179.
[354] Tillich, "Victory in Defeat," 23.
[355] The term *existence* is the real, the way things are; *essence* is the universal ideal, the way things ought to be.

brings the kingdom."[356] With the event of Jesus, the reality of the Kingdom of God appeared in a personal life and created a group with a historical consciousness, the church.[357] This symbol, which was instantiated in the person and life of Jesus and later His church, is the answer to the concrete ways in which the gap between the ideal and real is expressed in humanity's historical existence; it is the means by which we are saved. The symbol includes both "the struggle of unambiguous life with the forces which make for ambiguity, and the ultimate fulfillment toward which history runs."[358] Tillich's *Kingdom* grammar, then, includes both the inner-historical and transhistorical.

Tillich was dissatisfied with the typical, liberal definitions of the Kingdom that centered on progressivistic, utopian, and transcendental interpretations of history.[359] Tillich instead reinterpreted the Kingdom of God as the answer to the questions implied in historical existence, specifically the meaning of history,[360] though his ultimate answer seems as progressivistic and utopian as previous generations. In his own definition, Tillich's unique contribution to liberal *Kingdom* grammar lay in his immanent-transcendent dichotomy: "[The Kingdom of God] has an inner-historical and a transhistorical side. As inner-historical, it participates in the dynamics of history; as transhistorical, it answers the questions in the ambiguities of the dynamics of history."[361] Tillich's *Kingdom* grammar has both a

---

[356] Tillich, "Victory in Defeat," 25.
[357] Tillich, "Victory in Defeat," 25. Tillich also equates *existence* with ambiguity and *essence* with unambiguous life.
[358] Tillich, *Systematic Theology*, 3:108.
[359] Tillich, *Systematic Theology*, 3:356.
[360] Paul Tillich, "Victory in Defeat: Meaning of History in Light of Christian Prophetism," *Interpretation* 6 (1952): 23.
[361] Tillich, *Systematic Theology*, 3:357.

dynamic and static element, an immanent and transcendent element: "It works and struggles in history and it is the eternal fulfillment beyond history...The Kingdom of God is fighting in history and victorious above history."[362] Tillich insisted that in order for the symbol *Kingdom of God* to provide a proper answer to the questions concerning the meaning of history, it must be immanent and transcendent at the same time. The terms *Spiritual Presence* and *Eternal Life* both help Tillich's *Kingdom* grammar explain the Kingdom of God's activity in and above history and salvation of humanity.

The first side of the Kingdom of God is what Tillich called the *Spiritual Presence*. It is the inner-historical, immanent aspect of his *Kingdom* grammar. Tillich said the Spiritual Presence is "the presence of the Divine Life within creaturely life;"[363] it manifests itself in all history and "acts upon [Mankind] in every moment...there is always New Being in history;"[364] and the Spiritual Presence is a "meaning-bearing power which grasps the human spirit in an ecstatic experience."[365] This symbol stands as the power that brings meaning to bear upon the experience of an individual at the point the human mind is grasped by that which is of ultimate meaning.[366] Furthermore, the Spiritual Presence is the guide of what Tillich termed *essentialization*, the inner-historical process of regaining one's essence: "the Spiritual

---

[362] Tillich, "Victory in Defeat," 24.

[363] Tillich, *Systematic Theology*, 3:107.

[364] Tillich, *Systematic Theology*, 3:140.

[365] Tillich, *Systematic Theology*, 3:115. *Ecstasy* is the "state of being grasped by the Spiritual Presence," or the human spirit under the conditions of existence being under the control of the universal human ideal. Ibid, 3:114.

[366] Tillich, *Systematic Theology*, 1:111-12, describes ecstasy in this way: "Ecstasy ('standing outside one's self') points to a state of mind which is extraordinary in the sense that the mine transcends its ordinary situation...Ecstasy occurs only if the mind is grasped by the mystery, namely, by the ground of being and meaning."

Presence elevates the human spirit into the transcendent union of unambiguous life and gives the immediate certainty of reunion with God."[367] In tangible form, the Spiritual Presence embodies itself in the so-called *Spiritual Community,* created by the New Being under the conditions of finite existence,[368] which is really any group that embodies the universal human ideal of love. Spiritual Community isn't identical with Christian churches, but is a catch-all word for all who give themselves over to the Kingdom of God, the universal human ideal.

The second aspect of the Kingdom of God and symbol for the unambiguous life above history is *Eternal Life.* It is the transcendent side of the resolution to the problem of ambiguity, symbolizing the fulfillment of history and the "permanently present end of history."[369] In this fulfillment, Tillich argued that somehow the positive elements of history—which are taken as positive human progress, especially ethical—live on while the negative parts of humanity are removed. [370] He argued that which has been created will not be lost—including all humans— only the elements of existence that are contrary to the essence of life will be removed. This end, however, is actually not really an end at all. Instead, Tillich envisioned it as present; the future end is present now.

---

[367] Tillich, *Systematic Theology*, 3:128.

[368] Tillich, *Systematic Theology*, 3:150.

[369] Tillich, *Systematic Theology*, 3:396.

[370] Tillich, *Systematic Theology*, 3:397. As Tillich writes, "nothing which has been created in history is lost, but it is liberated from the negative elements with which it is entangled within existence. The positive becomes manifest as unambiguously positive and the negative becomes manifest as unambiguously negative in the elevation of history to eternity. Eternal Life, then, includes the positive content of history, liberated from its negative distortions and fulfilled in its potentialities."

Tillich re-interpreted *eternal* to mean *right now*, hence his well-known phrase the *eternal now*. He argued that the past and future meet in the present, that both are included in the "now." Accordingly, "the eschaton becomes a matter of present experience without losing its futuristic dimension: we stand *now* in the face of the eternal, but we do so looking ahead toward the end of history and the end of all that is temporal in the eternal."[371] What is clear is that there is no terminus to history, in the classical Christian sense; history is not fulfilled but rather history continues to unfold and is elevated to the eternal—that which is of ultimate meaning in existence. What happens now, then, is a progressive "burning" of that which is negative in favor of that which is positive, which is symbolized by the idea of ultimate judgment. Tillich argued that *judgment* means "here and now, in the permanent transition of the temporal to the eternal, the negative is defeated in its claim to be positive, a claim it supports by using the positive and mixing ambiguously with it."[372] Notice that people are not in view here, but non-entities called "the positive" and "the negative," which might include the negative outcomes of human progress like pollution and ethical actions like war. While both terms are incredibly vague, they must be synonyms for the *essential* and *existential* that Tillich argues throughout his works. In other words, *Eternal Life*—the transhistorical side of the Kingdom of God—is the *telos*, the aim of human development; it is that which is essentially positive in place of the existentially negative. This aspect of the Kingdom is a present experience of future ends, a transition from essence to

---

[371] Tillich, *Systematic Theology*, 3:396.
[372] Tillich, *Systematic Theology*, 3:397.

existence right here and now in which humanity is saved through right-now human progress.

As with Schleiermacher, Ritschl, and Rauschenbusch before him, human progress right now is central to Tillich's *Kingdom* grammar and human salvation. Tillich wrote, "The hope of the Kingdom of God is not the expectation of a perfect stage at the end of history...The hope of mankind lies in the here and now, whenever the eternal appears in time and history," whenever the universal human ideal shows up in human existence.[373] In many ways, the Kingdom is an ongoing activity that "is happening always in history, the fight of the divine and the demonic, the defeat and the ultimate victory of the kingdom of God"[374] in our human existence in which we recover our essence from existence in history. The Kingdom and the salvation it brings is manifested historically whenever there is human progress and development, including pre-Christianity with Israel's exodus from Egypt, "the East-West encounter in present-day Japan," and development of Western culture in the last 500 years.[375] Tillich's *Kingdom* grammar is the historical progressive gap-closing process between essence and existence, which seems to cash-out as humanistic progress. Ending racism, curing cancer, and building the United Nations—all good things for sure—are modern day marks of human progress, marks of the unambiguous life in history and expressions of the Kingdom of God. Fundamental to this human progress and unambiguous life is love.

Tillich insisted that the Kingdom progressively unfolds through acts of love, a consistent element of the Kingdom

---

[373] Paul Tillich, "The Right to Hope," *The Christian Century* 107 no 33 (1990): 1066.
[374] Tillich, "Victory in Defeat," 26.
[375] Tillich, *Systematic Theology*, 3:365.

grammar that has developed from Schleiermacher thus far: "The Kingdom of God does not come in one dramatic event sometime in the future. It is coming here and now in every act of love...."[376] Tillich states plainly that "the Kingdom of God is the universal actualization of love."[377] Furthermore, he states that the communal expression of the Kingdom—the Spiritual Community—is fundamentally a community of love.[378] Likewise the church, one form of the Spiritual Community that embodies the Kingdom, is fundamentally a community of love.[379] Love is fundamental to the Kingdom because, as Tillich argued, faith and love cannot be separated because faith is the "state of being grasped by the Spiritual Presence," by the inner-historical side of the Kingdom, which is the universal human ideal of love.[380] Thus, love is central to one's religious experience and communal expression of that experience, because when one exercises faith one exercises love. Because the Kingdom comes here and now in every act of love, Tillich's Kingdom grammar has the familiar ring of universalism.

Tillich makes it clear that anything that brings meaning to history counts as Kingdom activity. Using the Greek word *kairos* to describe the in-breaking event of the central manifestation of the Kingdom, Tillich argued that this appearance "is again and again re-experienced through relative '*kairoi*' in which the Kingdom of God manifests itself in a particular breakthrough," [381] suggesting the Kingdom manifests itself

---

[376] Tillich, "The Right to Hope," 1066. (emph. mine)
[377] Tillich, *Systematic Theology*, 3:413.
[378] Tillich, *Systematic Theology*, 3:156.
[379] Tillich, *Systematic Theology*, 3:177, 178.
[380] Tillich, *Systematic Theology*, 3:177.
[381] Tillich, *Systematic Theology*, 3:370.

universally in various ways. As he says, the "Kingdom of God and the Spiritual Presence are never absent in any moment of time...The Kingdom of God is always present..." reinforcing the universal symbol *Kingdom*.[382] Furthermore, his use of the terms *Spiritual Community* and *the churches* suggests a universalism. As Tillich explains, "The predicate of intensive universality keeps the churches wide open—*as wide as life universal*. Nothing that is created and essentially good is excluded from the life of the churches and their members." He goes on to say "There is nothing in nature, nothing in man, and nothing in history which does not have a place in the Spiritual Community and, therefore, in the churches of which the Spiritual Community is the dynamic essence."[383] *The churches* do not seem to correlate with The Church,[384] but instead function as a catch-all for any "spiritual presence" that helps progress historical existence toward the universal human ideal and fights against the forces that impede this transition from existence to essence.[385] There are Christian varieties that stand as the "manifest church," but also "latent churches" that seem to have no connection with Christianity, yet have always manifested the Kingdom in embodied form [i.e. Spiritual Community] throughout history.[386] Everyone, then, can solve our problem by advancing humanity through acts of love. In the end everyone wins because love wins through the saving power of the Kingdom.

---

[382] Tillich, *Systematic Theology*, 3:317, 372.
[383] Tillich, *Systematic Theology*, 3:170. (emph. mine)
[384] In *Systematic Theology*, 3:377.
[385] Tillich, *Systematic Theology*, 3:375.
[386] Tillich, *Systematic Theology*, 3:376.

CONCLUSION

Like Schleiermacher, Ritschl, and Rauschenbusch before him, Tillich defined the Kingdom of God as a progressive unfolding of the universal human ideal within historical existence that ultimately saves humanity. Though his own *Kingdom* grammar was shaped by Existentialism, it was still consistent with three prior generations of Protestant liberal grammar. Humans are affected by their miserable, meaningless existence, which causes them to actualize the universal state of sin in their own existence. They are not the problem; their environment and existence is. The solution to that problem of bad existence must do something to help re-construct a meaningful existence. That meaningful existence came with the person of Jesus, who successfully conquered human existence by living the universal human ideal. He didn't just found the Kingdom, as other liberals have suggested; He *was* the Kingdom by nature of His loving life, which climaxed in His death.

As with three liberal generations, the Kingdom is the mode by which humanity is saved, rather than the work of Jesus on the cross. Jesus saves insofar as He brings in the Kingdom, rather than through His atoning death. Thus, the Kingdom itself is what saves us, and all of humanity can and will benefit from this saving power. Humanity as a whole, in light of the historic actualization of the universal human ideal in the life of Jesus in human existence, can conquer their own estrangement from the universal human ideal. What all people must do is accept that they are already accepted. A person must simply accept that he already has all that he needs to live his best meaning-filled life right now, in this life.

6

McLaren's Grammar

Thus far, we have traced the generational development of Protestant liberal *Kingdom* grammar. McLaren's grammar includes several of their features. He teaches that sin is social and environmental, rather than an inherited sinful nature and guilt; Jesus is the moral, rather than metaphysical, Son of God; in founding the Kingdom of God, it was necessary that Jesus lived but he gives no compelling reason that Jesus' death was necessary; the Kingdom of God is concerned with humanity's progress; the Kingdom comes into the here-and-now through the power of loving human action; it is inclusive, in that every act counts as Kingdom acts; it is universalistic, in that everyone will be saved; the Kingdom centers on the words, deeds, and suffering of Jesus—His inspiring personality provides humanity the proper example of the universal human ideal; and ultimately, the Kingdom is concerned with bringing the universal human ideal to bear on human existence, empowering individuals and society to reach their fullest potential and live their best life right now.

Our purpose in tracing the development of Protestant liberal kingdom grammar is to show how a progressive form of contemporary evangelicalism is the twenty-first century expression of that grammar. Here, we turn toward the task of proving the original thesis of this examination: the *Kingdom* grammar of the Emergent Church movement is continuous with four previous generations of Protestant liberalism, including how it defines the Kingdom of God, who is in, how one gets in, and how it solves for our human problem. From Schleiermacher through Ritschl, Rauschenbusch, and Tillich, one can trace the general themes of Protestant liberalism to the Emerging Church movement, particularly to one of its most well-known articulators, Brian McLaren. While he might eschew the "liberal" label,[387] he has obviously perpetuated Protestant liberal *Kingdom* grammar. And though some may say no single voice speaks for the Emergent Church movement,[388] it is clear he is one of the most significant theological voices in the movement, someone who is referred to as the "grandfather" of the Emergent Church. Therefore, it is appropriate to examine his *Kingdom* grammar in order to understand how the generational development of liberal *Kingdom* grammar is impacting contemporary Evangelicalism.

MCLAREN'S HISTORICAL CONTEXT

In 2001 Brian McLaren, a little known pastor just north of Washington D.C., began influencing street-level theological

---

[387] See McLaren, *A Generous Orthodoxy*, 131-143.
[388] Tony Jones, *The New Christians: Dispatches from the Emergent Frontier* (San Francisco: Jossey-Bass, 2008), 231. The reference is included in Appendix B: "A Response to Our Critics," from 2005.

conversations within evangelicalism with his landmark book, *A New Kind of Christian.* [389] Through the book's two protagonists—Pastor Dan and Neo—McLaren took the reader on a redefining journey through evangelical's core theological doctrines. God, creation, sin, Christ, the cross, resurrection, and judgment were all addressed and countered with alternative possibilities that formed the foundation for the Emerging Church conversation. It was also a reflection of his own spiritual journey, one that began with fundamentalism via the Plymouth Brethren and culminated in "a quest for honesty, for authenticity, and for a faith that made more sense to me and to others...learning that there is a kind of faith that runs deeper than mere beliefs."[390] Many in our post-9/11, recession-racked, socially-upended world who entered this church conversation found resonance with McLaren's own spiritual quest.

Those seeking to do Christianity on the other side of modernity have found solace in the questions and alternative answers offered by McLaren in response to what many perceive to be stogy, stuffy, stale theology that has outlived its lifecycle. In place of a theology he claims is beholden to modernity, McLaren insists "we need a new way of believing, not simply new answers to the same old questions, but a new set of questions. We are acknowledging that the Christianities we have created deserve to be reexamined and deconstructed...so that our religious traditions can be seen for what they are...they are evolving,

---

[389] McLaren has since retired from pastoring *Cedar Ridge Community Church* and been named one of the "25 Most Influential Evangelicals In America," *Time Magazine*, February 7, 2005.

[390] McLaren, *A New Kind of Christianity*, 6, 8.

embodied, situated versions of the faith." [391] Like other Emergents, McLaren has set out to construct a new, fresh, alternative Christianity in light of postmodernity, because he like others realized "something isn't working in the way we're doing Christianity any more."[392]

Of postmodernism, McLaren writes, "I see the postmodern conversation as a profoundly moral project in intension at least, a kind of corporate repentance among European intellectuals in the decades after the Holocaust."[393] In embracing the *generous orthodoxy* descriptor of Hans Frei, McLaren embraces a post-foundationalism posture characteristic of postmodernism to describe his flavor of Christianity. [394] Postmodernism as an intellectual movement surfaced in the late 1960s as a surrogate to the post-structuralism of France, which itself was rooted in Kantian philosophy. [395] As Carl Raschke explains, "Postmodernism in this sense was nothing more or less than a theory of language that served to demystify previous theories of language routinely utilized to undercut the language of belief,"[396] particularly the "language of belief" rooted in modernity. Stanley Grenz notes, "postmodernism signifies the quest to move beyond modernism. Specifically, it involves a rejection of the modern-mindset, but launched under the conditions of

---

[391] McLaren, *A New Kind of Christianity*, 18, 27.
[392] McLaren, *A New Kind of Christianity*, 9.
[393] Brian McLaren, "Church Emerging: Or Why I Still Use the Word *Postmodern* but with Mixed Feelings," in *An Emergent Manifesto of Hope* (Ed. Doug Pagitt and Tony Jones; Grand Rapids: BakerBooks, 2007, 144.
[394] See McLaren, *A Generous Orthodoxy*.
[395] Carl Raschke, *The Next Reformation: Why Evangelicals Must Embrace Postmodernity* (Grand Rapids: Baker Academic, 2004), 35, 37.
[396] Raschke, *The Next Reformation*, 37.

modernity."[397] Grenz goes on to describe how the modern mind is defined by the Enlightenment project, which exalted the individual rational man to the center of the universe. The goal of the human intellectual quest was "to unlock the secrets of the universe in order to master nature for human benefit and create a better world," an ethos that particularly characterized the twentieth century through technology.[398] Postmodernism, on the other hand, says there can be no objective, autonomous knower because knowledge is not mechanistic and dualistic, but historical, relational, communal, and personal; reality is relative, indeterminate, intuited and participatory.[399] Three names are almost routinely associated with the postmodern project: Jacque Derrida, Jean François Lyotard, and Michael Foucault.

Derrida is considered the father of French deconstruction, a method for rethinking long held beliefs and intellectual assumptions. One of his primary contributions to postmodern philosophy was his often repeated phrase: "there is nothing outside the text." Here, Derrida champions the postmodern sentiment that interpretation is an inescapable part of being human and experiencing the world; life is interpretation all the way down because we all bring something to the table out of our cultural, economic, and religious context. For postmoderns, no realm of pure reading exists beyond the realm of interpretation. Lyotard is known for his "incredulity toward metanarratives," which isn't so much a rejection of grand stories, but the manner in which those stories legitimize themselves. In other words, it is

---

[397] Stanley Grenz, *A Primer on Postmodernism* (Grand Rapids: Eerdmans Publishing, 1996), 2.

[398] Stanley Grenz, *A Primer on Postmodernism*, 3.

[399] Stanley Grenz, *A Primer on Postmodernism*, 7-8.

not the stories themselves that are the problem, but the way they are told (and to a degree why they are told). As James K. A. Smith argues, "For Lyotard, metanarratives are a distinctly modern phenomenon: they are stories that not only tell a grand story, but claim to be able to legitimate or prove the story's claim by an appeal to universal reason."[400] Smith continues, "What characterizes the postmodern condition, then, is not a rejection of grand stories in terms of scope or in the sense of epic claims, but rather an unveiling that all knowledge is rooted in some narrative or myth. The result, however, is what Lyotard describes as a 'problem of legitimation' since what we thought were universal criteria have been unveiled as just one game among many."[401] All claims to universal truth are reduced to one story among many stories. These stories are conditioned by their own sets of cultural and historical rules, a point McLaren and other Emergent Christians are quick to point out. Finally, Foucault, the master institutional de-constructor was famous for his often quoted phrase, "power is knowledge." Foucault led the charge in cultivating a "deep hermeneutic of suspicion" that marks our postmodern culture's relationship to Institutions of Power, including and especially the institution of the Church. Like Nietzsche, Foucault traced the lineage of secret biases and powerful prejudices that lay submerged beneath institutional truth claims, especially those ideas deemed "moral" or "normal" by institutions like Christianity. According to Foucault, nothing that is "true" is innocently and purely discovered. Instead, what those institutions (State and Religious) deem normal and moral

---

[400] James K. A. Smith, *Who's Afraid of Postmodernism* (Grand Rapids: Baker Academic, 2006), 65.
[401] Smith, *Who's Afraid of Postmodernism*, 69.

are covertly motivated by various interests of power. It is out of this historical milieu that McLaren's Kingdom grammar has been constructed.

THE PROBLEM WHICH THE KINGDOM SOLVES

Like four generations preceding him, McLaren defines the problem at the root of his *Kingdom* grammar differently than the historic Christian faith's conception of the problem defined by original sin. Through his protagonist Neo in his *New Kind of Christian* trilogy, McLaren contends the Christian story has been distorted, because early Christianity imported "the Greek idea of a fall from a perfect, unchanging, ideal, complete, harmonious, fully formed world into a world of change, challenge, conflict..."[402] McLaren rejects original sin; he insists there is no event of "the Fall" or corresponding "original sin" and "total depravity" in which humanity plunged into rebellion and alienation, resulting in an inherited sinful nature.[403] Instead, the framing narrative of humanity is one of systemic progression and ascent, with corresponding descent resulting in "new depths of moral evil and social injustice."[404] Accordingly, human nature has not "fallen" but is still fundamentally good,[405] progressing

---

[402] McLaren, *The Story We Find Ourselves In*, 52. This is later affirmed and further developed in *A New Kind of Christianity*, 33-45.
[403] McLaren, *A New Kind of Christianity*, 43. In an endnote McLaren asserts that these terms "frequently derive their meaning from a story that is, I believe, inherently un-Jewish and unbiblical, and so when they are read into the biblical story, they distort and pollute it." 266n.15.
[404] McLaren, *A New Kind of Christianity*, 51.
[405] McLaren, *Story We Find Ourselves*, 52: As McLaren says, "the God-given goodness in creation isn't lost...God's creative fingerprint or signature is still there, always and forever. The evil of humanity doesn't eradicate the goodness of God's creation, even though it puts all of that goodness at risk."

from an embryonic stage to a higher stage of existence. As one can see, McLaren's understanding of human nature reflects Rauschenbusch's own strong appropriation of evolutionary doctrine. As the Earth's story is one of emergence, so too is humanity's; our story is not a fall from perfection into a state of imperfection, but "unfolds as a kind of compassionate...classic coming-of-age story."[406] McLaren does not see just one single cataclysmic crisis but "an avalanche of crises." [407] As humans "come of age" they grow beyond God, and their relationship deteriorates in progressive, fitful "experiences of alienation." McLaren equates sin with "stagnation and decay," saying, "Because of this counter-emergent virus we call sin, the stages, episodes, and levels do not always unfold as they should. There are setbacks, stagnations, false starts, premature births, retardations, impatient rebellions, emergence defects, and failed attempts at emergence."[408] Sin is anti-progress, it is the opposite of the type of human progress (i.e. emergence) the Kingdom of God promotes, and for which we will see solves our human problem. What impedes human progress are bad systems and stories.

In his re-imagined framing narrative, individuals are no longer the issue, but human systems: Rather than individuals acting out of their sinful nature and sinning, "socioeconomic and technological advances" lead to moral evil and social

---

[406] McLaren, *A New Kind of Christianity*, 49, 51.
[407] McLaren, *The Story We Find Ourselves*, 53-54, 56. He writes, "all involve human beings gaining levels of intellectual and technological development that surpass their moral development—people becoming too smart, too powerful for their own good...Human beings leave their identity, their life, their story as creatures in God's creation...As they become more independent, they lose their connection to God, their sense of dependence...So they experience alienation from God."
[408] McLaren, *A Generous Orthodoxy*, 282.

injustice.[409] In the words of McLaren, "it's a story about the downside of 'progress'—a story of human foolishness...the human turn toward rebellion...the human intention toward evil."[410] The problem is not that humans rebelled against God and are rebels or that humans did evil and are evil. For McLaren, the story is one where humans collectively create evil, damaging and savaging God's good world; it is a story where "humans have evil intent" instead of being evil themselves. Those evil intentions are not the result of an evil nature, but the bad systems and stories that consume humanity. McLaren believes the main dysfunctions of humanity are existential; he frames the crisis of the human condition as an existential crisis of prosperity, equity, and security.[411] These three crises form the "cogs" in what McLaren terms the *suicide machine*.[412] The suicide machine is a metaphor for "the *systems* that drive our civilization toward un-health and un-peace."[413] McLaren envisions the driving force behind our broken, problematic condition to reside in the systems of the world rather than in the individual person. According to him, humanity suffers from a "dysfunction of our societal machinery," which is operated not by single individuals but by humanity acting together."[414] In other words, individual sinful human nature is not the problem, but rather a universal sin of society, which of course is how four generations of liberals defined the human problem: Rauschenbusch said sin was social, Schleiermacher and Ritschl

---

[409] McLaren, *A New Kind of Christianity*, 51.
[410] McLaren, *A New Kind of Christianity*, 54.
[411] McLaren, *Everything Must Change*, 5.
[412] McLaren, *Everything Must Change*, 53.
[413] McLaren, *Everything Must Change*, 53. (emphasis mine)
[414] McLaren, *Everything Must Change*, 65.

said our problem was a kingdom or systemic "web" of sin and evil.

In *A New Kind of Christianity*, McLaren illustrates this explanation of the human condition and reality of so-called "social sin." Using the story of the Israelites in Exodus, he explains that it is a story of "liberation from the external oppression of social sin," while also celebrating "liberation from the internal spiritual oppression of personal sin."[415] Because McLaren does not believe that sin is part of human nature because of an event of rebellion, he must mean something different by "internal spiritual oppression of personal sin." It seems even this internal oppression is related to the social systems of sin, because he asserts that the Israelites were freed from "the *dominating powers* of fear, greed, impatience, ingratitude, and so on."[416] The power of Fear and Ingratitude were the oppressors, which in this Exodus narrative apparently resulted from years of being "debased by generations of slavery."[417] This slave framing story, then, is what contributed to the Israelites communal and individual commitment to "fear, greed, impatience, ingratitude, and so on." The internal compulsion toward greed, for example, was an internal power that resulted from the external system of slavery and the bad framing narrative out of which Israel was liberated. Thus, our ultimate problem is bad systems and stories.

Unlike the traditional historic faith that locates the problem of the human condition in individual sinfulness and an inherited sinful nature, McLaren believes humans are in trouble because

---

[415] McLaren, *A New Kind of Christianity*, 58.
[416] McLaren, *A New Kind of Christianity*, 58. (emphasis mine.)
[417] McLaren, *A New Kind of Christianity*, 58.

we are in bondage to the "dominant societal machinery," which entices us to keep faith in its systems of wealth, security, pleasure, and injustice.[418] This faith and bondage has led to a sort of universal consciousness that is driven by destructive, dysfunctional framing stories. The global crises of which McLaren says we must be saved are the symptoms and consequences of the dysfunction, resulting in a collection of human evil. Dysfunctional societal machinery, destructive framing narratives, and collective human evil are our problems. Rather than sinning out of an inner, natural compulsion, innately good humans are compelled to act badly because of these environmental forces; bad systems and bad stories cause us to misbehave. Thus, we need a better system and a better story to solve for our human problem. We find both in the alternative system and story of the Kingdom which came through the person and life-work of Jesus of Nazareth.

THE BEARER OF THE KINGDOM: THE PERSON & WORK OF JESUS

At the heart of liberal *Kingdom* grammar is the person of Jesus of Nazareth, whose chief work was founding the historical movement of the Kingdom of God through His loving life example. The same is true for McLaren: the man Jesus is important because of His revolutionary Kingdom movement and model of loving life. While the historic Christian faith recognizes Jesus Christ as God and in some way a penal substitutionary sacrifice for the sins of the world, McLaren

---

[418] McLaren, *Everything Must Change*, 271.

recognizes neither. Instead, Jesus is merely the best teacher of a better way of living, the one who lived the best way to be human, and one who is our best picture of the character of God. In *The Story We Find Ourselves In*, McLaren describes Jesus as a "revolutionary" who was a "master of living."[419] According to McLaren, "Jesus really is in some mysterious and in a unique way sent from God and full of God."[420] Notice McLaren does not say Jesus *is* God, but merely a messenger of sorts from God. His fellowship with God comes from His ethical way of living; Jesus is Divine because He *acts* divinely. As with four generations of liberals before him, McLaren seems to view Jesus as the moral not the metaphysical Son of God.

McLaren affirms this characterization in his most recent book, *A New Kind of Christianity*, by insisting that Jesus "brings us to a new evolutionary level in our understanding of God...the experience of God in Jesus requires a brand-new definition or understanding of God," because He "gives us the highest, deepest, and most mature view of the character of the living God."[421] McLaren's emphasis on the "character of God" finds substantial resonance with four generations of liberalism: "When you see [Jesus], you are getting the best view afforded to humans of the character of God;" "Jesus serves as the Word-made-flesh revelation of the character of God;" and "the invisible God has been made visible in his life. 'If you want to know what God is like,' Jesus says, 'look at me, my life, my ways, my deeds, my character.'"[422] Elsewhere he writes that Jesus simply identifies

---

[419] McLaren, *The Story We Find Ourselves In*, 115, 121, 122.
[420] McLaren, *The Story We Find Ourselves*, 122.
[421] McLaren, *A New Kind of Christianity*, 114, 115.
[422] McLaren, *A New Kind of Christianity*, 118, 128, 222.

Himself *with* God, telling His disciples that those who had seen Him had in "some real way" also seen God.[423] In a "mysterious and unique way" Jesus is full of God. He shows, images and expresses God's character. This view of the person of Jesus is liberal in general and starkly Ritschlian in particular.

From McLaren's earliest writings one can detect his theological trajectory and emphasis of Jesus as "teacher" and "liver." In explaining Jesus as "Lord," McLaren argues this means Jesus "was the master of living...it would mean that no one else could take the raw materials of life...and elicit from them a beautiful song of truth and goodness. [The disciples] believed Jesus' way was higher and more brilliant, and the right way to launch a revolution of God."[424] Elsewhere he writes that Jesus' message and teachings is an "alternative framing story" that can "save the system from suicide," a message that focuses "on personal, social, and global transformation in this life."[425] Furthermore, "Jesus' life and message centered on the articulation and demonstration of a radically different framing story—one that critiques and exposes the imperial narratives as dangerous to itself and others."[426] The best teacher, way, and picture of God is the perfect solution to McLaren's problem, because as we already saw we need a better example to follow in order to live differently and avert dysfunction and destruction. Jesus' mastery over life through His higher, more brilliant way of living and alternative message provides the existential solution to our existential problem. Fundamentally, the solution Jesus

---

[423] McLaren, *The Secret Message of Jesus*, 31.
[424] McLaren, *The Story We Find Ourselves In*, 121.
[425] McLaren, *Everything Must Change*, 73, 22.
[426] McLaren, *Everything Must Change*, 154-155.

provides through His work is the Kingdom of God, which is exactly how liberal *Kingdom* grammar has framed the solution for four generations.

Central to the work of Jesus is His vocation as the founder of the Kingdom of God, the one in whom the original way of human existence was found, taught and modeled to the world. McLaren insists that Jesus did not come to start a new religion, but to announce a new kingdom, a new way of life;[427] He was the founder of a new countermovement to all other human regimes.[428]Through His life and teachings, Jesus "inserted into human history a seed of grace, truth, and hope that can never be defeated," a seed that will "prevail over the evil and injustice of humanity and lead to the world's ongoing transformation into the world God dreams of."[429] Because the human problem is bad systems and stories, we need a new system and a new story to repair and heal us. Jesus provides humanity the solution through his teachings on the Kingdom of God and example of living out the way of that Kingdom. McLaren makes it clear that the central point of Jesus is the Kingdom of God: "[Jesus] came to launch a new Genesis, to lead a new Exodus, and to announce, embody, and inaugurate a new kingdom as the Prince of Peace. Seen in this light, Jesus and his message has everything to do with poverty, slavery, and a 'social agenda.'"[430] He insists that Jesus himself "saw these dynamics at work in his day and proposed in word and deed a new alternative. Jesus' creative and transforming framing story invited people to change the world

---

[427] McLaren, *A New Kind of Christianity*, 139.
[428] McLaren, *The Secret Message of Jesus*, 66.
[429] McLaren, *Everything Must Change*, 79-80.
[430] McLaren, *A New Kind of Christianity*, 135.

by disbelieving old framing stories and believing a new one: a story about a loving God who calls all people to live life in a new way."[431] We are called to follow Jesus in this new way by following His teachings and example of love.

McLaren believes our problem is the dysfunctional systems and destructive stories of our world. Therefore, our solution came when God called Jesus as a messenger to show us a better way of living and teach us a better story: the Kingdom system and Kingdom story. McLaren agrees with Schleiermacher, Ritschl, Rauschenbusch and Tillich before him that the work of Jesus is fundamentally rooted in founding and living the Kingdom of God. Furthermore, Jesus is the vehicle of the Divine because of the way He lived and taught. Through His vocation as founder of the Kingdom of God Jesus was filled with God—meaning He acted like God would act on earth—and ultimately revealed the character of God by what He did and with what He said. In so acting and revealing, Jesus is the vehicle for an existential solution to our existential problem. As McLaren rhetorically asks, "Is Jesus' healing and transforming framing story really powerful enough to save the world?"[432] Because McLaren believes our systems and stories are the problem, our solution is found in an alternative system and story, which we find in Jesus' message on the Kingdom of God. McLaren answers his question thusly:

> if we believe that God graciously offers us a new way, a new truth, and a new life, we can be liberated from the vicious, addictive cycles of our suicidal framing stories.

---

[431] McLaren, *Everything Must Change*, 237-274.
[432] McLaren, *Everything Must Change*, 269.

> That kind of faith will save us...our failure to believe
> [Jesus' good news] will keep us from experiencing its
> saving potential, and so we'll spin on in the vicious
> cycles of Caesar. 433

According to McLaren, Jesus' teachings on the Kingdom provides the liberation we need from the systems and stories of the world by providing an alternative new system and story, a new way, truth, and life. We find salvation when we "transfer our trust from the way of Caesar to the way of Christ."[434] Notice that McLaren calls people to transfer their trust to the *way* of Christ rather than *person* of Christ. McLaren urges us to transfer our trust from the world's systems and stories—from our bad *existence*—to the system and story of Christ's Kingdom, because the Kingdom is the actual work of Jesus. As with four generations preceding him, McLaren's *Kingdom* grammar fundamentally insists that human salvation isn't found in a *name* (i.e Jesus Christ), but a *movement*—the Kingdom of God.

THE SALVATION OF THE KINGDOM

In one of his clearest definitions of the Kingdom, McLaren defines the Kingdom of God as "a reality into which we have been emerging through the centuries, which is bigger than whatever we generally mean by 'Christianity' but at the same time is what generously orthodox Christianity is truly about."[435] In the same section he equates the Kingdom to "the way of

---

[433] McLaren, *Everything Must Change*, 270.
[434] McLaren, *Everything Must Change*, 271.
[435] McLaren, *A Generous Orthodoxy*, 288.

Jesus," which is "the way of love and the way of embrace."[436] The Way of Jesus and Kingdom of God "integrates what has gone before so that something new can emerge."[437] And toward what are we emerging? The universal human ideal, the essence of what it means to human: McLaren writes, "Jesus invitation into the Kingdom of God was an invitation into *the original universe, as it was meant to be.*"[438] In this definition are several features consistent with liberal *Kingdom* grammar: the Kingdom is transcendent in that it is equated with an ultimate reality that supersedes any particular religion, representing the universal ideal, the essence of human existence; it is immanent in that it is most closely embodied in humanity in the life and way of Jesus and is concerned with historical transformation; it is progressivistic in that the Kingdom takes humanity from a lower level of living to a higher level of existence; it is fundamentally about love-inspired action; finally, it is universal, in that McLaren's grammar has all of humanity squarely in view.

Like the four generations preceding McLaren, his Kingdom grammar is inherently defined by love-inspired action: he suggests the only way for the Kingdom of God to save humanity is through "weakness and vulnerability, sacrifice and love;"[439] McLaren argues that the central governing "policy" of the Kingdom is universal love;[440] he insists the way of Christ, the way of the Kingdom, is inherently the "way of love;"[441] the mission of the Church itself is defined by the single goal of "forming

---

[436] McLaren, *A Generous Orthodoxy*, 287.
[437] McLaren, *A Generous Orthodoxy*, 287.
[438] McLaren, *The Secret Message of Jesus*, 53. (emph. mine)
[439] McLaren, *The Secret Message of Jesus*, 69.
[440] McLaren, *A New Kind of Christianity*, 154.
[441] McLaren, *A New Kind of Christianity*, 168.

Christlike people, people who live the way of love, the way of peacemaking, the way of the kingdom of God, the way of Jesus;"[442] and finally, the Kingdom of God advances, gains ground "with reconciling, forgiving love: when people love strangers and enemies…"[443] This love activity flows from Jesus Himself who was the first Master at loving activity, which culminated at the cross. For McLaren, the cross is a stage upon which Christ renders a grand performance illustrating God's love, acceptance, and new Kingdom way of sacrifice and suffering. Jesus' life and message has been one of non-violence and triumph over enemies through peace and self-sacrifice. Like the other liberals, the cross is the culmination of those teachings as an exposé on love. Rather than joining in with the "'shock and awe' display of power as Roman crucifixions were intended to do," McLaren says Jesus gives us a "'reverence and awe' display of God's willingness to accept rejection and mistreatment…"[444] In this display of "Christ crucified," McLaren says "we see that the lowly way of Christ, the vulnerable way of love, is the only way of life."[445] And this life is Kingdom-life. This love-inspired life is what transforms and saves humanity.

Consistent with the four previous generations of liberals, McLaren's *Kingdom* grammar is inherently progressivistic vis-à-vis humanistic change. As he says, "God stands ahead of us in time, at the end of the journey…and washes over us with a ceaseless flow of new possibilities, new options, new chances…This newness, these possibilities are always 'at hand,

---

[442] McLaren, *A New Kind of Christianity*, 171.
[443] McLaren, *The Secret Message of Jesus*, 69.
[444] McLaren, *A New Kind of Christianity*, 158-159.
[445] McLaren, *A New Kind of Christianity*, 169.

'among us,' and 'coming' so we can 'enter' the larger reality and transcend the space we currently fill." He goes on to say, "We constantly *emerge from what we were* and are into *what we can become*,"[446] equating the Kingdom of God with emergence, with humanistic progress. McLaren rhetorically asks, "What does the future hold? the answer begins, '*That depends on you and me.* God holds out to us at every moment a brighter future; the issue is whether we are willing to receive it and work with God to create it. We are participating in the creation of what the future will be.'"[447] That the future depends on you and me is patently consistent with Rauschenbusch's *social gospel*. Along with Schleiermacher, Ritschl, and Tillich, McLaren believes that we are the makers of our best life now, we are responsible for bringing into existence the best version of ourselves, the universal human ideal; we are responsible for saving ourselves. This is the case because humanity—individuals and as a community—is the actual *medium* that contains the Kingdom of God, right here and now.[448] Furthermore, all people are called, through their own power and choice, to live in the radical new way of the Kingdom. As McLaren states, "we do indeed have the choice today and every day to seek it, enter it, receive it, live as citizens of it, invest in it, even sacrifice for it," which, depending on this choice, will create two very different worlds and futures: one hellish and one heavenly.[449] Thus, McLaren urges everyone to "start doing the next good thing now," so that the good of the Kingdom will prevail by love, peace, and endurance of suffering,

---

[446] McLaren, *A Generous Orthodoxy*, 283, 284. (emph. mine)
[447] McLaren, *A New Kind of Christianity*, 196. (emph. mine)
[448] McLaren, *The Secret Message of Jesus*, 101.
[449] McLaren, *The Secret Message of Jesus*, 181.

while bad ethical acts like domination, violence, and torture will be overcome through our collective human effort.[450]

Ultimately, salvation is participation in the Kingdom of God, which McLaren calls participatory eschatology. While McLaren contends conventional eschatologies have cultivated resignation, fear, and aggression, participatory eschatology inspires much more:

> a passion to do good, whatever the suffering, sacrifice, and delay because of a confidence that God will win in the end; courage, because God's Spirit is at work in the world and what God begins God will surely bring to completion; a sense of urgency, because we are protagonists in a story; and humility and kindness, because we are aware of our ability to miss the point, lose our way, and play on the wrong side. 451

Furthermore, McLaren argues that the death and resurrection of Jesus are paradigms for this salvation in which we ourselves are to participate in anticipation of God's coming Kingdom: we join with Jesus in dying (metaphorically to our pride and agendas, literally in martyrdom as a witness to God's Kingdom and justice); we rise again in triumph "through the mysterious but real power of God. In this cruciform way, we participate in the ongoing work of God, and we anticipate its ultimate success."[452] For McLaren, our dying and rising with Christ are symbolic of our rejection of and triumph over the dysfunctional systems and destructive stories of our world; we are called to die to the bad ethics of the world and rise to new life by living like Jesus. Thus, salvation is entirely existential, in that

---

[450] McLaren, *Everything Must Change*, 146.
[451] McLaren, *A New Kind of Christianity*, 200.
[452] McLaren, *A New Kind of Christianity*, 200-201.

His loving example is what saves us from our bad existence, an existential salvation that extends to the whole human race.

In this definition of humanistic progress, we find the familiar ring of universalism present in liberal *Kingdom* grammar. McLaren believes God's wish and hope is for all of humanity to grow toward Christlikeness, because we are *all* children of God.[453] In fact, McLaren believes that "a person can affiliate with Jesus in the kingdom-of-God dimension without affiliating with him in the religious kingdom of Christianity. In other words, I believe that Christianity is not the kingdom of God. The ultimate reality is the kingdom of God…"[454] Because the Christian faith is not the single container of God's reign, the Kingdom is universal; it is a universal human ideal instantiated in the person and life of Jesus whom all may join simply by emulating Him. McLaren insists that everyone is a potential agent of the Kingdom by nature of people's loving activity, like the taxi cab driver McLaren references who treated his guests with special care and respect; Carter had within him the spirit of the Kingdom of God and was a secret agent of the Kingdom.[455] For McLaren this can be true because the Kingdom is about our daily lives, it is a daily way of life centered around Jesus' loving message and life example. He stresses the Kingdom is about so-called *purposeful inclusion*, because it "seeks to include all who want to participate in and contribute to its purpose,"[456] which of course is humanistic progress toward bringing the universal human ideal—in McLaren's words, the original universe as it

---

[453] McLaren, *A Generous Orthodoxy*, 283.
[454] McLaren, *A Generous Orthodoxy*, 282n.141.
[455] McLaren, *The Secret Message of Jesus*, 85-89.
[456] McLaren, *The Secret Message of Jesus*, 167.

was meant to be—to bear on human existence. Consequently, McLaren finds it "fascinating" to think that thousands of Muslims, Buddhists, Hindus, and even former atheists and agnostics could come from the east and west and north and south "to enjoy the feast of the kingdom in ways that those bearing the name Christian have not."[457] McLaren would believe this possible because he believes that anything that contributes to humanistic progress counts as Kingdom activity; any loving-act that subverts the prevailing systems and stories solves for our human problem and provides individual salvation.

In the end, because we are called to live in the system and story of the Kingdom by living the teachings of Jesus, McLaren says ultimate salvation at judgment will be based on behavior, not beliefs: "God will examine the story of our lives for signs of Christlikeness...These are the parts of a person's life that will be deemed worthy of being saved, remembered, rewarded, and raised to new beginnings."[458] Giving food and water to the needy, showing mercy, welcoming the stranger, and being generous like Jesus is what God cares about, what will result in salvation. Conversely, "all the unloving, unjust, non-Christlike parts of our lives...will be burned away, counted as unworthy, condemned, and forgotten forever." [459] Notice the implicit universalism embedded in McLaren's soteriology: in the end, everyone will find salvation, because, as Tillich taught, the positive will live on while the negative will not. Ultimately, then, our salvation depends upon our *existence*, it depends upon how we live, whether we walked the path of Jesus in word, deed, and

---

[457] McLaren, *The Secret Message of Jesus*, 217.
[458] McLaren, *A New Kind of Christianity*, 204.
[459] McLaren, *A New Kind of Christianity*, 204.

suffering. Since "no good deed will be forgotten," we are urged to "start doing the next good thing now and never give up until the dream comes true," until God's Kingdom comes. [460] Therefore, in reality, salvation comes not through *Jesus'* saving act on the cross, but through every *human* act that lives out Jesus' way of life. In many ways, each person is his own savior, because every act of love counts as Kingdom acts, as saving acts that bring the universal ideal to bear on existence. In reality, the *Kingdom* saves us through humanistic progress, rather than through Jesus.

CONCLUSION

This *Kingdom* salvation of which McLaren and Emergent grammar speaks is wholly consistent with four generations of liberal *Kingdom* grammar. In this *grammar*, our human problem is not a sinful nature but dysfunctional systems and destructive stories. Rather than bound by sin on the inside, we are oppressed on the outside by bad social and spiritual systems and stories. Jesus is the antidote, the cure for these bad systems and stories because He provided the alternative system and story of the Kingdom through His life and teachings. For McLaren, the Kingdom of God is "A life that is radically different from the way people are living these days, a life that is full and over flowing, a higher life that is centered in an interactive relationship with God and with Jesus...an extraordinary life to the full centered on a relationship with God."[461] He contends this is what the Apostle

---

[460] McLaren, *Everything Must Change*, 146.
[461] McLaren, *The Secret Message of Jesus*, 37.

John termed "eternal life," or "life of the ages." Through his Kingdom message and Kingdom way of living, "Jesus is promising a life that transcends 'life in the present age'...[he] is offering a life in the new Genesis, the new creation that is 'of the age' not simply part of the current regimes, plots, kingdoms, and economies created by humans."[462] Jesus came, then, to liberate us from these old regimes (i.e. dysfunctional systems) and plots (i.e. destructive stories), to teach and show us the highest, best way found in the Kingdom. He came to end *life-as-we-know-it* and usher in *life-as-it-ought-to-be*; Jesus' life saves, rather than His death and resurrection. This essence of what it means to be human is rooted in universal brotherly love. The Kingdom represents this ultimate reality, which comes when anyone does any act of love, whether cleaning a local river, launching an adult literacy program, or returning a dropped set of keys to a stranger on a busy city sidewalk. Somehow these love-inspired acts collectively bring in the future we all long for, burning up the negative in the process and enveloping all of humanity in its arms of inclusion. And in the end, while Jesus' life provides the example and way, humanity is its own savior. That is the obvious, logical conclusion to liberal *Kingdom* grammar, which McLaren recites *in toto*.

---

[462] McLaren, *A New Kind of Christianity*, 130.

7

Conclusion

This examination has demonstrated that the Emergent Church's *Kingdom* grammar is continuous with four previous generations of Protestant liberal theologians. This grammar teaches that sin is social and environmental, rather than an inherited nature and guilt—their view of sin is Pelagian; Jesus of Nazareth, the person who bore the solution to our problem, is not God, but merely divine by nature of living out the universal human ideal; the work of Jesus is His life, rather than His atoning death—His death is important insofar as it was the climax of his life of love; and the Kingdom of God is the means by which humanity is saved—humanity is beckoned to place their faith in this *way* of Jesus rather than His person and work. In the end, the gospel of the Emergent Church is identical with the good news of liberalism: the Kingdom of God, the universal human ideal and essence of human existence, has come near in the life of Jesus; live your best existence now by turning from the destructive stories and dysfunctional systems of this world and turning toward everyday acts of brotherly love. We conclude this examination by considering an observation and a few implications that contemporary appropriations of liberal Kingdom grammar are already having within evangelicalism.

First, an observation: in tracing the generational development of liberal Kingdom grammar it was interesting to note the ways in which the focus on the Church itself shifted and waned. When Schleiermacher introduced the language of the Kingdom back into the Church's theological discourse, the Church was squarely in view: He equated the Kingdom with the Church. Ritschl maintained such a connection, yet broadened the Kingdom to include those well beyond its borders. By the time Tillich formulated his own theological enterprise, the Church had become a symbol and mostly unnecessary. Likewise, in McLaren's theological missive arguing for a new kind of Christianity, the Church is roundly ignored in favor of the Kingdom as the ultimate religious reality. This gradual downplaying and dismissal of the Church makes sense, as the Church is simply one faith community that embodies the universal human ideal and is important only insofar as it was the original religious organization that perpetuated Jesus' teachings. Now in our postmodern polytheistic context, there is even more pressure to downplay and negate the role of the Church as the particular embodiment of Christ and agent of the Kingdom. Such maneuvers have two implications for the future of mainstream evangelicalism.

First, it was noted at the beginning how the terms *mission*, *evangelism*, and *gospel* seem to have shifted over the past few years in light of the resurgent use of the Kingdom of God. While perhaps the nature of Jesus and His substitutionary work on the cross is not in danger of losing their meaning and significance in such circles, one has to wonder how using the Kingdom in ways liberals have for generations will begin to affect mainstream evangelical commitment to core evangelical convictions, mainly conversionism and activism—particularly evangelistic. Popular Evangelical magazines such as *RELEVANT,* books on Christian cultural engagement such as *AND: The Gathered and Scattered Church*[463] and *For the City: Proclaiming and Living Out the Gospel,*[464] and young church leader conferences like *Catalyst* emphasize doing good by living like Jesus. Not that this emphasis is necessarily a bad thing. It seems, however, that in so emphasizing the Kingdom in ways that liberals have for years— mainly transforming human existence through mundane and supramundane acts of love—mainstream evangelicals are in danger of losing sight of what has always been central to evangelicalism, and authentic, historic Christianity.

Furthermore, evangelicals should think twice about appropriating the grammar of the Kingdom in ways liberals have because of the implications that grammar has for the Christian faith itself. How liberals arrive at their definition of *Kingdom* depends on how they define sin, the person and work of Jesus, and other aspects of historic orthodoxy. In light of that grammar, then, what is to say mainstream evangelicals will not join progressives in transforming, say, the meaning of the cross itself? Already some have accused proponents of substitutionary

---

[463] Hugh Halter and Matt Smay, *AND: The Gathered and Scattered Church* (Grand Rapids: Zondervan, 2010).
[464] Darin Patrick and Matt Carter, *For the City: Proclaiming and Living Out the Gospel* (Grand Rapids: Zondervan, 2010).

atonement of holding a view akin to "divine child abuse."[465] And while some do not go as far as this language they wonder whether we should speak of the cross in language that side-steps traditional substitutionary language altogether in favor of alternative atonement views, such as *Christus Victor*. What is to stop mainstream evangelicals from eventually downplaying the significance of Jesus' death in favor of Jesus' significant life? Perhaps more importantly, if the deeds and teachings of Jesus are all that matter, then what would stop some evangelicals from fudging on the *person* of Jesus, including His deity? Without sounding apocalyptic, if evangelicals continue to use the language of the Kingdom in ways that liberals have for generations, they risk the potential of joining them in the other beliefs that supplied the context and definition of that grammar. So the first implication in adopting liberal *Kingdom* grammar is the danger of losing sight of the historic Christian faith.

Secondly, the Kingdom grammar of liberals and the Emergent Church has massive implications for the future of missions and evangelism. As the introduction noted, a new generation is thinking differently about the nature of evangelism at home and missions abroad. For instance, in times past the typical evangelical college would take students on Spring Break trips to key beaches around the country to share the gospel with Spring Break revelers. While such methods of evangelism could be contested, it is worth noting that now it is more common for such colleges to take trips to serve the homeless in Seattle or build wells in Africa than it is to share the gospel with people in need of a Savior. Missions is now about acts of love in the

---

[465] McLaren, *The Story We Find Ourselves*, 102.

interest of serving our neighbor, rather than acts of gospel proclamation in the interest of seeing our neighbor saved. Furthermore, alongside a shift in emphasis in missions has been a shift in evangelism, the hallmark of mission work of yore. Rather than evangelism being the proclamation of the gospel, people now define evangelism using the maxim often ascribed to St. Francis of Assisi: preach the gospel at all times, if necessary use words. Words that urge repentance, belief, and confession are considered unnecessary, being abandoned in favor of actions of acceptance, service, and love.

The gospel is now framed as the Kingdom coming to our here-and-now rather than justification by faith in Christ. While the Kingdom is part and parcel of the gospel of Jesus Christ, it is being pronounced at the expense of the justification provided through Jesus' death and resurrection. Such pronouncement not only has implications for the future of mission and evangelism, but the gospel itself. Therefore, it behooves evangelicals to reconsider their *Kingdom* grammar in order to guard their *gospel* grammar. Yes, we must pray for God's Kingdom-rule to break into our existence in increasing measure. But we do so with the realization that it was God Himself through His Son's life, death, and resurrection that made it possible in the first place. It is not the *Kingdom* that saves us, but Jesus Christ alone.

Afterword

If I have learned anything in this academic exercise it's this: theology matters. Getting the "pieces" of theology right, as much as we can in our finiteness, matters because when we get one of those pieces "wrong," the rest fall in lockstep.

How one defines our human problem has great bearing on how one defines our human solution. How one defines our human solution has great bearing on how one defines the One who bore that solution. This book has demonstrated as much in its overview of the generational development of Protestant liberal theology. When you define our human problem environmentally, then our solution must do something with our environment; when you define our human problem as having to do with bad examples, then our solution must provide a better example; when you define our human problem as narratively driven, then our solution must provide a better narrative to live and lean into.

Perhaps more significantly, our definition of the One who bore our solution, Jesus of Nazareth, is reduced to a prophet-like character who came simply to provide us a better example and better story to live; He came to change our environment in order to change us. So what's important about Jesus becomes His life and way of living. This means He doesn't have to be God and doesn't have to actually be alive.

If I have learned anything in the last few years, it's that theology matters, and when you get the pieces of theology wrong you ultimately get the gospel wrong. Of late, my generation is all a flutter with reimagining the Christian faith—reimagining the *pieces* of the Christian faith. I understand this pull toward reimagining the Christian faith, because I have been there myself. But what I have learned, especially at the end of my Th.M. and thesis project, is that what my generation needs is not to reimagine the Christian faith, but *rediscover* it. We need to rediscover what and how the Church of Jesus Christ has always believed about our problem, solution, and the One who bore that solution. We need to rediscover the gospel.

To be frank, that rediscovery effort is not going to come through the Emergent Church. It is clear their reimagination enterprise is simply one iteration in a long line of Protestant liberal leavers—Emergents have left the historic Christian faith in the same way liberals have every generation since Schleiermacher, yet in a way that's palatable for our postmodern, post-Christian day. Which, for this post-Emergent who had high hopes of a genuine third way that cuts through the malaise of contemporary liberal-conservative theological discourse, is sad indeed.

As is probably evident at this point, this book and the thesis project that went into it is deeply personal. It's personal because I myself was involved with and hoodwinked by the Emergent

Church. And it's personal because I myself still long for a third way. I realize this term is over used, yet as I survey our current evangelical landscape that is split between progressive Emergent evangelicals on the one side and traditional Young Calvinist evangelicals on the other, I'm left wanting. I—and my gut tells me plenty more people—want an alternative that cuts through the current evangelical malaise and recaptures the gospel in all of its grandeur and majesty and revolutionary character—a gospel that includes the Kingdom in all of its already-not-yet glory in order to provide new life right now.

Now more than ever the Church is in need of passionate ambassadors of Christ who take seriously their calling as ministers of reconciliation, in the fullest sense of that Kingdom calling. Yet, I hope that a new generation of Christians will rediscover what the Church has always believed regarding God's magical, revolutionary Story of Rescue in order to bring the type of right-now transformation for which our world longs—without reimagining the Kingdom, and consequently the gospel, along the way.

In closing this book, I would be remise if I didn't acknowledge the real "man behind the curtain" who made this work possible: my advisor, mentor, and friend Michael E. Wittmer, who graciously provided the foreword to this work. In many ways, Mike's patience, push-backs, and prodding launched my journey beyond Emergent. Several conversations over several Chinese lunches and even more conversations in my academic program challenged me to search the scriptures, hold on to tradition, and rediscover—rather than reimagine—what the Church has always believed.

So thanks, Mike. I would not have made it this far if it was not for you. And I will make it even further thanks to your care and friendship—and some more Chinese lunches.

Bibliography

Barth, Karl. *Protestant Thought: From Rousseau to Ritschl.* New York: Harper and Brothers, 1959.

Belcher, Jim. *Deep Church: A Third Way Beyond Emerging and Traditional.* Downers Grove: IVP Books, 2009.

Clements, Keith W. *Friedrich Schleiermacher: Pioneer of Modern Theology.* London: Collins Liturgical Publications, 1987.

Cooper, John W. *Panentheism: The Other God of the Philosophers.* Grand Rapids: BakerAcademic, 2006.

Dorrien, Gary. "Kingdom Coming: Rauschenbusch's Christianity and the Social Crisis." *Christian Century* 124 no 24 (2007): 25-29.

Fries, Paul Roy. "Religion and the Hope for a Truly Human Existence." PhD diss., Utrecht University, 1979.

Garvie, Alfred Ernest. *The Ritschlian Theology, Critical and Constructive*. Edinburgh: T & T Clark, 1899.

Gibbs, Eddie and Ryan K. Bolger. *Emerging Churches: Creating Christian Community in Postmodern Cultures*. Grand Rapids: BakerAcademic, 2005.

Grenz, Stanley J. and Roger E. Olson. *20th Century Theology: God and the World in a Transitional Age*. Downers Grove: InterVarsity Press, 1992.

Grenz, Stanley J. *A Primer on Postmodernism*. Grand Rapids: Eerdmans Publishing, 1996.

Jones, Tony. *The New Christians: Dispatches from the Emergent Frontier*. San Francisco: Jossey-Bass, 2008.

Killen, R. Allan. *The Ontological Theology of Paul Tillich*. Kampen, J. H. Kok, 1956.

Livingston, James C. *Modern Christian Thought: From the Enlightenment to Vatican II*. New York: Macmillian, 1971.

McLaren, Brian. *The Story We Find Ourselves In*. San Francisco: Jossey-Bass, 2003.

_____. *A Generous Orthodoxy*. Grand Rapids: Zondervan, 2004.

_____. *The Secret Message of Jesus*. Nashville: Word Publishing, 2006.

_____. *Everything Must Change*. Nashville: Thomas Nelson Publishers, 2007.

_____. "Church Emerging: Why I Still Use the Word Postmodern but with Mixed Feelings." Pages 141-152 in *An Emergent Manifesto of Hope*. Edited by Doug Pagitt and Tony Jones. Grand Rapids: BakerBooks, 2007.

_____. *A New Kind of Christianity*. New York: HarperOne, 2010.

Mueller, David L. *An Introduction to the Theology of Albrecht Ritschl*. Philadelphia: The Westminster Press, 1969.

Nelson, Derek R. "Schleiermacher and Ritschl on Individual and Social Sin." *Journal of the History of Modern Theology*. 16 no 2 (2009): 131-154.

Niebuhr, Richard R. *Schleiermacher on Christ and Religion*. New York: Scribner's, 1964.

O'Neill, Andrew. *Tillich: A Guide for the Perplexed*. New York: T & T Clark, 2008.

Olson, Roger. *The Story of Christian Theology*. Downers Grove: IVP Academic, 1999.

Orr, James. *The Ritschlian Theology and the Evangelical Faith*. London: Houghton and Stoughton, 1897.

Pauk, Wilhem and Marion. *Paul Tillich: His Life and Thought*. New York: Harper and Row, Publishers, 1989.

Raschke, Carl. *The Next Reformation: Why Evangelicals Must Embrace Postmodernity*. Grand Rapids: Baker Academic, 2004.

Rauschenbusch, Walter. *Christianity and the Social Crisis*. New York: HarperOne, 2007.

_____. *A Theology for the Social Gospel*. Nashville: Abingdon Press, 1945.

_____. *The Righteousness of the Kingdom*. Nashville: Abingdon Press, 1968.

Ritschl, Albrecht. *Instruction In The Christian Religion*. London: Longmans, Green, and Co., 1901.

_____. *The Christian Doctrine of Justification and Reconciliation*. Edinburgh: T & T Clark, 1902.

Schleiermacher, Friedrich. *On Religion: Speeches to Its Cultured Despisers*. New York: Harper Torchbooks, 1958.

_____. *The Christian Faith*. Philadelphia, Fortress Press, 1928.

_____. *Schleiermacher's Soliloquies: An English Translation of the Monologen with a Critical Introduction and Appendix*. Translated by Horace Leland Friess. Chicago: The Open Court Publishing Company, 1926.

Smith, James K. A. *Who's Afraid of Postmodernism: Taking Derrida, Lyotard,and Foucault to Church*. Grand Rapids: BakerAcademic, 2006.

Stackhouse, Max L. Introduction to *The Righteousness of the Kingdom*, by Walter Rauschenbusch. Edited by Max L. Stackhouse; New York: Abingdon Press, 1968.

Swing, Albert Temple. *The Theology of Albrecht Ritschl*. London: Longmans, Green, and Co., 1901.

Tillich, Paul. *The Shaking of the Foundations*. New York: Charles Scribner's Sons, 1948.

_____. *Systematic Theology* 3 vols. Chicago: The University of Chicago Press, 1951.

_____. "Victory in Defeat: The Meaning of History in Light of Christian Prophetism." *Interpretation* 6 (1952):17-26.

_____. *The Courage to Be*. New Haven: Yale University Press, 1952.

_____. *The New Being*. New York: Charles Scribner's Sons, 1955.

_____. *The Eternal Now*. New York: Charles Scribner's Sons, 1963.

_____. "The Right to Hope." *The Christian Century* 107 no 33 (1990): 1064-1067.

Welch, Claude. *Protestant Thought in the Nineteenth Century*. 2 vols. Eugene, OR: Wipf & Stock Publishers, 2003.

West, Cornell. "Can These Dry Bones Live?" Pages 231-234 in *Christianity and the Social Crisis in the 21st Century*. Edited by Paul Rauschenbusch; New York: HarperOne, 2007.

Wyman, Walter E. "Sin and Redemption." Pages 129-149 in *The Cambridge Companion to Friedrich Schleiermacher*. Edited by Jaqueline Mariña. Cambridge: Cambridge University Press, 2005.

Reimagining

THE

Christian
Faith

**EXPLORING THE EMERGENT THEOLOGY
OF DOUG PAGITT, PETER ROLLINS
SAMIR SELMANOVIC, & MCLAREN**

Introduction

I remember the exact date when my journey toward taking Emergent theology to task began: August 2, 2008. It was the day my church hosted the *Church Basement Roadshow*, an innovative book tour featuring Emergent megastars Tony Jones, Doug Pagitt, and Mark Scandrette. Each of them released a new book that year that was instrumental in the ongoing Emergent effort to reimagine the Christian faith.

Because I was still thoroughly immersed in and connected to the Emergent Church movement, I jumped at the chance to host these Emergent heavyweights in my hometown and my church. I was so dedicated that I even donned red long johns—which I later found out to be pear-shaped Victoria's Secret lingerie—and a top-hat to play my part as the country bumpkin emcee.

Tony, Doug, and Mark didn't disappoint with a rousing performance of angsty post-evangelical faith-deconstruction ensconced in the garb of Grand Ole Opry showmanship. While most of my parishioners weren't in on the joke, there was a large contingent of post-everything Christians from the Grand Rapids area who positively lapped up their performance. Including a young high school graduate from my church who had been struggling with his faith.

I clearly remember the moment when I began moving toward taking Emergent theology to task, because I remember the moment when I saw this young high school graduate from my church walking around with a copy of Doug's new book, *A Christianity Worth Believing*, in tote.

You see, that summer I had read Doug's book and had begun to see some warning signs that things were not quite right with his theological enterprise. There was a time I would have applauded his efforts at reimagining the Christian faith, and the fruit of that reimagination. But after a year of seminary I began to see cracks in the facade of Emergent's new kind of Christianity. I began to became increasingly uncomfortable with not only the deconstruction efforts of Emergent, but also their re-construction efforts. While that discomfort had not fully blossomed, it was there and I began to see the danger signs.

After reading Doug's book, I began to see the dangers the book and its theology posed. Yet, I invited Doug, Tony, and Mark, anyway. I hosted them and promoted them. And for selfish reasons: I wanted to be known as the guy who brought these three national authors and leaders to West Michigan; and I wanted to be known by these Emergent leaders so that I could, in someway, become an Emergent insider.

Lame, I know. Self-serving, really.

When I saw this young guy toting around Doug's book a tinge of regret washed over me—after I spent a graduate paper more closely examining Doug's theology, that tinge turned into full-on regret. I never did get around to talking to this young high school graduate about Doug's Christianity worth believing. After that experience, and subsequently examining Doug's book through the lens of historical theology, I began a journey toward taking the theology of the Emergent Church movement to task.

I also vowed I would never again trade my pastoral responsibility for stewarding theological truth for personal ambition or gain. Perhaps the past three years of writing in response to the Emergent Church has been a subconscious form of recompense for that August 2 moment—a sort of punishment-by-keyboard. Regardless, since that moment I have spent much of my academic career more closely examining the theology at root to the Emergent Church movement, the fruits of which are presented in this short book in a series of three essays, culled from my Master of Theology (ThM) program in historical theology.

The first essay came directly out of my August 2 experience. For a few years I had heard the charge that

Doug Pagitt was a Pelagian, which was a not-so-subtle way of saying he was a heretic (Pelagianism is the heresy of Pelagius, a 5th century Church thinker condemned a heretic by the early church.) After reading his book I had a sense something was theologically off, and I wanted to see if Pagitt really was a Pelagian. So I spent a semester reading all of Pelagius' known letters and comparing his thoughts with Pagitt's. The result was an academic treatment of one of the Emergent Church's most vocal theological voices. That's the first essay, titled "Pagitt and Pelagius."

The second essay, "Rollins, Selmanovic, and Barth," came from a summer studying Karl Barth, the famous Swiss theologian often cited as a friend of Emergent. After reading four volumes of his massive *Church Dogmatics* I was struck by how little Barth actually has in common theologically with the Emergent Church. In fact, Barth would vociferously oppose much, if not most, Emergent theology for the same reasons he opposed liberal theology, particularly around the key doctrine of revelation. In this essay I revisited Emergent darling Peter Rollins and his book *How (Not) To Speak of God*, a pivotal book for my own Emergent predilections back in the day. After reading Barth I saw some problems with Rollins' hyper-transcendent view of God, and so I used Barth as a theological dialogue partner to respond to his views which seem to deny an actual revelation from God to humanity.

From there, I took a second prominent voice to task for his views of God's revelation outside of Jesus Christ: Samir

Selmanovic. As the director of a prominent interfaith organization, Selmanovic is on the leading edges of the pluralism conversation within the Emergent Church. His views do not disappoint that leadership as he strongly suggests God's revelation isn't solely contained to Jesus Christ alone. Again, Barth has something to say about that, and I let him in theological dialogue with Selmanovic.

The final essay is reserved for the most prominent voice within Emergent, the so-called "grandfather"—or maybe it's "godfather"—of the Emergent Church movement: Brian McLaren. Love him or hate him, he is undeniably the most shaping voice in this movement, in many ways giving rise to it through his famous *New Kind of Christian* trilogy. For years, charges of theological liberalism were met with "he's just asking questions" dismissals. That changed in 2010, however, with the publication of *A New Kind of Christianity*, McLaren's theological opus that put to rest any questions that he and his friends were indeed reimagining the Christian faith.

But this reimagining effort wasn't in a way that was actually new and different. It was new and different to theologically ignorant evangelicals whom this reimagining enterprise was largely directed. McLaren's kind of Christianity is a very old kind of Christianity. About 200 years old, actually. His kind of Christianity is simply liberal Christianity repackaged for a new day.

Because I had heard for years the charge of liberalism leveled against McLaren, I wanted to see for myself if it was true, if he really was just a new kind of theological liberal. So one semester, during my course on the Modern Church in my Master of Theology program, I read every English translation from one of the most prominent voices in historical theological liberalism: Albrecht Ritschl. In this final essay, "McLaren and Ritschl," I show how McLaren follows footprint for footprint the path Ritschl tread long ago. How McLaren frames our problem, our solution, and the bearer of our solution are the ways in which liberalism has framed them for four generations. His is indeed an old kind of Christianity. (I should note that some of the content from McLaren's essay was revised and extended for a bigger work on historical theological liberalism that was published in May 2012: my Master's thesis, *Reimagining the Kingdom: The Generational Development of Liberal Kingdom Grammar from Schleiermacher to McLaren*.)

If I have learned anything in the last few years at the end of my ThM program it's that theology matters. And when you get the pieces of theology wrong you ultimately get the gospel wrong. Of late, my generation is all a flutter with reimagining the Christian faith—reimagining the pieces of the Christian faith. I understand this pull toward reimagining the Christian faith, because I have been there myself. What my generation needs, however, isn't to reimagine the Christian faith, but rediscover it. We need to rediscover what and how the Church of Jesus Christ has always believed about our problem, solution, and the One who bore that solution. We need to rediscover the gospel.

To be frank, that rediscovery effort is not going to come through the Emergent Church. As you will see through these short essays, it has become clear that their reimagination enterprise is simply one iteration in a long line of Protestant liberal leavers—Emergents have left the historic Christian faith in the same way liberals have every generation since Schleiermacher, yet in a way that's palatable for our postmodern, post-Christian day. Which, for this post-Emergent who had high hopes of a genuine third way that cuts through the malaise of contemporary liberal-conservative theological discourse, is sad indeed.

I hope this short book will help expose some of the major theological thinkers in the Emergent Church movement for what they are: Purveyors and peddlers of recycled foreign theology other-than the historic Christian faith for a new, postmodern day. And I hope it will inspire some in the Church to take theology seriously and rediscover what the Church has always believed.

1

Pagitt & Pelagius

Tony Jones, author and former National Coordinator of Emergent Village, wrote in a recent book, The New Christians, "We are not becoming less religious, as some people argue. We are becoming differently religious. And the shift is significant. Some call it a tectonic shift, others seismic or tsunamic. Whatever your geographical metaphor, the changes are shaking the earth beneath our feet." [466] Those changes include not only the shifting religious sentiments within the broad American religious landscape, but those within Protestantism itself. Specifically, a particular earth-shaking tectonic shift burst onto the stage of Evangelicalism nearly ten years ago in a "conversation" called Emergent. Over the last ten years books, conferences, and local conversations have given way to a national movement known as the Emerging Church. [467] In fact,

---

[466] Tony Jones, *The New Christians: Dispatches from the Emergent Frontier* (San Francisco: Jossey-Bass, 2008), 2.
[467] Two terms need clarification at the beginning: 1) Emergent (also known as Emergent Village) is the national 501(c)3 nonprofit organization that acts as a coordinating 'hub'

one of its leaders, Brian McLaren, was named one of Time Magazine's 25 most influential evangelicals in America. [468]Consequently, many publishers now publish entire series of books by leading Emergent authors, in addition to the thousands of weblogs and community cohort meetings that drive local conversations. This conversation, then, is now a significant contemporary fixture in the broader evangelical community and national Christianity, making it necessary for the academy to take a serious examination of this movement's theology.

The Emerging Church was born out of a need to both contextually engage our shifting postmodern culture with the teachings, way, and person of Jesus Christ, and rethink traditional doctrines of the Church. Thus, this movement within Evangelicalism is both missional and theological. It is the second facet with which many have taken issue. In true postmodern form, it appears that nothing is off the table when it comes to the in-vogue postmodern deconstructive process: penal substitutionary atonement is altogether dismissed as "divine child abuse;" [469] the apostle John's testimony regarding the need to "believe in" Jesus is replaced with an "opt-out" program of universal inclusivism; [470] and a Grand Rapids pastor frequently

for 2) the Emerging Church, a broader movement within mostly evangelicalism to rethink Christian Spirituality both missionally and theologically in light of postmodernism. I will use the two terms in these separate forms to delineate between the broad conversation and a specific organization.

[468] "25 Most Influential Evangelicals In America," *Time Magazine*, February 7, 2005.

[469] Brian McLaren, *The Story We Find Ourselves In* (San Francisco: Jossy-Bass, 2003) 102.

[470] See Spencer Burke, *A Heretic's Guide to Eternity* (San Francisco: Jossey-Bass, 2006).

insists that "as far as we know the tomb is empty."[471] While their penchant for dialogue over church, spirituality, and theology is appreciated—we certainly should not shy away from re-thinking and re-learning theology—the question remains, however, at what point is this conversation no longer Christian?

One of the most significant facets of Emerging Church theology that pushes the limits of the (non)Christian conversational label is its perspective on human nature after the Fall. Jones himself represents a growing consensus within this conversation that rejects the historic doctrine of original sin. He suggests that nothing in the biblical account of creation or Paul's examination of human nature suggests a change at the genetic, fundamental level nor is a tainted spiritual nature passed from mother to child biologically.[472] He goes so far as to suggest the Apostle Paul was wrong about human nature in Romans 5 and rejects original sin altogether, insisting that this doctrine is "neither biblically, philosophically, nor scientifically tenable."[473] Clearly, a national deconstructive effort is underway to re-define a doctrine that has been part of historic Christian orthodoxy for centuries. No one within the Emerging Church has come as close, however, to setting forth an alternative to this historic Christian doctrine than pastor and emergent leader Doug Pagitt.

---

[471] While Rob Bell, pastor of Mars Hill Bible Church, may not himself deny the bodily resurrection of Jesus Christ, this statement certainly leaves open the possibility that the tomb might, for all we know, *not* be empty.

[472] While Rob Bell, pastor of Mars Hill Bible Church, may not himself deny the bodily resurrection of Jesus Christ, this statement certainly leaves open the possibility that the tomb might, for all we know, *not* be empty.

[473] Tony Jones, *Original Sin: A Depraved Idea*, 26 January, 2009. http://blog.beliefnet.com/tonyjones/2009/01/original-sin-a-depraved-idea.html and *Was Paul Wrong?* 18 February, 2009, http://blog.beliefnet.com/tonyjones/2009/02/was-paul-wrong.html.

Pagitt is the founding and teaching pastor of an emerging church community outside Minneapolis, Minnesota called Solomon's Porch. Aside from his duties as teaching pastor for his church, Pagitt has helped navigate and position Emergent as an alternative to existing, traditional versions of Christianity through radio interviews, conferences, blogs, and books. Last year, Pagitt solidified those navigation and positioning efforts with his theological opus, A Christianity Worth Believing. In the book's opening page, Pagitt sets forth the purpose for writing his book:

> I don't believe in the versions of Christianity that have prevailed for the last fifteen hundred years, the ones that were perfectly suitable for their time and place but have little connection with this time and place. The ones that answer questions we no longer ask and fail to consider questions we can no longer ignore. The ones that don't mesh with what we know about God and the world and our place in it...I am conflicted because I want to believe differently. 474

While Pagitt may believe he is believing differently—and consequently believe he is offering the world a different Christianity that is more believable than the current form—in reality he is simply believing *otherly*; the form of Christianity that Pagitt pushes is neither innovative nor different: it is a form of Christianity other-than the versions that *currently* exist but mirrors those that have *already* existed. Whether by intention or accident, the Christian faith that Pagitt believes "feels alive,

---

[474] Doug Pagitt, *A Christianity Worth Believing* (San Francisco: Jossey-Bass, 2008), 2.

sustainable, and meaningful in *our* day" [475] is really a form of faith from an *other* day. This paper examines that other faith and theology of Pagitt in relation to two thinkers from that other day (the late early church), Pelagius and Augustine. In true postmodern, Emergent form, Pelagius and Augustine will act as theological dialogue partners with this contemporary self-proclaimed theologian in order to assess his theology on human nature and sin, and the consequences of those thoughts for the gospel. While Pagitt may conclude that a person does not "have to be a fifth-century Augustinian in order to be a follower of Jesus,"[476] our study will reveals how closely Pagitt resembles an other belief from the same period of time: the beliefs of Pelagius. From his view of human nature and sin, salvation, discipleship, and judgment, this paper explores how Pagitt mirrors the theology of Pelagius, while describes the responses of Augustine to Pelagius as a means of responding to Pagitt today.

While Pagitt rejects the versions of Christianity that have prevailed, he resurrects an other form of Christianity from the past that was deemed a threat to the gospel: Pelagianism. In the story of Christian theology, the 5th century is known mostly for the doctrinal dispute between Pelagius of Britain and Augustine of Hippo. The controversy stemmed largely from the differing concepts of humanity's relation to God which both men had been preaching for a generation. [477] Pelagius' outlook regarding human nature was the opposite of Augustine's: the trouble was not nature, but habit, thus every person is responsible for his or

---

[475] Pagitt, *Christianity*, xii. (Emphasis mine).
[476] Pagitt, *Christianity*, 49.
[477] W. C. Frend, *The Rise of Christianity* (Philadelphia: Fortress Press, 1984.), 675.

her own sin, not because Adam infected the human race.[478] Led by Augustine, Pelagius' opponents charged him and his followers with three things: 1) denying original sin; 2) denying God's grace as essential for salvation; and 3) preaching sinless perfection through free will apart from grace.[479] For the next twenty years, the two would argue over the the nature of humanity post-fall, the nature of sin, the ability to be sinless through personal effort, and the role of grace in the life of a person. Ultimately, however, the battle was over the nature of salvation itself. As Roger Olson says, "The story of Christian theology is the story of Christian reflection on salvation."[480] The same is true today.

As the Emerging Church has grown in prominence, some have begun to label it a "conversation of heresy," especially a conversation steeped in the so-called Pelagian heresy. Likewise, some have charged Pagitt with the so-called heresy of Pelagianism. Therefore, because the Emerging Church is becoming a dominant alternative within broader Evangelicalism it is important to understand the significance of this movement's theology. Furthermore, because Pagitt is a significant leader and thinker within the Emerging Church, it behooves the academy to examine how his "hope-filled, open-armed, alive-and-well-faith for the left out, left behind, and let down in us all"[481] is a repackaged previously existing version of Christian spirituality. In the end, interacting with Pagitt's, Pelagius', and Augustine's

---

[478] Frend, *Rise of Christianity*, 674.
[479] Roger E. Olson, *The Story of Christian Theology* (Downers Grove, IL: IVP Academic, 1999), 269.
[480] Olson, *Christian Theology*, 13.
[481] The subtitle to Pagitt's book.

works will reveal that Pagitt embraces an other form of faith that both the Communion of Saints and Spirit of God have deemed foreign to the Holy Scriptures, Rule of Faith, and gospel of Jesus Christ.

HUMAN NATURE & SIN

Like Pelagius, it appears that Pagitt has reacted to Augustinian theology. For Pagitt, Augustine's doctrine of depravity was based on cultural readings and understandings of certain biblical passages; the doctrine of original sin isn't biblical, it is cultural. [482] In fact, after citing sections from the Westminster Confession of Faith, Augsburg Confession, and *Book of Common Prayer* on Original Sin, Pagitt asserts that these "versions" as "extreme theology" that do not fit the Christian story. [483] The starting point for these confessions and explanations of human nature flow from a source (Augustinian theology) that started with a view of humanity born out of a Greco-Roman world that centered on dualism and separation from God.

According to Pagitt, this theology could not reconcile its assumptions of human frailty and limitations with the story from the Scriptures that said humans were created in the image of God. "So the theology of depravity made sense to people who held a view of humans as being something less than God had intended." [484] For Pagitt, original sin was a cultural response to a wrongly held assumption that the current condition of humanity

---

[482] Pagitt, *Christianity*, 127.
[483] Pagitt, *Christianity*, 123-124.
[484] Pagitt, *Christianity*, 128.

was less than the condition at which they were originally created. This false assumption about the starting place of human nature led to a "false doctrine" on how human nature is now, later resulting in distortions of the doctrine of salvation and judgment. Pagitt believes "the rationale for this view of humanity has expired, and so ought the theology that grew out of it." [485] Because Augustinian theology begins with the false assumption that humans are now, post-Fall, different than they were intended at Creation, the Church should abandon it.

Pagitt insists we need to tell a better story, a story (read: theology) that explains we are still created in the unbroken Image of God as partners and collaborators with Him who are still His people; this story never loses "sight of what it means to be created in the Image of God." [486] The Imago Dei plays a central role in Pagitt's theology of human nature. He insists that the story of God says the Imago Dei is the same as it ever was. While we were created to partner with God as Images of God, we still are; the Image of God has not changed. Most Christians who hold to the historic belief of the doctrine of the Imago Dei believe that image is cracked, broken, and tainted at some level. Pagitt, however, believes nothing has inherently changed about that Image—about human nature—from the very beginning of Creation. Referencing the Genesis 3 narrative of Adam and Eve, Pagitt says, "Their state of being did not change, their DNA didn't change...This story never suggests that the sin of Adam and Eve sends them into a state of depravity." [487] In fact, "we are still capable of living as children of God" because we can still

---

[485] Pagitt, *Christianity*, 128.
[486] Pagitt, *Christianity*, 129-130.
[487] Pagitt, *Christianity*, 129-130.

regard human nature as being "inherently godly." [488] This strong belief in the original Imago Dei plays strongly into Pagitt's belief in the fundamental goodness of humanity and capacity to choose good over evil.

Taking his cues from Celtic Christians, Pagitt believes that all humans "posses the light of God within them. That light might brighten or dim as a person lives well with God or moves away from God, but the light is never extinguished." [489] The chief end of humanity isn't to simply glorify God, as the Westminster Confession suggests, but to *"live* like God," [490] a capacity Pagitt believes is inherent within our nature. It is clear that for Pagitt, we are still good and can still choose to live godly. Nothing changed within human nature because of Adam, we are still the way we intended, though "we are invited to live free from sin and destruction, to seek lives lived in harmony with God." [491] But as Pagitt asks, if we are not born sinners, why do we sin? If we are still born as we were intended to be at Creation, why don't we live "in harmony with God?"

Instead of starting out rotten, "the systems, hurts, and patterns of this world create disharmony with God and one another. It is life that creates illness and sin." [492] While we are born good and godly, examples, habits, and ignorance from our life taint our in-born goodness. Pagitt offers an example of a newborn baby to argue his case. In the case of a newborn, we should not view him or her as full of evil, but instead should

---

[488] Pagitt, *Christianity*, 136, 137.
[489] Pagitt, *Christianity*, 141, 142.
[490] Pagitt, *Christianity*, 143. Emphasis mine.
[491] Pagitt, *Christianity*, 160.
[492] Pagitt, *Christianity*, 165.

understand that this newborn begins life entirely good. That good child is affected, trained, and drawn into sin because of the examples other sin-trained models provide. Children sin because they practice what is modeled for them by adults or older siblings, continue in those practices and form habits, and simply do not know better. [493] Sin manifests itself and affects people from the outside in, rather than the inside out; our nature is not broken, but our examples, habits, and knowledge are.

But as Pagitt suggests, "when sin is active, we must deal with it; the good news is we can." [494] Because we were created good, and still are, we are invited and capable of living free from sin and destruction, to seek to live in harmony with God. Pagitt goes further by suggesting, "We can live lives in a collective way, so the systems that cause disharmony with God can be changed. We can change the patterns wired into us from our families and create new ways of relating and being. In other words, we can be born-again, new creations." [495] While the implications of this quotation for salvation and the Gospel will be addressed later, what is clear is that Pagitt believes that humans on their own can change, in their own power; by themselves they can become new creations. During this discourse on changing and being "born-again," Pagitt mentions neither the power of Christ nor the presence of the Holy Spirit. Instead, when sin comes to tempt us, *we* are the ones who flee from, plot against, and eradicate it. [496] In other words, people can by *nature*, through their own inner capacity, choose to be "in sync" or "out of sync" with God. They

---

[493] See Pagitt, *Christianity*, 165 for the author's complete illustration.
[494] Pagitt, *Christianity*, 163.
[495] Pagitt, *Christianity*, 167. (Emphasis mine).
[496] Pagitt, *Christianity*, 164.

themselves challenge and change the systems and patterns which impinge upon their still-intact Imago Dei. These ideas on human nature and sin are not merely different than current versions of Christianity, they simply mirror an *other*. That other is Pelagius.

Like Pagitt, Pelagius begins with anthropology. His view of human nature can be summarized by a section from his letter *On Chastity*:

> Reflect carefully then, I beg you, on the good which is yours if you always remain such as God created man from the beginning and as he sent him forth thereafter, when he had brought him into the world. Observe what a blessing it is to be always in the state in which you were created and to preserve the features of your first birth. For no one is born corrupt nor is anyone stained by corruption before the lapse of an appointed period of time. Every man is seen to posses among his initial attributes what was there at the beginning, so that he has no excuse thereafter if he loses through his own negligence what he possessed by nature. 497

For Pelagius, the original Imago Dei has not changed; God created humans good and uncorrupt, and they still exist in this good, uncorrupted state. We are to remain and live out of the originally created good nature by pursuing the virtues of God. Like Pagitt, Pelagius places great emphasis on the original Image of God after which humans were (and still are) fashioned together. We are still to measure the good of human nature by reference to its Creator, supposing He has made people

---

[497] Pelagius. "On Chastity," from *The Letters of Pelagius and His Followers*, ed. by B. R. Rees. (Suffolk, England: The Boydell Press, 1991), 259. (Emphasis mine).

exceedingly good.[498] Pelagius (like Pagitt) reacted to any notion that humanity was corrupt and incapable of choosing to follow the commands of God.

Pelagius believed that God bestowed on His rational human creatures the gift of "doing good out of (the creature's) own free will and capacity to exercise free choice."[499] God the Creator gave humans the inner capacity to do good or evil. Even now we can choose to do either out of our natural capacity and ability. Embedded within us is a "natural sanctity in our minds which administers justice equally on the evil and the good and...distinguishes the one side from the other by a kind of inner law."[500] Using this inner capacity, natural sanctity, and inner law, humans are naturally capable of living "in sync with God" or "out of sync with God," to choose honorable and upright actions or wrong deeds. The reason people can live *in* or *out* of sync with God is because nature does not determine their ability to do so; this "living" is a product of choice. As Pelagius argues, "When will a man guilty of any crime or sin accept with a tranquil mind that his wickedness is a product of his own will, not of necessity, and allow what he now strives to attribute to nature to be ascribed to his own free choice?"[501]

In fact, it is God himself who presupposes our unfettered inner ability to choose good or evil. According to Pelagius' logic, if God has commanded us to love God and love people—if God has commanded us not to sin—then we must by nature have the

---

[498] B. R. Rees. "To Demetrias," from *The Letters of Pelagius and His Followers.* (Suffolk, England: The Boydell Press, 1991), 37.

[499] Pelagius, "To Demetrias," 38.

[500] Pelagius, "To Demetrias," 40.

[501] Pelagius. "On the Possibility of Not Sinning," from *The Letters of Pelagius and His Followers.* Ed. B. R. Rees. (Suffolk, England: The Boydell Press, 1991), 167-168.

capacity to choose good. "No one knows better the true measure of our strength than He who has given it to us nor does anyone understand better how much we are able to do than He who has given us this very capacity of ours to be able; nor has He who is just wished to command anything impossible or He who is good intended to condemn a man for doing what he could not avoid." [502] In typical Pelagian form, he insists that if humans are naturally incapable of being without sin, then there would be no command to be holy. Consequently, if God commanded us to be good, then we must be able to choose good; if we are able to choose good, then we must able to do good. Because God created us good we are good and are capable of doing good.

How then would Pelagius answer Pagitt's question, "Why do we sin?" We sin for three reasons: examples, habits, and ignorance. Both Pagitt and Pelagius view human nature as fundamentally flawless, still good even post-Fall. No one has a corrupted nature. Pelagius defended the goodness of nature and ability to choose either goodness or wickedness. In his letter *To Demetrias*, Pelagius declares that our nature is capable of doing good and evil and that he wants to "protect it from an unjust charge, so that we may not seem to be forced to do evil through a fault in our nature." [503] Pelagius insists we do things by choice through the exercise of our will, and he wants to make sure that we are not forced to do evil but have the freedom to choose. He doesn't want anything to stand in the way of our will's ability to choose good or evil. Sinning is the product of our will, not of

---

[502] Pelagius, "To Demetrias," 53-54.
[503] Pelagius, "To Demetrias," 43.

necessity of nature. [504] If this is true, if our nature is good, why then do we sin? For Pelagius, the answer begins with Adam.

Pelagius makes clear that "through Adam sin came at a time when it did not yet exist...through the former's sin (Adam's) death came in; Adam is the source of sin." [505] Adam is the archetype not only for sin, but also for sinning. He was the first example of disobedience that later influenced generations into sinning. [506] In fact, "all are condemned for following his example." [507] From Adam's pattern and example of disobedience, his descendants modeled for others what Adam modeled for them. Since then, generations of humans have perpetuated that original pattern for disobedience, which has petrified into habits of sin; patterns has led to habits.

In his letters and commentary, it is clear Pelagius believes generations of humans have been "instructed" and "educated in evil." We possess a "long habit of doing wrong which has infected us from childhood and corrupted us little by little over many years and ever after holds us in bondage and slavery to itself, so that it seems somehow to have acquired the force of nature." [508] While nature is not corrupt, the example set by Adam and subsequent generations has formed corrupting habits. Now, humans are "drunk with the habit of sins" so that we do not know what we do. [509] In commenting on Romans 7:17 and the "Sin that lives in me," Pelagius says, "[Sin] lives as a guest

---

[504] Pelagius, "On the Possibility of Not Sinning," 167-168.
[505] Pelagius, *Romans*, 92, 93.
[506] Pelagius, *Romans*, 95.
[507] Pelagius. "On the Christian Life," from *The Letters of Pelagius and His Followers*. Ed. B. R. Rees (Suffolk, England: The Boydell Press, 1991), 121.
[508] Pelagius, "To Demetrias," 44.
[509] Pelagius, *Romans*, 104.

and as one thing in another, not as one single thing; in other words, as an accidental quality, not a natural one." [510] Our sin is not natural, it is accidental because of the "guest of habit" that has formed within all of us. As Pagitt suggests, we are influenced by systems that model for us disintegration and patterns that are wired into us by others. In the end, Pelagius exclaims, "I who am held prisoner in this way—who will set me free from this fatal, corporeal habit?" [511]

Not only has the example of Adam and others influenced us and our habits, ignorance has, too. "The thick fog of folly and ignorance has so blinded our mind that it is incapable of feeling or saying anything divinely inspired." [512] Over time, human reason and nature has been "buried beneath an excess of vices" because of a "long habituation of sinning," and is "tainted with the rust of ignorance." [513] We no longer know what we are doing, because we are ignorant about what we should be doing. Though Pelagius does not go into detail about how we become ignorant or from where this ignorance comes, it makes sense it would arise from the confusion which disobedient examples and patterns cause and the habits that are formed from following those disobedient patterns. Ignorance, then, comes from the foreign example of Adam and others and both arises from and influences our habits. Through our freedom of choice, we respond to the example of Adam and others, leading to the formation of habits and ignorance of correct living. Now out of ignorance and habit we host the "guest of sin" and live as if

---

[510] Pelagius, *Romans*, 104.
[511] Pelagius, *Romans*, 105.
[512] Pelagius, "To Demetrias," 45.
[513] Rees, "To Demetrias," 44.

drunk on those perpetual carnal habits. While Pelagius still believes we are responsible to choose righteously, examples, ignorance, and poor habits impinge upon our natural ability to choose.

In summation, neither Pagitt nor Pelagius believe anyone is born corrupt or stained by corruption. They both appeal to the original Imago Dei and the Creator as a defense for this belief. They believe God made us as good Image Bearers and our sin doesn't change this good nature. Both insist that our inner nature (and according to Pagitt, our DNA) did not change after the Fall; we still posses God's spark of godliness within us. Instead of the necessity of nature forcing us to sin, Pelagius and Pagitt insist that we sin when we follow the example of Adam and others into living lives of disintegration from God. Following those patterns, habits formed out of doing wrong from childhood have corrupted us to the point that sin inhabits our lives as a guest to the point we are drunk on those habits of sin. Sin is not natural, but accidental. Through bad examples and habits, we have been educated in ignorance, so that we now do not know what we do nor what we should do. In the end, both Pelagius and Pagitt believe we are not born depraved and nothing internal causes us to sin. Instead, systems, patterns, and habits outside of us lead us into living lives of disharmony with God and one another. The good news, according to both, is that we can change these patterns and live out of our natural good capacity. Pelagius' and Pagitt's theology of humanity and sin have great bearing on another, greater theology: the theology of salvation.

SALVATION, DISCIPLESHIP, & JUDGMENT

Pagitt, like much of the Emerging Church, rejects penal substitutionary atonement as a framing narrative for understanding humanity's reconciliation with God. Instead, he supplies what might be considered a moral example theory of atonement, though he rejects any atonement theory and would cringe at such a comparison. Because human nature is fundamentally godly and merely impinged upon by broken, sinful systems, humanity can be saved merely by following a better example. Since humans have the inner, natural capacity to do good or evil, their salvation comes not through a sacrifice but through a new model and set of teachings by which they can know how to act and form new habits. Consequently, the life, Way, pattern, and teachings of Jesus are the center of Emerging Church theology and form the core of Pagitt's views on salvation, too.

Broadly speaking, Pagitt believes Jesus came to call people to join in with God, rather than the systems of disintegration. Pagitt writes concerning the early Christians: "The Messiah was their map, their guide to what true partnership with God looked like" through His example and teachings; Jesus "restored them to the lives for which they were created." [514] Salvation comes, then, when people "follow Jesus as Joshua into the promised land of freedom and release," because he is the new pattern of harmony for humanity by showing us what full integration with God looks like and fulfilling what people are meant to do and be. [515] According to Pagitt, the problem is not that humanity is

---

[514] Rees, "To Demetrias," 44.
[515] Pagitt, *Christianity*, 182, 208.

depraved, that human nature is marked and tainted by sin which causes people to sin. Instead, human nature is marked and defined by a sound *Imago Dei* that carries with it the capacity to choose integration with God or disintegration from God. Sinful choices from the outside, through sinful systems and patterns, influence that sound Image into forming ongoing habits, which lead to ongoing sin. What humanity requires, then, is someone to model for us integration with God, to show us a better more *original* way of being human. Jesus is that person. As Pagitt argues, "He tells his followers, *shows* his followers, what it looks like to live in harmony with God. Because Jesus is the Son of God, he is the *very model* of complete integration with the Creator. And because Jesus is the Son of humanity, he is the *very model* of living out that integration in the midst of war, pain, joy, conflict, love, loss, and fear." [516] According to Pagitt, then, humanity has corrupt, sin-tainted patterns that model sin and influence sin-formed habits.

Salvation, then, comes not through a sacrifice that does something with the objective, natural realities of rebellion, evil, and death. [517] Instead, salvation comes through an example, a new pattern that models for us integration with God. For Pagitt, the cross was not about the suffering, bloodshed, and death of Jesus, for that was the old "Greek blood god" version of atonement. [518] Instead, "Jesus is the core of Christianity because it is through Jesus that we see the fullness of God's hopes for the

---

[516] Pagitt, *Christianity*, 182, 208.
[517] As evidenced in the previous section, humanity does not possess a sin-tainted nature; our "DNA hasn't changed." Instead, examples, patterns, and systems press against our will, influencing our choices and forming sin habits.
[518] Pagitt, *Christianity*, 194.

world. Jesus is the redemption of the creation plan. He *shows* us what is means to live in partnership with our creator. He *leads* us into what it means to be integrated with God." [519] Salvation is found in the example and model that Jesus shows humanity; we find redemption through the the leadership of Jesus into better patterns and better habits that are integrated with God. Because human nature is untainted and still intact, we merely need a better model than the one that failed us before. Thus, Jesus is a new Adam for creation, a new example and model. For Pagitt, "Just as Adam was the pattern of disobedience, so Jesus is the new pattern of harmony." [520]

Interestingly, Pelagius in his commentary on Romans translates "pattern" as "type" and offers this commentary: "Adam is the source of sin, so too is Christ the source of righteousness." Elsewhere in commentary on 5:12, Pelagius says that sin came into the world "by example or by pattern." And in 5:19 he says, "Just as by the example of Adam's disobedience many sinned, so also many are justified by Christ's obedience." [521] Clearly, Pagitt mirrors Pelagius' contrast between the example/pattern of Adam's disobedience vs. the example/pattern of obedience, or "harmony" to use Pagitt's language. Because of the disobedient example of Adam, "generations of disintegration" followed his pattern and developed habits of

---

[519] Pagitt, *Christianity*, 195.
[520] Pagitt, *Christianity*, 208. Interestingly, Pelagius in his commentary on Romans translates "pattern" as "type" and offers this commentary: "Adam is the source of sin, so too is Christ the source of righteousness." Elsewhere in commentary on 5:12, Pelagius says that sin came into the world "by example or by pattern." And in 5:19 he says, "Just as by the example of Adam's disobedience many sinned, so also many are justified by Christ's obedience." Pelagius, *Romans*, 92-95. Clearly, Pagitt mirrors Pelagius' contrast between the example/pattern of Adam's disobedience vs. the example/pattern of obedience, or "harmony" to use Pagitt's language.
[521] Pelagius, *Romans*, 92-95.

disintegration. Jesus came to provide a new, better model after which new generations of humans could pattern their lives, developing habits of "integration with the Creator." Salvation is found in the example, model, and pattern of Jesus Christ, not His suffering, bloodshed, and death on a cross.

This theology of "salvation by example" influences how Pagitt views discipleship and eschatology. Those who decide to follow this new pattern are invited into God's work now, for "the kingdom-of-God gospel calls us to partner with God, to be full participants in the life God is creating, to follow in the way of Jesus as we seek to live as people who are fully integrated with our Creator." [522] Instead of choosing to live lives of disintegration, we are called to be fully integrated with God now. This is possible because 1) we are "inherently godly," having the "light of God" within us; and 2) "we can change the patterns wired into us from our families and create new ways of relating and being." [523] Discipleship, then, is about choosing to live well with God in this life.

The problem comes when the question, "Why?" is asked. Why must we live lives of integration? Pagitt does not address judgment or what happens when one does not choose to live a life of integration with God, or better put, when a person intentionally chooses not to "partner with God" or seek to live as a person who is fully integrated with their Creator. Instead, Pagitt assures the world that "God will dwell among us, that God will be with us, that the whole of creation will be healed and restored and fully integrated with God. Earthly life will be made

---

[522] Pagitt, *Christianity*, 226.
[523] Pagitt, *Christianity*, 137, 141, 167.

new as it is transformed into the Kingdom of God." [524] While Pagitt reflects Pelagius in calling people to find salvation and life in the example of Jesus and calls all people to follow Jesus' pattern of integration with God, he does not go as far as Pelagius does soteriologically and eschatologically.

Pelagius both reflects and contrasts Pagitt's theology of salvation. Like Pagitt, Pelagius looks to Christ as a new example and model. In *On the Christian Life*, Pelagius says, "let no man judge himself to be a Christian, unless he is one who both follows the teachings of Christ and imitates His example."[525] Elsewhere he says, "Men are not Christians unless they follow the pattern and teaching of Christ. A Christian is one who lives by Christ's example." [526] In his commentary on Romans Pelagius says Christ "offered, by way of grace to overcome sin, *teaching and example*." [527] While a Christian is certainly called to follow the example of Jesus and live out his teachings—no person can be called a Christian unless they both believe in Christ and live in Him through obedience—this emphasis on the teachings and example of Christ makes more sense when Pelagius' view of salvation comes into focus.

For Pelagius, the teachings and example of Christ are of utmost importance to ensure salvation in the end. A person is forgiven of sins and becomes a Christian initially at baptism. Baptism is the event at which a person becomes a son or daughter of God and is reborn. [528] A person believes with his

---

[524] Pagitt, *Christianity*, 230-231.
[525] Rees, "On the Christian Life," 123.
[526] Pelagius. "To an Old Friend," from *The Letters of Pelagius and His Followers*. Ed. by B. R. Rees (Suffolk, England: The Boydell Press, 1991), 151.
[527] Pelagius, *Romans*, 98. Emphasis mine.
[528] Pelagius, "To Demetrias," 56.

heart and is justified and he confesses with his lips and is saved, all of which is fulfilled at baptism when sins are washed away. [529] Forgiveness and justification, then, happens during baptism, but for past sins. This is clear from Pelagius' letter, *On Bad Teachers*: "Faith is an aid in ridding us of sin...that is to say, it releases us from sins already committed but does not grant pardon and immunity for those which we commit in the future." [530] People come to Christ by faith and find forgiveness for sins committed thus far through baptism, but not for sins committed afterwards. "If there is to be sinning thereafter, what does it profit us to have washed it away?" [531] Here Pelagius warns Christians not to sin after they have received the forgiveness of sins and justification through baptism. In fact, he goes so far to say "If you sin [in the future], you will not be under grace." [532] According to Pelagius, in order not to sin into the future, post-baptism we need the example of Christ.

Unlike Pagitt—who's soteriology does not incorporate suffering and bloodshed, believing "Jesus was not sent as the selected one to appease the anger of the Greek blood god" [533]— Pelagius actually believes Christ carried our sins and suffered for us to provide justification, forgiveness, and freedom from future sin. This suffering and death on the cross provides forgiveness from past sins and releases us from being "drunk with the habit

---

[529] Pelagius, "On the Christian Life," 122.
[530] Pelagius. "On Bad Teachers," from *The Letters of Pelagius and His Followers*. Ed. by B. R. Rees (Suffolk, England: The Boydell Press, 1991), 217.
[531] Pelagius, "On the Christian Life," 122.
[532] Pelagius, *Romans*, 99.
[533] Pagitt, *Christianity*, 194.

of sin" [534] so that we can follow the example of Christ and choose not to sin. In his analysis of Romans 5:10 Pelagius says, "If we have been saved by Christ's death, how much more shall we glory in his life, if we imitate it!" [535] Furthermore, in 5:11 he writes, "[Paul] means to show that Christ suffered so that we who had forsaken God by following Adam might be reconciled to God through Christ." [536] Finally, in 5:12 Pelagius says:

> "Therefore just as through one person sin came into the world, and through sin death. By example, or by pattern. Just as through Adam sin came at a time when it did not yet exist, so in the same way through Christ righteousness was recovered at a time when it survived in almost no one. And just as through the former's sin death came in, so also through the latter's righteousness life was regained." 537

The context of all three verses is examples and patterns. Since humanity fell into sin through the example of Adam and formed habits of sin based on his pattern, we need a new example and a new pattern after baptism in order not to sin in the future. Christ, then, is compared to the example of Adam. While sin came through the example of Adam, righteousness was recovered through His example; whereas through the example of Adam's sin death arrived, through the example of Christ's righteousness life was regained. Even though the event of the cross—an event that somewhat mirrors Reformed expressions of

---

[534] Pelagius, *Romans*, 102. In reference to Rom. 7:15, Pelagius says that we on our own accord after subjecting ourselves to sin and the habit of sin act as if "drunk with the habit of sin," so that we do not know what we do.
[535] Pelagius, *Romans*, 92.
[536] Pelagius, *Romans*, 92.
[537] Pelagius, *Romans*, 92.

penal substitutionary atonement—was the catalyst for forgiveness, it seems to be the example of Christ that actually provides for life, eternal life.

Although Pelagius doesn't explicitly articulate it, it seems that he believes salvation occurs by following the example of Christ. Unfortunately, the depth of understanding of Pelagius' soteriology pales in comparison to our understanding of his anthropology and hamartiology. Considering how important the example of Adam and subsequent generations of humans are to influencing human nature to sin, however, it seems plausible that the example of Christ would provide the needed antidote to humanity's sin-drunk habit. While "Christ has redeemed us with His blood from death" and actually Himself conquered death in the process, if we stop sinning only then will our redemption be profitable. [538] We are redeemed and forgiven through his death from past sins, but attain the profit of that redemption in the future (eternal life) by stopping our habit of sinning. Pelagius makes this clear in his letter *On the Christian Life* when he says, "How can [a person] hope for everlasting life from God, if he has not earned it by good deeds...whoever has not been good has not life; whoever has not performed works of righteousness and mercy cannot reign with Christ." [539] This makes more sense when one realizes that Pelagius believes both faith and deeds are important.

While Pagitt mirrors Pelagius' theology of the example of Christ for attaining (eternal) life, Pelagius contrasts with Pagitt by insisting that faith is also required. Throughout his book,

---

[538] Pelagius, *Romans*, 82.
[539] Rees, "On the Christian Life," 117.

Pagitt never says that faith is required for the forgiveness of sins and salvation. Instead, "the way to God is to walk the path Jesus walked, the path of obedience, of integration, of partnership." [540] Unlike Pagitt, Pelagius believes that faith is important, but not faith alone. In his commentary on Romans 3:28 Pelagius indicates that a person in coming to Christ is saved when he first believes by faith. [541] Elsewhere Pelagius said we are saved by Christ's death and are forgiven of our sins by Christ. As he says in his letter *On the Christian Life*, "the faith of all holds that sins are washed away by baptism," which occurs when someone believes in his heart and confesses with his lips. [542] Presumably, Pelagius holds that a person believes in Jesus' redemption for sins and defeat of death through the cross when he comes by faith to be cleansed of his sins through baptism. At the moment of baptism, belief, confession and faith leads to justification, salvation, and forgiveness. [543]

Unlike Pagitt, Pelagius believes a person first finds new life through faith. Pelagius does not believe, however, that a person can have hope in faith alone. "So, if a man sins after gaining faith and receiving the holy lather (baptism), let him no longer hope for pardon through faith alone, as he did before baptism, but let him rather entreat it with weeping and wailing, with abstinence and fasting, even with sackcloth and ashes, and all manner of lamentation."[544] After a person receives baptism and sins, she can no longer hope that the faith that brought her to baptism

---

[540] Pagitt, *Christianity*, 211.
[541] Pelagius, *Romans*, 83.
[542] Rees, "On the Christian Life," 122.
[543] To understand all the "pieces" of this argumentation, see Rees, *The Letters*, 117, Pelagius, *Romans*, 82.
[544] Rees, "On Bad Teachers," 217. (Emphasis mine).

and belief in Christ to begin with will pardon her for those future sins; faith alone does not pardon for sins committed after the initial event of faith (read: baptism). In *On the Christian Life*, Pelagius argues, "For if faith alone is required, it is superfluous to order the commandments be kept." Since God has commanded people to keep his commandments, Pelagius surmises that eternal life is gained by both faith and deeds. Unless a person follows the example of Christ post-baptism, unless he chooses to keep the commands of Christ he has not life and will not share life with Christ." [545]

Perhaps this is why Pelagius places such a premium on discipleship and takes judgment seriously. In *To Demetrias* he says, "The bride of Christ must be more splendidly adorned than anything else, since the greater one whom one is seeking to please the greater the effort which is required to please him." [546] The bride is called to live a life that is "blameless" and "guiltless" in order to reign with Christ in the end, "for nothing is worthier of God, nothing can be more dear to him, than the blamelessness should be maintained with all possible circumspect." [547] Why? What is the promise for those who fail to live such a life post-baptism? Judgment and hell. Pelagius makes plain in On Divine Law that those who believe in Christ and receive him through baptism and renounce the devil and the world are called to pay attention to the things which are forbidden and to diligently fulfill the things commanded, because "the punishment of hell is

---

[545] Rees, "On the Christian Life," 123.
[546] Rees, "To Demitrias," 123.
[547] Rees, "On the Christian Life," 118.

promised to all of us who do not live in righteousness." [548] Not only does Pelagius believe in hell for those who do not believe, he also believes hell is reserved for those who fail to choose righteousness, to live in sync with God after they first have faith in Christ through baptism. Pagitt does not go this far, however. Instead he merely suggests that "the afterlife isn't a place. It's a state of being." [549] That state of being is vaguely defined as the state in which God's hope and dreams for the world are fulfilled and come to fruition in the Kingdom right now, with no mention of judgment or a "state of being" for those who do not "faith" in Christ or even partner with God and His dreams. [550] While Pagitt agrees with Pelagius in that humans are called to "[align] their lives with the things of God, with the work of God," he does not go as far as Pelagius to suggest what happens to those who don't, or even those who were aligned and then fall out of alignment.

In summation, while Pelagius and Pagitt agree that the example and pattern of Christ is primary for our "salvation" and "integration with the life of God," they go about it in different ways. Pagitt denies the penal essence of the event of the cross by dismissing the suffering, bloodshed, and death of Christ as reflective of ancient Greek blood god myths. Pelagius on the other hand, acknowledges that Christ's suffering, shed blood, and death actually does something for us. While a more exhaustive study of Pelagius' soteriology is necessary, it appears likely that he believes the cross is penal in essence, recognizing

---

[548] B. R. Rees. "On Divine Law," from *The Letters of Pelagius and His Followers.* (Suffolk, England: The Boydell Press, 1991), 99.
[549] Pagitt, *Christianity*, 222.
[550] Pagitt, *Christianity*, 222.

Jesus' suffering and bloodshed provides justification for, salvation from, and forgiveness of sins, while needing the example of Christ to carry us to the end. Pagitt's theology of salvation reduces the cross to mere example. In fact, in so doing he is left only with the example, pattern, way, and teachings of Christ. This is likely why Pagitt and the broader Emerging Church focus on following the teachings and example of Jesus: without the penalty of the cross that is all that is left.

Here is where Pagitt agrees with Pelagius: in order to live a life of righteousness, a new example and pattern must replace the old ones found in Adam and others. The cross does not save, but the example of Jesus does. While Pelagius believes the cross provides for the forgiveness of past sins through faith and "the holy lather"of baptism, Pelagius does not stop with faith alone, but rather requires disciplined following after the example of Christ to provide for future salvation. Both Pagitt and Pelagius, then, rely upon the example of Christ for ultimate, eschatological salvation, in addition to the inner goodness of humanity to obey and choose integration with God.

CONCLUSION

According to Pagitt's own published work, it is clear he reflects much, if not most, of Pelagius' theology. Pagitt is a Pelagian. From human nature to sin, human will to grace, and salvation to judgment, much of Pagitt's theology mirrors Pelagius'. While Pagitt may want to believe differently, he simply believes *otherly*. Historically, this "other theology" was already addressed by another theologian: Augustine. Though the theological controversy between the two was rancorous and dramatic, Augustine and others already dealt with the "other theology" of Pelagius (and Pagitt) through numerous writings and councils in the 5th century. Back then, what was the response of Augustine to Pelagius and how might Augustine respond to Pagitt if he were alive today? This paper will conclude with Augustine's response to Pelagius' theology of human nature, sin, grace, and salvation.

First, regarding human nature, Augustine acknowledges that at first it was uncorrupt and without sin; at Creation, Adam was faultless. He argues, "But that nature of man in which every one is born from Adam, now wants the Physician, because it is not sound." [551] While Pelagius says all people are born sound, Augustine responds by saying that now, post-Fall, the nature of all people is corrupted. "Let us not suppose, then, that human nature cannot be corrupted by sin, but rather, believing, from the inspired Scriptures, that it is corrupted by sin." [552] Foundational to Pelagius' theology was the notion that we are good and untainted, and out of that untainted nature we are capable of not sinning. Pelagius "maintained that our human nature actually possesses an inseparable capacity of not at all sinning." [553] In arguing against this inner capacity, Augustine offers a line from the Lord's Prayer: "Lead us not into temptation, but deliver us from evil." Augustine wonders, "If they already have capacity, why do they pray? Or, what is the evil which they pray to be delivered from?" [554] In other words, why

---

[551] Augustine. "On Nature and Grace" from *A Select Library of Nicene and Post-Nicene Fathers*. Volume 5. Edited by Phillip Schaff. (Grand Rapids: Eerdmans Publishing, 1991), 122.
[552] Augustine, "On Nature and Grace," 128.
[553] Augustine, "On Nature and Grace," 141.
[554] Augustine, "On Nature and Grace," 142.

should a person pray to be delivered from evil if he, through his own capacity, can deliver himself and not sin? He goes on to say, "Behold what damage the disobedience of the will has inflicted on man's nature! Let him be permitted to pray that he may be healed! [The nature] is wounded, hurt, damaged, destroyed. It is a true confession of its weakness, not a false defense of its capacity, that it stands in need of. It requires the grace of God." [555] In response to Pelagius' belief that human nature is not corrupt and is capable on its own not to sin, Augustine replies that human nature must be delivered from evil because it must be healed. That healing comes not from self-will, but from the grace of God.

What disturbed Augustine and others most was Pelagius' view of grace. They objected most that Pelagius did not maintain that it is by the grace of God that a man is able to be without sin. [556] Pelagius and his followers argued that the grace of God actually *is* the nature in which we were created, which enables us to act righteously. [557] According to them, the grace of God is not dispensed through Christ, but through Creation; we are able to sin not because of Christ, but because of our human nature, which is in fact the grace of God. Augustine counters, "This, however, is not the grace which the apostle commends to us through the faith of Jesus Christ. For it is certain that we possess this nature in common with ungodly men and unbelievers; whereas the grace which comes through the faith of Jesus Christ

---

[555] Augustine, "On Nature and Grace," 142.
[556] Augustine, "On Nature and Grace," 139.
[557] Augustine. "On Grace and Free Will" from *A Select Library of Nicene and Post-Nicene Fathers*. Volume 5. Edited by Phillip Schaff. (Grand Rapids: Eerdmans Publishing, 1991), 454.

belongs only to them to whom the faith itself appertains." [558] While Pelagius equated grace with the God's creation of a good inner nature, Augustine said the grace of God to which the Scriptures attest comes through faith in Christ. Grace is not from Creation, but from Christ alone.

Augustine was also concerned that Pelagius maintained no other opinion than that the grace of God is given according to our merit. In response, Augustine declares, "God's grace is not given according to our merit...it is given not only where there are no good, but even where there are many evil merits preceding." [559] While Pelagius maintains that humans can choose to do good deeds out of an inner, naturally good capacity—and thus are rewarded by God because of those good deeds—Augustine insists that no man ought to attribute those good deeds to himself, but to God. [560] Furthermore, while Pelagius believes that a man is justified from and forgiven of sins by Christ only at the event of baptism, Augustine believes that the grace of God is with him even into the future to cover not yet committed sins. "It is necessary for a man that he should be not only justified when unrighteous by the grace of God...but that, even after he has become justified by faith, grace should accompany him on his way, and he should lean upon it, let he fall." [561] Augustine's view sharply contrasts with Pelagius who insists that the example of Christ is what "empowers" people to choose the righteous life after baptism. Instead of the grace of God empowering people to choose to live in Christ, people's good inner nature allows them

---

[558] Augustine, 'On Grace and Free Will," 454.
[559] Augustine, 'On Grace and Free Will," 449.
[560] Augustine, 'On Grace and Free Will," 449.
[561] Augustine, 'On Grace and Free Will," 449.

to choose integration with God. Augustine counters, "Man, even when most fully justified, is unable to lead a holy life, if he be not divinely assisted by the eternal light of righteousness." [562]

Finally, Augustine addressed the ultimate results of Pelagius' theology: salvation. Augustine responded by saying Pelagius' view of human nature "causes the grace of Christ to be 'made of none effect,' since it is pretended that human nature is sufficient for its own holiness and justification." [563] In reality, neither the cross of Christ nor the grace of God is necessary if humans, through their own inner nature, can pull themselves up by their own bootstraps. Augustine counters Pelagius' faith in human nature by saying, "if the righteousness came from nature, then Christ is dead in vain." [564] If the grace of God came through nature and out of our own inner capacity we can attain to right living, rather than through faith in Christ, then Christ's death was in vain. Augustine maintained that the same faith which restored the saints of old now restores us: "that is to say, faith 'in the one Mediator between God and men, the man Christ Jesus,'—faith in His blood, faith in His cross, faith in His death and resurrection." [565] While Pelagius believes a person is justified, saved, and forgiven when a person comes in faith to Christ through baptism, he does not believe that faith alone is sufficient for salvation. Instead, faith and deeds ultimately bring and secure eternal life into the future. Augustine wishes Pelagius would meditate on Acts 4:12, which says, "There is no other name under heaven given by which we must be saved," "and that

---

[562] Augustine, 'On Nature and Grace," 129.
[563] Augustine, 'On Nature and Grace," 141.
[564] Augustine, 'On Grace and Free Will," 454.
[565] Augustine, 'On Nature and Grace," 139.

[Pelagius] would not so uphold the possibility of human nature, as to believe that man can be saved by free will without the Name!" [566]

In many ways, the same conclusions arrived at by Augustine of Pelagius could be applied to Pagitt. Because Pagitt clearly mirrors a substantial amount of Pelagius' theology on humanity, sin, and salvation, one could imagine similar criticism from Augustine of Pagitt. Augustine might tell Pagitt that we do not have the light of God within us still, but rather are broken and tainted because of sin. In response to Pagitt's newborn analogy, Augustine would maintain that we are born sinners and are in need of healing from birth. Furthermore, Augustine might insist that the systems, hurts, and patterns of this world are not to blame for living lives of disintegration, rather we sin because we are naturally sinful; examples, habits, and ignorance does not lead us into sin, our nature does. Salvifically, Augustine would probably declare that the event of the cross, with all of its suffering, bloodshed, and death, is of the utmost importance because of the real, tangible expression and dispensation of grace it bore for the world. We need Christ, not simply for His example and pattern, but for the grace and salvation He brings us through the event of the cross. Christ is not simply our map, guide, and new example, He is our Savior and Redeemer. Augustine would maintain that we can live integrated lives with God by obeying Him, rather than living out of our sinful nature, because of the grace He gives us through faith in Jesus Christ alone, not because Jesus' example is better than the rest.

---

[566] Augustine, "On Nature and Grace," 137.

As quoted from Olson in the beginning, the story of Christian theology is about the historical reflection on the nature of salvation. Likewise, an examination of Pagitt, Pelagius, and Augustine is not simply an exercise in parsing theological positions on the nature of humanity and original sin, it's about the gospel of Jesus Christ. According to this examination, Pagitt's Christianity is not a different, more hopeful faith, it is an other form of faith that both the Communion of Saints and Spirit of God have deemed foreign to the Holy Scriptures, Rule of Faith, and gospel of Jesus Christ. One question remains, however: How will the contemporary American Communion deem this other faith?

BIBLIOGRAPHY

Augustine. "On Nature and Grace" from *A Select Library of Nicene and Post-Nicene Fathers.* Volume 5. Edited by Phillip Schaff. Grand Rapids: Eerdmans Publishing, 1991.

_____. "On Grace and Free Will" from *A Select Library of Nicene and Post-Nicene Fathers.* Volume 5. Edited by Phillip Schaff. Grand Rapids: Eerdmans Publishing, 1991.

Frend, W. C. H. *The Rise of Christianity.* Philadelphia: Fortress Press, 1984.

Jones, Tony. *The New Christians.* San Francisco: Jossey-Bass, 2007.

_____ "Original Sin: A Depraved Idea." 26 January 2009. http://blog.beliefnet.com/tonyjones/2009/01/original-sin-a-depraved-idea.html.

_____ "Original Sin: The Genesis of a Doctrine." 29 January 2009. http://blog.beliefnet.com/tonyjones/2009/01/ original-sin-the-genesis-of-a.html.

_____ "Original Sin: Paul, Romans 5, and the Heart of the Issue." 16 February 2009. http://blog.beliefnet.com/ tonyjones/2009/02/original-sin-paul-romans-5-and.html.

McLaren, Brian. *The Story We Find Ourselves In*. San Francisco: Jossey-Bass, 2003.

Olson, Roger. *The Story of Christian Theology*. Downers Grove, IL: IVP Academic, 1999.

Pagitt, Doug. *A Christianity Worth Believing*. San Francisco: Jossey-Bass, 2007.

Pelagius. "To Demetrias." Pages 29-70 in *The Letters of Pelagius and His Followers*. Translated by B. R. Rees. Suffolk, England: The Boydell Press, 1991.

_____. "On Divine Law." Pages 88-104 in *The Letters of Pelagius and His Followers*. Translated by B. R. Rees. Suffolk, England: The Boydell Press, 1991.

_____. "On the Christian Life." Pages 105-126. *The Letters of Pelagius and His Followers*. Translated by B. R. Rees. Suffolk, England: The Boydell Press, 1991.

_____. "To an Old Friend." Pages 147-154 in *The Letters of Pelagius and His Followers*. Translated by B. R. Rees. Suffolk, England: The Boydell Press, 1991.

_____. "On Bad Teachers." Pages 214-235 in *The Letters of Pelagius and His Followers*. Translated by B. R. Rees. Suffolk, England: The Boydell Press, 1991.

_____. *Pelagius' Commentary on St. Paul's Epistle to the Romans*. Translated by Theodore De Bruyn. Oxford: Clarendon Paperbacks, 1998.

2

Rollins, Selmanovic, & Barth

In 2007, Doug Pagitt and Tony Jones co-edited a book called *An Emergent Manifesto of Hope*. At the time, Tony Jones was the National Coordinator of Emergent Village, a national coordinating organization for the progressive Evangelical "conversation" known as the emerging church. Likewise, Doug Pagitt was one of the founding members of Emergent and editor of the newly-minted Emersion line of books from Baker Publishing Group out of which this title was published. The book was a collection of "voices" within the broader conversation "attempting to sing a song together" (whether or not the harmonies matched) in order to provide context for and explain what exactly was being sung within the Emergent

Church. [567] One such voice was Chris Erdman who wrote a piece on the venerable Swiss theologian Karl Barth.

In the Emergent Church conversation Barth is considered a so-called "Friend of Emergent" who supposedly supports the key questions and answers percolating within the Emerging conversation. In his article, "Digging Up the Past: Karl Barth (the Reformed Giant) as Friend to the Emerging Church," Erdman attempts to establish that Barth is Emergent's friend and theological ally. Erdman likes Barth because he insisted that "the theological enterprise must never be the sole realm of academic theologians" and because he believed "the theological imperative was never finished." [568] Similarly, leaders in the Emergent Church call on the Church as it currently exists to wrench theological work from the hands of the elite and put it firmly into the hands of the people, in order to ensure theological inquiry and development is "never static, never dull, never fixed, always open." [569] As Erdman insists, "We now, like Barth then, are dissatisfied with the established and entrenched theology that has produced our present crisis. We seek another way; we want to 'begin all over again,' to work in a state of 'constant emergency.'" [570] The only problem is that the theological work and "other way" born out of that dissatisfaction would be questioned and confronted by Barth himself, rather than supported.

---

[567] Tony Jones, "Introduction: Friendship, Faith, and Going Somewhere Together" in *An Emergent Manifesto of Hope* (ed. by Doug Pagitt and Tony Jones; Grand Rapids: Baker Books, 2007), 14.

[568] Chris Erdman, "Digging Up the Past: Karl Barth (the Reformed Giant) as Friend to the Emerging Church" in *An Emergent Manifesto of Hope* (ed. Doug Pagitt and Tony Jones; Grand Rapids: Baker Books, 2007), 238.

[569] Erdman, "Digging Up the Past," 239.

[570] Erdman, "Digging Up the Past," 240.

Though the Emergent Church may find companionship in Barth's own theological journey, he is much more a foe than friend to what that journey has produced. Upon surveying the theological fruit birthed from two influential emerging church thinkers—Peter Rollins and Samir Selmanovic [571]—and digging into the particulars of Barth's own theology, [572] this essay will reveal how Barth is an adversary to the emerging church in a particularly important area of theological discourse, the doctrine of revelation. Rollins understands the revelation of God in two key ways: 1) the hiddenness and hyper-transcendence of God, resulting in a thickly veiled God who isn't truly knowable; and 2) our inability to say anything directly of God Himself, resulting in speech that never speaks of God but merely our understanding of God. While Selmanovic does believes God is revealed and known to humanity, that revelation and knowledge is neither contained within the "Christian religion" nor exclusively in Jesus Christ. Consequently, God is trans-religious and is also revealed beyond the person of Jesus Christ. Barth will counter both

---

[571] Hailing from Belfast, Ireland, Peter Rollins is an up-and-comer within the Emergent Church conversation who has written on our (in)ability to speak of God by exploring the doctrine of the revelation of God. His book, *How (not) to Speak of God* (Brewster, MA: Paraclete Press, 2006.) is described as offering "an unprecedented message of transformation that has the potential to revolutionize the theological architecture of Western Christianity."

Samir Selmanovic is a founder and Christian co-leader of Faith House Manhattan, an interfaith community that brings together "forward-looking Christian, Muslims, Jews, atheists, and others who seek to thrive interdependently." He has also served on the Coordinating Group for Emergent Village, is the director of a Christian community in New York City called *Citylights*, and serves on the Interfaith Relations commission of the National Council of Churches.

[572] Karl Barth, *Church Dogmatics*, vol. I,1: *The Doctrine of the Word of God* (trans. G.T. Thomson. Edinburgh: T.&T. Clark, 1936); Karl Barth, *Church Dogmatics*, vol. II,1: *The Doctrine of God* (ed. G.W. Bromiley and T.F. Torrance; trans. T.H.L Parker, W.B. Johnson, Harold Knight, and J.L.M. Haire. Edinburgh: T.&T. Clark, 1957).

theologians by insisting the revelation of God is "clear and certain" and is exclusively in Jesus Christ.

While Barth insists that theology is "nothing but human 'language about God'" [573] he still insists there is something to say. In fact, a whole lot to say. And because the theological discipline of dogmatics is the servant of Church proclamation, [574] that "something" should be proclaimed well and in accordance with the Holy Scriptures, for the glory of God and good of the world. In the end, Barth will reveal how what Rollins and Selmanovic are saying is neither in one accord with the Scriptures nor part of the historic Christian faith.

GOD CAN BE KNOWN

In *How (Not) to Speak of God*, Rollins operates from the assumption that, "That which we cannot speak of is the one thing about whom and to whom we must never stop speaking." [575] Though we are called to continually speak of God, we cannot actually speak of or describe Him. Throughout this rhetorical tour de force, Rollins' book attempts to re-understand the traditional understanding of the nature of God's self-disclosure. As Rollins explains, traditionally Christianity has rested upon the idea that God has communicated to humanity through revelation, a concept that has been known as "that which reveals," is the opposite of concealment, and God has graciously disclosed to us something about himself. [576] In other words, in

---

[573] Barth, *Church Dogmatics*, vol. I,1:3.
[574] Barth, *Church Dogmatics*, vol. I,1:92.
[575] Pete Rollins, *How (Not) to Speak of God* (Brewster, MA: Paraclete Press, 2006, xii.
[576] Rollins, *How (Not) to Speak of God*, 7.

the past the historic doctrine of revelation that meant God has actually revealed, de-concealed, and graciously disclosed Himself to the world. In fact, Rollins suggests it is thought that "Christianity...has privileged access to the mind of God," an access which is contained and controlled by Christianity alone. [577] Rollins believes otherwise.

According to Rollins, this idea of revelation came through the Enlightenment after Christianity (falsely) embraced the Age of Reason, believing that "God was open to our understanding insomuch as God was revealed to us through the scripture." [578] For these Enlightenment Christians, it was simple: God gave us a document (the Holy Scriptures) and the ability to understand and explore that document (the mind), thus providing access to God's full, real Self (revelation). For Rollins, however, this notion of theistic accessibility is nothing short of "conceptual idolatry." He insists the idea of any system of thought which the individual or community takes to be a visible rendering of God—in this case an intellectual rendering—is neither God nor of God, but is instead an anthropocentric construct, an idol. [579] Rollins insists that Western theology has reduced God to conceptual idols by the very exercise of naming God. Instead, Rollins suggests God is not only unnameable, He is "omninameable," he cannot be revealed through human words and at the site of revelation, even when we think we can see God revealed to us, "we can only speak of God's otherness and

---

[577] Rollins, *How (Not) to Speak of God*, 7.
[578] Rollins, *How (Not) to Speak of God*, 9.
[579] Rollins, *How (Not) to Speak of God*, 12.

distance; Revelation has concealment built into its very heart."
[580]

Rollins believes that Christianity has far too much confidence in a full divine self-disclosure, too much confidence in an actual complete revelation at God's own behest, resulting in an overly defined, imbued "God" term. As Rollins insists, "If we fail to recognize that the term 'God' always falls short of that towards which the word is supposed to point, we will end up bowing down before our own conceptual creations forged from the raw materials of our self-image, rather than bowing before the one who stands over and above that creation." [581] According to Rollins, Christianity—especially the Western variety—has and is bowing before self-made revelatory "blocks of wood" in the form of theological constructs. He believes these constructs never really point to God Himself, however, because God blinds us with too much information about Himself. We must realize that our understanding of God comes as a result of One who overflows and blinds our understanding; God's incoming blinds our intellect, saturates our understanding with a blinding presence, and gives us far too much information, resulting in an intellectual "short-circuiting" by the excess of presence. [582] Ironically, while he argues God blinds us with the light of His presence, Rollins also agrees with Gregory of Nyssa that the more we move toward God we journey into divine darkness. While religious knowledge begins as an experience of entering into the light, the deeper we go the more darkness we find in that

---

[580] Rollins, *How (Not) to Speak of God*, 12.
[581] Rollins, *Speak of God*, 19.
[582] Rollins, *Speak of God*, 22, 24.

light; God is beyond the reach of all thinking. [583] In short, "Christianity testifies to the impossibility of grasping God because of the hyper-presence of God." [584] Barth would suggest otherwise, however.

For Barth, humanity has actual, genuine knowledge of God because God has chosen to actually, genuinely disclose Himself to us. Through His own purpose and volition, God made the decision to encounter man. As Barth argues, "God encounters man in such a way that man can know Him. He encounters him in such a way that in this encounter He still remains God, but also raises man up to be a real, genuine knower of Himself." [585] Rather than being hyper-hidden and overly concealed, God sets Himself before man in such away that he can actually and genuinely speak of and describe God. In other words, God is "graspable" by the very fact He has placed Himself before man to be grasped. In fact, though Barth does acknowledge a hiddenness and mystery to even His revelation, he also insists that God has made Himself "clear and certain to us;" God does not remain hidden to us, but we have a knowledge from God Himself. [586] We can actually, genuinely know God because He has chosen to show Himself to us in such a way that we can consider and conceive Him. [587] What we must understand, however, is that this knowledge is not from us, but from God.

This knowledge of which we speak "cannot at any moment or in any respect try to understand itself other than as the

---

[583] Rollins, *Speak of God*, 27.
[584] Rollins, *Speak of God*, 46.
[585] Barth, *Church Dogmatics*, II,1:32.
[586] Barth, *Church Dogmatics*, II,1:39.
[587] Barth, *Church Dogmatics*, II,1:10.

knowledge made possible, realized and ordered by God alone." [588] Like Barth, this is somewhat the point Rollins attempts to make: the source of our desire (God) is set as an object that we reflect upon in order to grasp it, hold it. [589] In an effort to maintain God's "otherness" and "beyondness," however, Rollins ultimately makes God unreachable and unknowable. Furthermore, Rollins argues that even when we describe God and claim a knowledge of Him, that claim and knowledge isn't even God Himself, but merely our *understanding* of God. [590] Barth would strongly insist otherwise, however. In fact he did: "there is a readiness of God to be known as *He actually is known* in the fulfillment in which the knowledge of God is a fact." [591] Rather than being hyper-hidden and our God-talk other than God Himself, God can be known because God wants to be known and what we say of God, by His grace, actually speaks of God. Barth continues: "'God is knowable' means God can be known—He can be known of and by Himself; in His essence, as it is turned to us in His activity, He is so constituted that He can be known by us." [592] In sharp contrast to Rollins, Barth rightly asserts that God has in fact set Himself before man in such away that we can confidently say "God can be known."

While human efforts at accurately and exhaustively describing God are fraught with inconsistencies, fragility, and incompleteness because man is fallen and sinful, we can know God because He has revealed Himself to humanity to be known.

---

[588] Barth, *Church Dogmatics*, II,1:41.
[589] Rollins, *Speak of God*, 1-2.
[590] Rollins, *Speak of God*, 98.
[591] Barth, *Church Dogmatics*, II,1:65. (emph. mine)
[592] Barth, *Church Dogmatics*, II,1:65.

As Barth explains, "God makes Himself known and offers Himself to us, so that we can in fact love Him as the one who exists for us...and He creates in us the possibility—the willingness and readiness—to know Him; so that, seen from our side also, there is no reason why this should not actually happen." [593] Actual, genuine knowledge of God can "actually happen" because we have a revelation from Him that comes to us in a manner that is intelligible, accessible, and clear. This revelation is clear, accessible, and intelligible not because we ourselves are capable of thinking our way to God through our own gumption and ingenuity, though. Barth makes it clear that, "it is by the grace of God and only by the grace of God that it comes about that God is knowable to us...He gives Himself to us to be known, which establishes our knowledge of Him. God's revelation is not at our power and command, but happens as a movement 'from God.'" [594] Barth also makes it incredibly clear that this ultimate movement of God to reveal Himself to humanity was through Jesus Christ, an assertion that is as questioned as our ability to even know God.

GOD'S REVELATION IS JESUS CHRIST

Not only does the Emergent Church question our ability to know God and challenge the extent to which God has truly spoken, the center of that knowledge and speaking is questioned, too. From the beginning, the historic Christian faith has taken seriously Jesus' own claim in John 14:9 that, "Anyone who has seen me has seen the Father." In the past, it was believed that

---

[593] Barth, *Church Dogmatics*, II,1:33.
[594] Barth, *Church Dogmatics*, II,1:69.

God the Father was revealed in God the Son, the One True God is only found in Jesus Christ. Now, however, even this central claim of historic Christian orthodoxy is questioned. In an essay in An Emergent Manifesto of Hope, Samir Selmanovic spearheaded this questioning when he claims, "We do believe that God is best defined by the historical revelation in Jesus Christ, but to believe that God is limited to it would be an attempt to manage God. If one holds that Christ is confined to Christianity, one has chosen a god that is not sovereign." [595] He writes elsewhere that the revelation of the grace of God through Jesus Christ, which has always been central to the historic Christian faith, is not exclusively limited to that faith or Jesus Christ. As Selmanovic claims, "We Christians have insisted that our revelation is the only container and only dispenser of grace. The rest of the world, graced from within, has been steadily proving us wrong. Grace is independent." [596] Selmanovic baldly asserts that the revelation that has come through the Holy Scriptures and Jesus Christ himself are not the only containers of God's grace; grace is also found outside the Christian Story. According to Selmanovic, neither the revelation of God Himself nor of His grace is contained or confined to Jesus Christ.

In *It's Really All About God: Reflections of a Muslim Atheist Jewish Christian,* Selmanovic revises and extends these initial thoughts on God's Christian containment. He argues, "to say God has decided to visit all humanity through only one particular religion is a deeply unsatisfying assertion about God."

---

[595] Samir Selmanovic, "The Sweet Problem of Inclusivism," (ed. Doug Pagitt and Tony Jones; Grand Rapids: BakerBooks, 2007), 193. (emph. mine)

[596] Samir Selmanovic, *It's Really All About God: Reflections of a Muslim Atheist Jewish Christian* (San Francisco: Jossey-Bass, 2009), 52.

[597] In order to protect his argument in favor of religious pluralism, Selmanovic claims that none of us are in charge of God; God refuses to be owned and to comply with our religious constructs. [598] In fact Selmanovic argues strongly for a revelation beyond that of the Christian faith:

> As long as those of us who are Christians insist on staying enclosed in our own world of meanings, we have nothing more to say to the world. Without recognizing God, grace, and goodness outside of the boundaries we have made and without the possibility of expanding our understanding of God, grace, and goodness, we have come to a place where Christianity as we know it must either end or experience another Exodus. 599

Here Selmanovic insists that Christians must acknowledge that God is everywhere—in every person, every community, and all creation—otherwise we will loose the basis for seeing God anywhere. [600] Ultimately, Selmanovic believes that "the Christianity that claims exclusive possession of God's revelation in the person of Jesus has hijacked that same God from the world." [601] After reducing Christianity to one of three monotheistic "religions," Selmanovic shows his real hand: "People want God, but not one who is the captive of a religion. They want an unmanaged God. Free God. That's where hope

---

[597] Selmanovic, *All About God*, 9.
[598] Selmanovic, *About God*, 16, 18.
[599] Selmanovic, *About God*, 60-61.
[600] Selmanovic, *About God*, 60-61.
[601] Selmanovic, *About God*, 68.

comes from." [602] Apparently, Selmanovic also desires a God free from religion, Christianity, Jesus Christ.

Barth paints a very different picture in his *Dogmatics*, however. He boldly asserts that God's revelation is only, exclusively in Jesus Christ. While Selmanovic believes that God is simply best defined by the historical revelation in Jesus Christ, Barth insists God is *only* defined by Jesus Christ. To suggest that God is not limited to "the historical revelation in Jesus Christ" is foreign to the Holy Scriptures and historic Christian faith. Barth argues this very point when he writes, "[God] is wholly and utterly in His revelation in Jesus Christ." [603] He also makes plain that we must know Jesus in order to know God, because "in him are hid all the treasures of wisdom and knowledge (Col. 2:3)." [604] Furthermore, Barth makes clear that what he describes in his *Dogmatics* is the knowledge of God as found in the knowledge of Jesus; unless Jesus Christ is the reference point for the revelation of God, "we have not described it in faith, or as the knowledge of faith, and therefore not in any sense as the true knowledge of God." [605]

While Selmanovic believes that "Grace did not start with Christianity and will not end with Christianity. It is a common thing in this world." [606] Barth argues otherwise: "When we appeal to God's grace, we appeal to the grace of the incarnation and to [Jesus Christ] as the One in whom, because He is the eternal Son of God, knowledge of God was, is and will be present

---

[602] Selmanovic, *About God*, 90, 92.
[603] Barth, *Church Dogmatics*, II,1:75.
[604] Barth, *Church Dogmatics*, II,1:252.
[605] Barth, *Church Dogmatics*, II,1:252.
[606] Selmanovic, *About God*, 51.

originally and properly." [607] For Barth, the revelation of God through grace is intimately and only connected to Jesus Christ, because His own act of divine self-disclosure is bound up with Him. Jesus Christ is given to the whole being of God, not simply a part of Him, and God is not known at all unless He is known in His entirety as Father, Son and Holy Spirit, Creator, Reconciler, and Redeemer. [608] It is in His grace through Jesus Christ that God is known as Reconciler and Redeemer. Rather than experiencing the knowledge of God and His grace apart from Jesus Christ, both are intimately and only connected to *Him*. It is only in Jesus Christ that we know and understand God and His grace.

Selmanovic goes on to rhetorically wonder, however, "Is our religion the only one that understands the true meaning of life? Or does God place his truth in others too? Well, God decides, and not us. The gospel is not our gospel, but the gospel of the kingdom of God, and what belongs to the kingdom of God cannot be hijacked by Christianity." [609] In this argument Selmanovic does two things: 1) he argues that the Kingdom of God is not connect simply to Jesus; and 2) he argues the Kingdom of God itself is a vehicle of what Barth call's "divine immanence." Barth, however, makes it clear that God's Kingdom is not known at all apart from Jesus Christ, and attempting to do so is heretical. As Barth strongly warns, "Christian heresies spring from the fact that man does not take seriously the known ground of divine immanence in Jesus Christ, so that from its revelation, instead of apprehending Jesus Christ and the totality

---

[607] Barth, *Church Dogmatics*, II,1:252.
[608] Barth, *Church Dogmatics*, II,1:51-52.
[609] Selmanovic, "The Sweet Problem of Inclusivism," 194.

in Him, he arbitrarily selects this or that feature and sets it up as a subordinate centre: perhaps the idea of creation...or even the kingdom of God." [610] It seems clear that Selmanovic is in danger of making the very mistake Barth warns against for two reasons.

First, Selmanovic clearly describes the Kingdom of God in terms that are utterly disconnected from Jesus Christ alone. Secondly, he has selected the feature of the Kingdom of God and believes it as a revelatory ground of "divine immanence," instead of Jesus Christ alone. Barth counters such people with these words:

> [They are] oblivious of the fact that [divine] immanence both as a whole and in its parts has Christian truth and reality only in so far as it is founded in Jesus Christ and summed up in Him, so that if, as a whole and in its parts, it is affirmed, preached and believed as a centre in itself and alongside Christ, the Church will inevitably be led back into heathendom and its worship of the elements. 611

Unfortunately, Selmanovic affirms this devastating indictment by claiming the Kingdom is not exclusively limited to Jesus Christ. I quote him at length:

> Many Christians believe that the Kingdom of God that Jesus spoke about is inseparable from knowing the person of Jesus. If so, the question begs to be asked: Is the Kingdom of God present in all of life, among all people, throughout history, or is the Kingdom of God limited to the historical person of Jesus and thus absent from most of life, most people, and most history? The

---

[610] Barth, *Church Dogmatics*, II,1:319.
[611] Barth, *Church Dogmatics*, II,1:319.

answer to this question depends greatly on whether Christians are willing to make their religion take a backseat to something larger than itself. 612

It seems clear that Selmanovic completely disconnects God's revelation from the person of Jesus Christ, while making it no longer exclusively connected to him. In light of these observations it seems clear enough from Selmanovic's arguments that the Kingdom of God, as part of divine immanence, has been wrested from its moorings in Jesus Christ and is "affirmed, preached and believed as a centre in itself and *alongside* Christ." God is now revealed in the Kingdom of God and alongside Jesus Christ, rather than through Him alone.

Not only does he believe that the Kingdom of God apart from Jesus Christ reveals God, Selmanovic denies that God is revealed fully and exclusively in Christ. Selmanovic both favors another revelation of God apart from Jesus Christ (the Kingdom of God) and denies that the fulness of God's revelation is in Him alone. As Barth reminds us, though, "Any deviation, any attempt to evade Jesus Christ in favor of another supposed revelation of God, or any denial of the fulness of God's presence in Him, will precipitate us into darkness and confusion." According to Barth, then, Selmanovic's belief that God is revealed in a separate act of divine immanence (the Kingdom of God) apart from Jesus Christ "will precipitate us into darkness and confusion." 613 Likewise, Selmanovic assertion that God is not revealed wholly, simply, exclusively in Jesus Christ will have the same result. It is clear that Selmanovic's belief in the revelation and knowledge of

---

612 Selmanovic, *All About God*, 76-77.
613 Barth, *Church Dogmatics*, II,1:319.

God largely departs from the historic Christian faith. In response Barth would adamantly declare it is really not all about God. It is really all about Jesus Christ.

CONCLUSION

Thanks to these Emergent leaders, there is now growing confusion within the Church over both the extent to which we may know God and the manner in which He has revealed Himself. It seems clear that Rollins understands God as hyper-transcendent and Wholly Other, believing He is far more hidden and concealed than the Christian faith believes. For Rollins we can neither truly name God nor actually describe Him, because He is not actually, genuinely revealed. Practically, this cashes out as what Rollins calls an "a/theistic Christianity." An a/theistic Christian can be said to operate with a discourse that makes claims about God while simultaneously acknowledging that these claims are provisional, uncertain, and insufficient; our questioning of God isn't really questioning of God Himself but only a means of questioning our *understanding* of God. [614] By implication this would mean the revelation we have of God is not complete or actual enough to understand, question, and know Him. This is why Rollins ultimately insists that speaking of God is really only speaking about our understanding of God, rather than God himself. [615]

Selmanovic, while acknowledging a real revelation of God that can be experienced by humans, believes that revelation is neither exclusively tied to Jesus Christ nor contained within the

---

[614] Rollins, *Speak of God*, 98.
[615] Rollins, *Speak of God*, 32.

Christian faith. For Him, it's really all about "God," a vapid, generalized World-Spirit [616] that is encased in all religions, rather than exclusively revealed through Jesus Christ, on the one hand, and the Church, on the other. Selmanovic is unsatisfied with the assertion that the Christian faith testifies to God's Story of Rescue and that rescue is exclusively found in Jesus Christ. In fact, the grace of God to which the Holy Scriptures and Church have testified for generations isn't even unique to the Christ or the Christian faith. Instead, this grace is independent from both and common in the world's histories, stories, and religions. God is present everywhere and in every person, and the Christian faith cannot insist on an exclusive revelation in Jesus Christ or the Church. In the end, it is the Kingdom of God that reveals God to the world, an idea that is trans-religious and separate from even Jesus Christ Himself.

Upon surveying the writings of both Rollins and Selmanovic, one wonders why they are self-described Christians and committed to Christianity at all. If God doesn't really speak, why posture one's self as a listener? If God is not wholly and exclusively revealed in Jesus Christ, why commit one's self to Him and His Story? In response to both religious thinkers, Barth asserts God does speak and He is revealed in Jesus Christ. For Barth, there is real, genuine knowledge of God because God has chosen to reveal Himself to humanity. This divine self-disclosure is in such away that humans can actually, genuinely know Him. Barth declares that there is a readiness of God to be known, a knowledge that is "clear and certain." While the knowledge that we have is not through our own gumption and ingenuity, but

---

[616] This is the same language Fredrick Schleiermacher uses in his book, *On Religion*.

through grace, God is revealed in such a way that we can know Him. Though we cannot apprehend this revelation through our own power and will, it does happen and has happened. Barth makes clear that ultimately Jesus Christ is the point at which the world truly knows God. While others may suggest God is *best* defined by Jesus Christ, Barth insists He is *only* defined by Jesus. God is utterly and wholly revealed in Jesus Christ; to know Jesus is to know God. In fact, the only way to know God in intimate relationship is through the grace found in and through Jesus Christ. Barth maintains that God's grace is only and intimately connected to Christ, rather than other sources and other religious faiths. Finally, Barth warns of the danger of selecting competing centers of revelation apart from Jesus Christ, like the Kingdom of God.

In his *Church Dogmatics* volume on *The Doctrine of God*, Barth makes clear that "Theology guides the language of the Church, so far as it concretely reminds her that in all circumstances it is fallible human work, which in the matter of relevance or irrelevance lies in the balance, and must obedience to grace, if it is to be well done." [617] Here Barth acknowledges the difficult task of "theologizing," of speaking of God and His acts. While that speech is fallible and vacillates between relevance or irrelevance, requiring a healthy dose of grace along the way, it needs to happen nonetheless. Every generation needs to cherish, protect, and contend for the Rule of Faith given by our Lord once to the Church. If not, there is a real danger of precipitating into darkness and confusion. It is clear from the writings of these

---

[617] Karl Barth, *Church Dogmatics*, vol. I,1:2.

two theologians and thinkers that a shift is occurring within the Church regarding an important piece of that Rule, revelation.

Though historic Christian orthodoxy has consistently held to the real, genuine knowability of God and that knowledge being fully and exclusively revealed (outside of creation) in Jesus Christ, there are some who insist otherwise. There is a growing number who shove God so far into the clouds that nothing can be concretely said of Him. Others still, and perhaps more dangerously so, find God outside Jesus Christ, insisting God is in every person, every community, every religion. God and His grace is no longer exclusively revealed in Jesus Christ, but possessed by other faiths, too. It is worth ending with Barth's warning as a reminder for these theologians and other Christians: "Any deviation, any attempt to evade Jesus Christ in favor of another supposed revelation of God, or any denial of the fulness of God's presence in Him, will precipitate us into darkness and confusion." [618]

May this not be the end of these or others who claim Jesus Christ as Lord.

BIBLIOGRAPHY

Barth, Karl. Church Dogmatics, vol I, 1: *The Doctrine of the Word of God*. Translated by G.T. Thomson. Edinburgh: T&T Clark, 1955.

_____. Church Dogmatics, vol II, 1: *The Doctrine of God*. Edited by G.W. Bromiley and T.F. Torrance. Translated by

---

[618] Karl Barth, *Church Dogmatics*, vol. I,1:2.

T.H.L Parker, W.B. Johnson, Harold Knight, and J.L.M. Haire. Edinburgh: T&T Clark, 1957.

Erdman, Chris. "Digging Up the Past: Karl Barth (the Reformed Giant) as Friend to the Emerging Church," Pages 236-243 in *An Emergent Manifesto of Hope.* Edited by Doug Pagitt and Tony Jones. Grand Rapids: Baker Books, 2007.

Jones, Tony. "Introduction: Friendship, Faith, and Going Somewhere Together." Pages 11-15 in *An Emergent Manifesto of Hope.* Edited by Doug Pagitt and Tony Jones. Grand Rapids: Baker Books, 2007.

Rollins, Pete. *How (Not) To Speak of God.* Brewster, MA: Paraclete Press, 2006.

Selmanovic, Samir. "The Sweet Problem of Inclusivism." Pages 11-15 in *An Emergent Manifesto of Hope.* Edited by Doug Pagitt and Tony Jones. Grand Rapids: Baker Books, 2007.

_____. *It's Really All About God: Reflections of a Muslim Atheist Jewish Christian.* San Francisco: Jossey-Bass, 2009

3

Ritschl & McLaren

In 2001 Brian McLaren, a little known pastor author just north of Washington D.C., [619] began influencing street-level theological conversations within evangelicalism with his landmark book, *A New Kind of Christian*. Through the book's two protagonists—Pastor Dan and Neo— McLaren took the reader on a redefining journey through evangelical's core theological doctrines. God, creation, sin, Christ, the cross, resurrection, and judgment were all addressed and countered with alternative possibilities that formed the foundation for a broader conversation known as the Emerging Church. It was also a reflection of his own spiritual journey, one that culminated in "a quest for honesty, for authenticity, and for a faith that made more sense to me and to others...learning that there is a kind of faith that runs deeper than mere beliefs." [620] Many who entered this conversation found resonance with

---

[619] McLaren has since retired from pastoring and been named one of the "25 Most Influential Evangelicals In America," *Time Magazine*, February 7, 2005.
[620] Brian McLaren, *A New Kind of Christianity* (New York, HarperOne, 2010,) 6, 8.

McLaren's quest, finding solace in the questions and alternative answers offered by McLaren in response to what many perceived to be stogy, stuffy, stale theology that had outlived its lifecycle. While the *New Kind of Christian* trilogy simply offered possibilities, McLaren's latest book, *A New Kind of Christianity*, suggests concrete alternatives to the historic Christian faith.

A New Kind of Christianity, the culmination of McLaren's work, is a theological tour de force that continues the Emerging Church's theological challenge, while offering theological alternatives in the process. Now rather than simply translating the historic Christian faith into a present postmodern context, McLaren insists "we need a new way of believing, not simply new answers to the same old questions, but a new set of questions. We are acknowledging that the Christianities we have created deserve to be reexamined and deconstructed...so that our religious traditions can be seen for what they are...they are evolving, embodied, situated versions of the faith." [621] Like others, McLaren has set out to construct a new, fresh, alternative Christianity.

There isn't anything new, however, about the main tenets of this newly constructed version of Christianity. Instead, the version of Christianity offered by the Emerging Church and its leaders is a repackaged form of other versions that have appeared throughout the historical progression of the story of Christian theology. McLaren's newest theological missive to the church is no different. Though he believes a new kind of Christianity "is trying to be born among those of us who believe

---

[621] McLaren, *New Kind of Christianity*, 18, 27.

and follow Jesus Christ,"[622] McLaren's version of Christianity is an old one; specifically A New Kind of Christianity is a repackaged form of the Christian faith known as Ritschlianism, the theology of Albrecht Ritschl, a German theologian who followed in the theological footsteps of Fredrick Schleiermacher, the father of modern-day liberalism. [623]

Shortly after his death, Ritschl was said to have done "more than any other theologian to prepare the way for a fundamental and yet conservative reconstruction of the theology of the church." [624] Though perhaps not as well known as his predecessor, Schleiermacher, Ritschl has been a significant theological force within liberal Protestantism, having influenced a generation of Western theologians and theological movements through his theological reconstruction. He had a profound impact on Adolf von Harnack, [625] who is credited with inaugurating the century-long Historic Jesus Movement. Walter Rauschenbusch, a Baptist preacher from upstate New York, drew upon the theological themes of Ritschl while founding the so-called Social Justice Movement. [626] One also finds elements of Ritschl in Paul Tillich, one of the four most influential theologians of the 20th century who helped give rise to Christian existentialism. [627] Following in the theological tradition of these 19th and 20th century theologians is a 21st century voice, Brian McLaren.

---

[622] McLaren, *New Kind of Christianity*, 13.
[623] Olson, *The Story of Christian Theology* (Downers Grove: IVP Academic, 1999), 542.
[624] Albert Temple Swing, The Theology of Albrecht Ritschl (London: Longmans, Green, and Co., 1901), 1.
[625] Livingston, James C. *Modern Christian Thought*, (New York: Macmillian Publishing Co., 1971.), 257, 258.
[626] Livingston, *Modern Christian Thought*, 262.
[627] Livingston, *Modern Christian Thought*, 356-370.

Because of the nature and influence of the contemporary emerging church movement in general and McLaren in particular, it is necessary to engage his writings. Currently, very few are placing the writings of these leaders under the lens of historical theology; very few historical theologian gave engaged McLaren's newest theological work. Therefore, this examination will explore McLaren's writings, with special emphasis on A New Kind of Christianity, in light of the theology of Ritschl. This theological comparison will map the theological similarities between Ritschl and McLaren in three key theological categories: sin, Christology, and salvation.

First, we will explore how they view humanity's problem through their view on sin. Second, we will look at why they say Christ was necessary and how our sin problem is solved through His work. Finally, we will seek to understand how we find salvation and from what we are saved in the first place. In the end, this comparative analysis will reveal McLaren's Christianity is not new at all. It is a repackaged form of theological liberalism that reigned in the early 20th century. His is indeed an old kind of Christianity.

ON HUMAN NATURE & SIN

McLaren first provided hints to his theological understanding of human nature and sin in an early work, *The Story We Find Ourselves In*, which he later developed in *A New Kind of Christianity*. In this second part of his *New Kind of Christian* trilogy, McLaren establishes the framing narrative for his new kind of Christian, one that would eventually form the foundation for his new kind of Christianity. Through his protagonist Neo, McLaren contends that the modern telling of the Christian story has been distorted, because it imported "the Greek idea of a fall from a perfect, unchanging, ideal, complete, harmonious, fully formed world into a world of change, challenge, conflict..." [628] For McLaren, there was no fall, in the traditional sense of the historic doctrine of sin. Instead, "the God-given goodness in creation isn't lost...God's creative fingerprint or signature is still there, always and forever. The evil of humanity doesn't eradicate the goodness of God's creation, even though it puts all of that goodness at risk." [629] Instead of creating a perfect world that "falls" from a Platonic perfect ideal, it is "a story of emergence;" creation is evolutionary and "must go on creating itself." [630] Therefore, humanity has not fallen and is still good. This initial exploration of McLaren's view of Creation and the Fall is important when we begin exploring his understanding of humanity and sin.

As the Earth's story is one of emergence, so too is humanity's; our story is not a fall from perfection into a state of imperfection, but "unfolds as a kind of compassionate...classic coming-of-age story." [631] While the traditional doctrine of the Fall contends "there is one cataclysmic event in which the first humans descend—or fall, if you will—from their ideal, perfect state into the material, imperfect story of history," McLaren does

---

[628] Brian McLaren, *The Story We Find Ourselves In* (San Francisco: Jossey-Bass, 2003), 52. This is later affirmed and further developed in *A New Kind of Christianity*, 33-45.

[629] McLaren, *Story We Find Ourselves*, 52.

[630] McLaren, *Story We Find Ourselves*, 52. In fact, in *A New Kind of Christianity* McLaren asserts, "Evolution fits beautifully in the good world of Elohim." 267n.4.

[631] McLaren, *New Kind of Christianity*, 49, 51.

not see just one single cataclysmic crisis but "an avalanche of crises" that:

> all involve human beings gaining levels of intellectual and technological development that surpass their moral development—people becoming too smart, too powerful for their own good...Human beings leave their identity, their life, their story as creatures in God's creation...As they become more independent, they lose their connection to God, their sense of dependence...So they experience alienation from God." 632

In other words, as humans "come of age" they grow beyond God, and their relationship deteriorates in progressive, fitful "experiences of alienation." McLaren describes this progress and growth in his book, *The Secret Message of Jesus* in this way:

> [Adam's and Eve's] noble status quickly deteriorates as they disconnect from God and reject any limits placed upon their freedom by their Creator. The results of their disobedience are visible as the story unfolds—a sense of shame and alienation from God and one another, violence of brother against brother, disharmony with creation itself, misunderstanding and conflict among tribes and nations. 633

For McLaren, there is no event of "the Fall" or corresponding "original sin" and "total depravity" in which humanity plunged into rebellion and alienation, resulting in an inherited sinful nature. [634] Instead, the framing narrative of humanity is one of

---

632 McLaren, *Story We Find Ourselves*, 53-54, 56.
633 Brian McLaren, *The Secret Message of Jesus* (Nashville: Word Publishing, 2006), 27.
634 McLaren, *The Secret Message of Jesus*, 27.

systemic progression and ascent, with corresponding descent resulting in "new depths of moral evil and social injustice." [635] In his re-imagined framing narrative, individuals are no longer the issue, but the human systems; "socioeconomic and technological advances" lead to moral evil and social injustice, not individuals acting upon their sinful nature. [636] In the words of McLaren, "it's a story about the downside of 'progress'—a story of human foolishness...the human turn toward rebellion...the human intention toward evil." [637] The problem isn't that humans rebelled against God and are rebels or that humans did evil and are evil. For McLaren, the story is one of humans creating evil and damaging and savaging God's good world, it is a story where "humans have evil intent," instead of being evil themselves. Those evil intentions are not the result of an evil heart, but the bad systems and stories that consume humans.

This framing narrative first written in *The Story We Find Ourselves In* evolved into a later work in which McLaren addresses the big questions and problems that face our world, insisting that everything must change. In his similarly titled book, *Everything Must Change*, McLaren believes the main dysfunctions of humanity are ethical; he frames the crisis of the human condition as a crisis of prosperity, equity, and security. [638] These three crises form the "cogs" in what McLaren terms the *suicide machine*. [639] The suicide machine is a metaphor for "the systems that drive our civilization toward un-health and un-

---

[635] McLaren, *New Kind of Christianity*, 51.
[636] McLaren, *New Kind of Christianity*, 51.
[637] McLaren, *New Kind of Christianity*, 54.
[638] Brian McLaren, *Everything Must Change* (Nashville: Thomas Nelson Publishers, 2007), 5.
[639] McLaren, *Everything Must Change*, 53.

peace." [640] McLaren envisions the driving force behind our broken, problematic condition to reside in the systems of the world, rather than in the individual person. According to him, humanity suffers from a "dysfunction of our societal machinery," which is operated not by single individuals but by humanity acting together." [641] In other words, individual sinful human nature is not the problem, but rather a universal sin of society.

Primarily, the dysfunction and sin of society is measured by our collective framing story. No matter what group we belong to, we are under the influence of that group's framing story, where we learn our origin, our destination, and how we should act in between along the way. According to McLaren, our world's dominant framing story is failing for three main reasons: it does not "guide us to respect environmental limits, but instead inspires pursuit of as much resource use and waste production as possible," resulting in an unsustainable way of life; it does not "lead us to work for the common good," but instead encourage each group to become "a competing us/them faction that seeks advantage for 'us,' not a common good for all;" and "our framing story does not lead these competing factions to reconcile peacefully," instead locking our world "in a vicious cycle of tension between an anxious global empire of the rich and an angry global terrorist revolution of the poor." [642]

In *A New Kind of Christianity*, McLaren illustrates this explanation of the human condition and reality of so-called "social sin." Using the story of the Israelites in Exodus, he

---

[640] McLaren, *Everything Must Change*, 53. (emphasis mine)
[641] McLaren, *Everything Must Change*, 65.
[642] McLaren, *Everything Must Change*, 68-70.

explains that it is a story of "liberation from the external oppression of social sin," while also celebrating "liberation from the internal spiritual oppression of personal sin." Because McLaren does not believe that sin is part of human nature because of an event of rebellion, he must mean something different by "internal spiritual oppression of personal sin."[643] It seems even this internal oppression is related to the social systems of sin, because he asserts that people are freed from "the *dominating powers* of fear, greed, impatience, ingratitude, and so on." [644] The power of Fear and Ingratitude, then are the oppressors, which in the Exodus narrative apparently results from years of being "debased by generations of slavery." [645] This slave framing story, then, is what contributed to the Israelites communal and individual commitment to "fear, greed, impatience, ingratitude, and so on." The internal compulsion toward greed, for example, was an internal power that resulted from the external system of slavery and the bad framing narrative out of which Israel was liberated. Thus, our ultimate problem is bad systems and stories.

Unlike the traditional historic faith that locates the problem of the human condition in individual sinfulness and an inherited sinful nature, McLaren believes humans are in trouble because we are in bondage to the "dominant societal machinery," which entices us to keep faith in its systems of wealthy, security, pleasure, and injustice. [646] This faith and bondage has led to a sort of universal consciousness that is driven by destructive,

---

[643] McLaren, *New Kind of Christianity*, 58.
[644] McLaren, *New Kind of Christianity*, 58. (emphasis mine.)
[645] McLaren, *New Kind of Christianity*, 58.
[646] McLaren, *Everything Must Change*, 271.

dysfunctional framing stories. The global crises of which McLaren says we must be saved are the symptoms and consequences of the dysfunction, resulting in a collection of human evil. Dysfunctional societal machinery, destructive framing narratives, and collective human evil are our problems. They compel innately good humans to act badly, rather than in inner, natural compulsion.

McLaren's understanding of the human condition and sin finds several points of connection to the theology of Ritschl. First, McLaren reflects Ritschl's own rejection of the historic doctrine of original sin. In confronting the idea of original sin, Ritschl relegates it to the sphere of "doctrine," insisting it is an intellectual idea that does not conform to experience. [647] Like McLaren, Ritschl rejects the notion that there was both an original righteousness and fall from that original constitution. [648] In fact, the doctrine of original sin that developed in the early church and was codified by Augustine out of this assumption [649] is challenged by Ritschl to in no way reflect any New Testament authors: "Neither Jesus nor any of the New Testament writers either indicate or presuppose that sin is universal merely through natural generation." [650] Likewise, he disputed as unbiblical the Reformed assertion that humans are incapable of

[647] Albrecht Ritschl, *The Christian Doctrine of Justification and Reconciliation: The Positive Development of the Doctrine*. Edited by H.R. Mackintosh and A.B. Macaulay (Edinburgh: T & T Clark, 1902.), 328.
[648] Ritschl, *Justification and Reconciliation*, 331.
[649] Albrecht Ritschl, *Instruction in the Christian Religion*. Translated by Alice Mead Wing (London: Longmans, Green & Co, 1901), 203.n27. Here he writes, "Augustine's doctrine of original sin, ie., that the original inclination to evil transmitted in generation is for every one both personal guilt and subject to the divine sentence of eternal punishment, is not confirmed by any New Testament author."
[650] Ritschl, *Instruction in the Christian Religion*, 203.n27.

doing good because of their inherent sinfulness.[651] Furthermore, Ritschl argued that original sin is neither derived from the natural endowment of man [652] nor inherited from previous generations. [653] Instead, Ritschl argued that sin is acquired through human history and development.

McLaren describes such an acquisition by asserting that the human narrative as one that is a "classic coming of age story." In other words, the condition of humanity evolved. Instead of inheriting a sinful nature from Adam, the generations from our first human parents got trapped in an "avalanche of crises" that engulfed humanity in dysfunctional systems and destructive stories. In the words of Ritschl, humanity is now caught in a "whole web of sinful actions and reaction, which presuppose and yet again increases the selfish bias in every man." [654] Humans were created with the capacity to freely direct their impulses toward the "perfect common good" or highest good. [655] From the beginning humans were created with an internal goodness that was to be directed toward the highest common good, which the Kingdom of God reflects. Now we are caught in webs similar to McLaren's dysfunctional systems and destructive stories that have escalated over time, webs which compel every man toward selfish acts.

Was it inevitable that humans would use their freedom to choose the opposite of the common good? Ritschl wrote that "The possibility and probability of sinning...can be derived from

---

[651] Ritschl, *Instruction in the Christian Religion*, 206-207.n4.
[652] Ritschl, *Instruction in the Christian Religion*, 204.
[653] Ritschl, *Justification and Reconciliation*, 348.
[654] Ritschl, *Justification and Reconciliation*, 350.
[655] Ritschl, *Instruction in the Christian Religion*, 202.

the fact that the human will...is a constantly growing power whose activity also is not from the first accompanied by a complete knowledge of the good." [656] Like McLaren's assertion that human power grew and developed over time from hunter-gatherers to empire dwellers, Ritschl suggests that the capacity for humans to act grew and developed over time, which inevitably led to an abuse of freedom. This freedom from our first parents resulted in a "defect in reverence and in trust in God, or indifference and mistrust of Him," which is the basic form of their sin.[657] In other words they lost "their connection to God, their sense of dependence...So they experienced alienation from God." [658]

In Adam, there is a universal loss of connection, dependence, reverence, and trust in God, because every generation has actively participated in the transgression of freely mistrusting God and rejecting the perfect moral good. These collective acts have resulted in what Ritschl calls the "kingdom of sin" or "web of sin." For Ritschl, the kingdom of sin is an alternative hypothesis to original sin that explains the human condition. [659] This kingdom or universal sinfulness is the collective human sins that act as a collective conscious out of which individuals act. He also describes this kingdom and universality as "united action" which leads to a reinforcement of sin in every generation: "United sin, this opposite of the kingdom of God, rests upon all as a power which at least limits the freedom of the

---

[656] Ritschl, *Instruction in the Christian Religion*, 204.
[657] Ritschl, *Justification and Reconciliation*, 334.
[658] McLaren, *Story We Find Ourselves*, 56.
[659] McLaren, *Story We Find Ourselves*, 56.

individual to do good." [660] Like McLaren's dysfunctional systems and destructive stories, the sin that swirls around us compels us to sin, which cashes out as a sinful bias that is acquired by individuals because of bad examples. As Ritschl explains, "The sinful bias...is not described by [Paul] as inherited, and can with perfect reason be understood as something acquired. In the individual [the sinful bias] comes to be the principle of the will's direction."[661] This individual bias contributes to the larger whole of "wickedness and untruth" in what Ritschl terms a "web of sinful action." It is the collective contribution of individual actions and reactions and also "increases the selfish bias in every man." [662] This "web of sin" is the dysfunctional systems and destructive stories of which McLaren speaks.

Both McLaren and Ritschl believe our human problem is what we do and not who we are by nature—we do not sin because we're sinners; we are a sinner because we sin in concert with humanity and its web of sin. The web of sin that surrounds us creates a bias within us toward selfishness and compels us to sin; we are oppressed on the outside not affected on the inside. Therefore, our solution must address this evil web of systems, the person who came to bring us that solution had to do something with that web. We didn't need a savior to stand in our place of punishment; we needed someone to launch a better system, a better Kingdom.

---

[660] Ritschl, *Instruction in the Christian Religion*, 206.
[661] Ritschl, *Justification and Reconciliation*, 346, 347.
[662] Ritschl, *Justification and Reconciliation*, 350.

ON THE PERSON & WORK OF CHRIST

If our human problem is the dysfunctional societal machinery and destructive framing narratives—in other words the "web of sin" and bad ethics formed by the world's systems and stories—what is the solution? For McLaren Jesus is indeed the answer for the world today, but in a way that is different from historical Christian orthodoxy. While the historic Christian faith recognizes Jesus Christ as God and in some way a penal substitute sacrifice for the sins of the world, McLaren recognizes neither. Instead, Jesus is merely the best teacher of a better way of living, the one who lived the best way to be human, and one who is our best picture of the character of God. The best teacher, way, and picture of God is the perfect solution to McLaren's problem, because according to him we need a better example to follow in order to live differently and avert dysfunction and destruction. In *The Story We Find Ourselves In*, McLaren describes Jesus as a "revolutionary" who was a "master of living". [663] According to McLaren, "Jesus really is in some mysterious and in a unique way sent from God and full of God." [664] Notice McLaren does not say Jesus *is* God, but merely a messenger of sorts from God and *full* of Him, which is code for sharing in the divine. As it will be shown, His fellowship with God comes from his ethical way of living; He is the moral, not the metaphysical, Son of God. While McLaren doesn't outright deny His ontological divinity, he never says He is God Himself, either. Again, because the problem is bad systems and stories, our solution needed to be in the form of a better teaching, system,

---

[663] McLaren, *Story We Find Ourselves*, 115, 121, 122.
[664] McLaren, *Story We Find Ourselves*, 122.

way of life, and story. Jesus provides that new, better system and story as a messenger from God who founds His Kingdom.

McLaren affirms this characterization in his recent book by insisting that Jesus "brings us to a new evolutionary level in our understanding of God...the experience of God in Jesus requires a brand-new definition or understanding of God," because He "gives us the highest, deepest, and most mature view of the character of the living God." [665] This emphasis on the "character of God" is used throughout McLaren's description of the person of God in *A New Kind of Christianity*: "When you see [Jesus], you are getting the best view afforded to humans of the character of God;" "Jesus serves as the Word-made-flesh revelation of the character of God;" and "the invisible God has been made visible in his life. 'If you want to know what God is like,' Jesus says, 'look at me, my life, my ways, my deeds, my character.'" [666] Elsewhere he writes, that Jesus simply identifies Himself *with* God, telling His disciples that those who had seen Him had in "some real way" also seen God. [667] In fact, McLaren agrees with a Quaker scholar, Elton Trueblood, whom he quotes: "The historic Christian doctrine of the divinity of Christ does not simply mean that Jesus is like God. It is far more radical than that. It means that God is like Jesus." [668] Jesus, then, is not God Himself: Jesus is like God and God is like Jesus. In a "mysterious and unique way" Jesus is full of God. He shows, images and expresses God's character. McLaren suggests He accomplishes this primarily

---

[665] McLaren, *New Kind of Christianity*, 114, 115.
[666] McLaren, *New Kind of Christianity*, 118, 128, 222.
[667] McLaren, *Secret Message of Jesus*, 31.
[668] As quoted by McLaren, *New Kind of Christianity*, 114.

through his life and teachings. This is a good thing because humanity needs a better life and set of teachings.

From McLaren's earlier writings one can detect this theological trajectory and emphasis on Jesus as "teacher" and "liver." In explaining Jesus as "Lord," he argues this means Jesus "was the master of living...it would mean that no one else could take the raw materials of life...and elicit from them a beautiful song of truth and goodness. [The disciples] believed Jesus' way was higher and more brilliant, and the right way to launch a revolution of God." [669] Elsewhere he writes that Jesus' message and teachings is an "alternative framing story" that can "save the system from suicide," a message that focuses "on personal, social, and global transformation in this life." [670] Furthermore, "Jesus' life and message centered on the articulation and demonstration of a radically different framing story—one that critiques and exposes the imperial narratives as dangerous to itself and others." [671] Again, since the problem is bad systems and stories, Jesus' mastery over life through his higher, brilliant way of living and alternative message provides the existential solution to our existential problem.

What exactly was that message that Jesus articulated? The message of the Kingdom of God, or as McLaren puts it the "revolution of God." Through his life and teachings, Jesus "inserted into human history a seed of grace, truth, and hope that can never be defeated," a seed that will "prevail over the evil and injustice of humanity and lead to the world's ongoing

---

[669] McLaren, *The Story We Find Ourselves In*, 121.
[670] McLaren, *Everything Must Change*, 73, 22.
[671] McLaren, *Everything Must Change*, 154-155.

transformation into the world God dreams of." [672] Because the human problem is bad systems and stories, we need a new system and a new story to repair and heal us. Jesus provides humanity the solution through his teachings on the Kingdom of God and living out the way of that Kingdom. McLaren makes it clear that the central point of Jesus is the Kingdom of God. As he insists, "[Jesus] came to launch a new Genesis, to lead a new Exodus, and to announce, embody, and inaugurate a new kingdom as the Prince of Peace. Seen in this light, Jesus and his message has everything to do with poverty, slavery, and a 'social agenda.'" [673] He insists that Jesus himself "saw these dynamics at work in his day and proposed in word and deed a new alternative. Jesus' creative and transforming framing story invited people to change the world by disbelieving old framing stories and believing a new one: a story about a loving God who calls all people to live life in a new way." [674]

His newest book revises and extends these arguments by insisting that Jesus came to "lead the way in liberation from the social and spiritual oppression of his day;" He was chosen by God "to liberate His people from oppression." [675] As we have already seen, our human problem is not a sinful nature, but dysfunctional systems and destructive stories. Rather than being affected on the inside by a sinful nature, we are oppressed on the outside by bad social and spiritual systems and stories. Jesus is the antidote, the cure for these bad systems and stories by providing the alternative system and story of the Kingdom

---

[672] McLaren, *Everything Must Change*, 79-80.
[673] McLaren, *New Kind of Christianity*, 135.
[674] McLaren, *Everything Must Change*, 237-274.
[675] McLaren, *New Kind of Christianity*, 131, 132.

through His life and teachings. And what is the Kingdom of God? "A life that is radically different from the way people are living these days, a life that is full and over flowing, a higher life that is centered in an interactive relationship with God and with Jesus...an extraordinary life to the full centered on a relationship with God." [676] According to McLaren, this is what the Apostle John termed "eternal life," or "life of the ages." Through his Kingdom message and Kingdom way of living, "Jesus is promising a life that transcends 'life in the present age'...[he] is offering a life in the new Genesis, the new creation that is 'of the age' not simply part of the current regimes, plots, kingdoms, and economies created by humans." [677] Jesus has come, then, to liberate us from these old regimes (i.e. dysfunctional systems) and plots (i.e. destructive stories) and teach and show us the highest, best way found in the Kingdom. As liberator from the bad systems and stories of the world, this course of action culminates in the ultimate showdown between the system and story of Caesar and Christ: the cross.

In the traditional Christian faith, the cross occupies a central feature of God's saving plan and work of Christ, for upon it Christ breaks open his body and sheds his blood for our sins in our stead as a substitute. What place does the cross have in McLaren's Christology? As with the other parts of his theology, the cross does have a place in God's saving movement, but a different one from the historic understanding. In response to the existing theories of the atoning work of Christ he argues for

---

[676] McLaren, *Secret Message of Jesus*, 37.
[677] McLaren, *New Kind of Christianity*, 130.

what he terms the 'powerful weakness theory,' which hinges on the word vulnerable:

> by becoming vulnerable on the cross, by accepting suffering from everyone...Jesus is showing God's loving heart, which wants forgiveness, not revenge, for everyone. Jesus shows us that the wisdom of God's kingdom is sacrifice, not violence. It's about accepting suffering and transforming it into reconciliation, not avenging suffering through retaliation. So through this window, the cross shows God's rejection of the human violence and dominance and oppression that have spun the world in a cycle of crisis..." 678

Later he insists that "the cross calls humanity to stop trying to make God's Kingdom happen through coercion and force...and instead to welcome it through self-sacrifice and vulnerability." [679] For McLaren, the cross is a stage upon which Christ renders a grand performance illustrating God's love, wisdom, acceptance, and new way of sacrifice and suffering. Through the cross Jesus "exposes Roman violence and religious complicity, while pronouncing a sentence of forgiveness on his crucifiers." Throughout Jesus' life, his message has been one of non-violence and triumph over enemies through peace and self-sacrifice. The cross, then, is the culmination of those teachings as an exposé on love. Rather than joining in with the "'shock and awe' display of power as Roman crucifixions were intended to do," Jesus gives us a "'reverence and awe' display of God's willingness to accept rejection and mistreatment..." [680] The cross

---

[678] McLaren, *The Story We Find Ourselves In*, 105. (emphasis mine.)
[679] McLaren, *The Story We Find Ourselves In*, 106.
[680] McLaren, *New Kind of Christianity*, 158-159.

is not the point at which God objectively dealt with the objective reality of human sin and our sin nature, as the historic faith insists. Instead, the cross event gave us the example of love, self-sacrifice, peace, and way of God's alternative Kingdom in contrast to the prevailing system and story of Rome.

Like his views on the human sinful condition, McLaren mirrors Ritschl's Christology in significant ways, too. According to Ritschl, "Jesus, the Founder of the perfect moral and spiritual religion, belongs to a higher order than all other men;" "His unique worth lies in the manner in which He mastered His spiritual powers through a self-consciousness which transcends that of all other men..." [681] As a unique higher man, He was "conscious of a new and hitherto unknown relation to God." [682] As with McLaren, Ritschl does not describe Jesus as being God himself, only a unique man belonging to a higher order of humanity. In fact, in regard to his relationship with God Jesus is described as having a *"strength of a fellowship or unity with God such as no one before Him had ever known."* [683] Apparently, Jesus' "unity" with God is similar to the fellowship or unity a man has with his wife: he and she are not ontologically one, they simply possess a relationship with each other unlike anyone else they have had with another. For Ritschl the same is true of Jesus with God: Jesus is not ontologically one with God, but simply has a unique relationship with Him. This uniqueness cashes out in his higher ethical display through his life and teachings.

We see a fuller picture of the theological connections between their Christology by exploring how Ritschl describes

---

[681] Ritschl, *Justification and Reconciliation*, 2, 332.
[682] Ritschl, *Justification and Reconciliation*, 386.
[683] Ritschl, *Justification and Reconciliation*, 333. (emphasis mine)

Jesus' divinity. Like McLaren Ritschl does not indicate Jesus is God, but instead Jesus "brings the perfect revelation of God, so that beyond what He brings no further revelation is conceivable or is to be looked for;" He is the "Bearer of the final revelation of God." [684] In Jesus we also see "the complete revelation of God as love, grace, and faithfulness." [685] It is when we examine the life of Christ that we receive this image of God and come to a fuller understanding of His person: "when we have placed the one common material of Christ's life, His speech and conduct as well as his patience in suffering...we exhaust the significance of his person as Bearer of the Divine lordship, or founder of the Divine Kingdom." [686] As McLaren suggests, Jesus is the highest, most advanced view of God and His character. Both McLaren and Ritschl agree that through Jesus' life we see and experience God. They believe Jesus shares in the Divine and is "full of God" because of how he acted, not who he was.

Furthermore, Christ's ethical actions are what connect him to God and give him what Ritschl terms the attribute of Godhead and Godhood. "Christ's Godhead is understood as the power which Christ has put forth for our redemption...[the Godhead attribute] of Christ is to be found in the service He provided, the benefit He bestows, the saving work He accomplishes...it is an attribute revealed to us in His saving influence upon ourselves." [687] Christ is God because of what He does, not who He is. Jesus is not ontologically God, but ethically so: He shares in the Divine because of His ethical services and

---

[684] Ritschl, *Justification and Reconciliation*, 388, 397.
[685] Ritschl, *Instruction in the Christian Religion*, 197.
[686] Ritschl, *Justification and Reconciliation*, 482-483.
[687] Ritschl, *Justification and Reconciliation*, 395, 396-397, 398.

action. In the words of McLaren, "Jesus is in some mysterious and unique way...full of God." Jesus is not God, but uniquely participates in the Divine through his higher ethical living and teaching.

As Ritschl makes clear, it is through the ethical activity of Jesus we find God. While Ritschl does say "[Jesus] is equal to God," it is clear from his writings that this equality is ethical, rather than ontological. He is equal with God because of his moral and ethical activity. [688] This activity is primarily the fulfillment of his vocation as the founder of the Kingdom. As Ritschl asserts, Jesus is the "personal vehicle of the Divine self-end;" He is "that Being in the world Whose self-end God makes effective and manifest after the original manner His own eternal self-end, Whose whole activity, therefore, in discharge of His vocation, forms the material of that complete revelation of God which is present in Him, in Whom, in short, the Word of God is a human person." [689] Jesus reveals God through His vocation as the founder of the Kingdom of God, as a "teacher" and "liver" of the "universal ethical kingdom of God," which is the "supreme end of God Himself in the world." [690] Jesus' ethical teachings and kingdom vocation, then, constitute Him as participating in the "Godhead," in the Divine. In fact, his "Divine" authority as Ruler does not come from being God Himself, but "by His morally effective teaching and by His gracious mode of conduct..."[691]

Finally, the significance of the work of Jesus is "'related to the moral organization of humanity through love-prompted action,"

---

[688] Ritschl, *Justification and Reconciliation*, 483.
[689] Ritschl, *Justification and Reconciliation*, 451.
[690] Ritschl, *Justification and Reconciliation*, 451.
[691] Ritschl, *Instruction in the Christian Religion*, 195.

[692] which is the Kingdom of God. His vocation was founding, living, and teaching the love-prompted actions of the Kingdom as triumph and transcendence over the ethically bad systems of the world. Through this vocation he provided the prototypical example of self-sacrifice, discipline, and attainment of virtue for others to follow. This was especially acute through His work on the cross, which served as confirmation and codification of that vocation for the rest of the world. Ritschl argued—which McLaren himself later affirmed and recycled—that the significance of Jesus' work on the cross for others served as an example to the rest of the world: "It is not mere fate of dying that determines the value of Christ's death as a sacrifice; what renders this issue of his life significant for others is His willing acceptance of the death inflicted on Him by His adversaries as a dispensation of God, and the highest proof of faithfulness to His vocation." [693] Thus, His sufferings served as a means of testing His faithfulness to His vocation, while also confirming and codifying it. [694] Both Ritschl and McLaren affirm that the work of Christ centered on founding, living, and teaching the Kingdom, and the cross was the culmination of that vocation in that this highest ethical common good was tested and displayed for all the world to see and follow, which is where we find our salvation.

ON SALVATION

---

[692] Ritschl, *Justification and Reconciliation*, 13.
[693] Ritschl, *Justification and Reconciliation*, 477, 4779
[694] Ritschl, *Justification and Reconciliation*, 480.

As this examination has already illustrated, Ritschl and McLaren believe our problem is the dysfunctional systems and destructive stories of our world. Our solution came when God called Jesus as a messenger to show a better way of living and teach a better story: the Kingdom system and Kingdom story. McLaren and Ritschl agree that he is the vehicle of the Divine because of the way he lived and taught. Through his vocation as founder of the Kingdom of God Jesus was filled with God— meaning He acted like God would act on earth—and ultimately revealed the character of God. In so acting and revealing he is the vehicle for an existential solution to our existential problem. McLaren has written of his journey toward better understanding the dynamics of this solution. Perhaps this theological exploration was most expressed in Everything Must Change when he asked, "Is Jesus' healing and transforming framing story really powerful enough to save the world?" [695] Because McLaren believes our systems and stories are the problem, our solution is found in an alternative system and story, which we find in Jesus' message on the Kingdom of God. McLaren answers his question on the following page:

> if we believe that God graciously offers us a new way, a new truth, and a new life, we can be liberated from the vicious, addictive cycles of our suicidal framing stories. That kind of faith will save us...our failure to believe [Jesus' good news] will keep us from experiencing its saving potential, and so we'll spin on in the vicious cycles of Caesar. 696

---

[695] McLaren, *Everything Must Change*, 269.
[696] McLaren, *Everything Must Change*, 270.

According to McLaren, our salvation is found in being liberated from the systems and stories of the world and believing in the new system and story—the new way, truth, and life—found in Jesus' teachings on the Kingdom. We find salvation when we "transfer our trust from the way of Caesar to the way of Christ." [697] Notice that McLaren doesn't call people to trust Christ Himself, but instead trust the *way of Christ*. McLaren urges us to transfer our trust from the world's systems and stories—represented by Caesar—to the system and story of Christ, which is the Kingdom of God. Ultimately, salvation is participation in the Kingdom of God, which he calls *participatory eschatology.*

While conventional eschatologies have cultivated "resignation, fear, and arrogant aggression," participatory eschatology inspires "a passion to do good, whatever the suffering, sacrifice, and delay because of a confidence that God will win in the end; courage, because God's Spirit is at work in the world and what God begins God will surely bring to completion; a sense of urgency, because we are protagonists in a story; and humility and kindness, because we are aware of our ability to miss the point, lose our way, and play on the wrong side." [698] In fact, the death and resurrection of Jesus are paradigms for this salvation in which we ourselves are to participate in anticipation of this coming Kingdom: we join with Jesus in dying (metaphorically to our pride and agendas, literally in martyrdom as a witness to God's Kingdom and justice); and rising again in triumph "through the mysterious but real power

---

[697] McLaren, *Everything Must Change*, 271.
[698] McLaren, *New Kind of Christianity*, 200.

of God. In this cruciform way, we participate in the ongoing work of God, and we anticipate its ultimate success." [699] For McLaren, our dying and rising with Christ are symbolic of our rejection of and triumph over the dysfunctional systems and destructive stories of our world. Salvation comes not from dying to the old sinful nature by believing in Jesus' death and rising to new life by believing in his resurrection. Instead, we are called to die to the bad ethics of the world and rise to new life by living like Jesus. Thus, salvation is entirely existential, in that His loving example is what saves us from our bad existence, an existential salvation that extends to the whole human race.

Because we are called to live in the system and story of the Kingdom by living the teachings of Jesus, ultimate salvation at judgment will be based on behavior, not beliefs. "God will examine the story of our lives for signs of Christlikeness...These are the parts of a person's life that will be deemed worthy of being saved, remembered, rewarded, and raised to new beginnings." [700] Rather than believing in Jesus' sacrifice on the cross and God resurrecting the Son, giving food and water to the needy, showing mercy, welcoming the stranger, and being generous like Jesus is what God cares about, what will lead to salvation. Conversely, "all the unloving, unjust, non-Christlike parts of our lives...will be burned away, counted as unworthy, condemned, and forgotten forever." [701] In the end ultimate salvation is dependent upon our ethics, whether we walk the path of Jesus in word and deed. Since "no good deed will be forgotten," we are urged to "start doing the next good thing now

---

[699] McLaren, *New Kind of Christianity*, 200-201.
[700] McLaren, *New Kind of Christianity*, 204.
[701] McLaren, *New Kind of Christianity*, 204.

and never give up until the dream comes true," until God's Kingdom comes. [702] Human salvation is not found in the broken body and shed blood on the cross, but in the new system and story of the Kingdom coming to earth as founded by Jesus' life and teachings.

It is important to note that the cross carries little soteriological significance for McLaren beyond pointing to an example of love and suffering in the face of the oppressive system and story of Caesar. [703] In fact, in his counter narrative to the traditional view of the cross—which maintains "God sent Jesus into the world to absorb all the punishment for our sins" [704]—one of McLaren's characters insists this view "sounds like divine child abuse,"[705] as if God the Father was abusing His Son on the cross. Instead, the cross is about Jesus' vulnerability and accepting suffering, showing God's loving heart, and showing us that Kingdom sacrifice is not violent but reconciliation through suffering. [706] For McLaren, salvation comes when we follow Jesus' example of non-violent vulnerability and suffering, which culminated at the cross.

His view of salvation agrees with the theologian Jürgen Moltmann, whom he quotes: "The one [Jesus] will triumph who first died for the victims and then also the executioners, and in so doing revealed a new righteousness which breaks through the vicious circles of hate and vengeance and which, from the

---

[702] McLaren, *Everything Must Change*, 146.
[703] In fact, in the part of *A New Kind of Christianity* that is designed to answer the *Narrative Questions* (Ch. 4-6) the event of the cross is neither emphasized nor mentioned.
[704] McLaren, *Story We Find Ourselves*, 101.
[705] McLaren, *Story We Find Ourselves*, 102.
[706] McLaren, *Story We Find Ourselves*, 105.

victims and executioners, creates...a new humanity." [707] This view does not stem from the apostle Paul's, which viewed the death and resurrection of Christ revealing a new righteousness from God that comes through faith in that death and resurrection. [708] Likewise, a new humanity is not born out of the defeat of sin through death and the resurrection, as Paul argues. [709] Instead, this new righteousness and new humanity is ethical; salvation from the dysfunctional systems and destructive stories comes because of Jesus' acts of love in the face of hate and suffering in the face of vengeance. Likewise, an alternative community is born through similar ethical acts of love and suffering; a new humanity happens when people participate in the righteous ethic of Jesus.

Like McLaren, Ritschl rejects the traditional substitutionary view of the cross as providing the means of salvation for humanity: "The view that Christ, by the vicarious endurance of the punishment deserved by sinful men, propitiated the justice or wrath of God, and thus made possible the grace of God, is not found on any clear and distinct passage in the New Testament." [710] And like McLaren, Ritschl does not believe the solution to man's problem of alienation comes through faith in the substitution of Christ on the cross. Instead, salvation comes through attaining the Kingdom of God. According to Ritschl, "The kingdom of God is the divinely vouched-for highest good of the community...the ethical ideal for whose attainment the

---

[707] Jürgen Moltmann, *The Crucified God* (London: SCM, 1974), 178. As quoted in McLaren, *New Kind of Christianity*, 206
[708] See Rm. 3:21-26.
[709] Rm. 5:12-20.
[710] Ritschl, *Instruction in the Christian Religion*, 220.n3.

members of the community bind themselves together through their definite reciprocal action." [711] Ritschl explicitly claims that the Kingdom of God is the solution to the problem of mankind when he writes:

> [the kingdom of God] offers the solution to the question propounded or implied in all religions: namely, how man, recognizing himself as a part of the world, and at the same time as being capable of a spiritual personality, can attain that dominion over the world, as opposed to limitation by it, which this capability gives him the right to claim. 712

Here Ritschl reveals that the problem is very similar to McLaren's: humanity must rise above the world, which is the bad systems and stories. In fact, "A universal ethical Kingdom of God is the supreme end of God Himself in the world," [713] and thus the end toward which all of humanity is to move. This movement toward attaining the ethical ideal of the Kingdom is possible through the justification Christ provides, two concepts which are in reality one in the same.

While others often separate justification and the Kingdom of God, claiming that "justification and reconciliation concern men as sinners, while the Kingdom of God concerns them as reconciled," Ritschl insists this dichotomy is "not quite exact." [714] Instead, "the conception of the Kingdom of God and justification are homogeneous," they are one and the same idea.

---

[711] Ritschl, *Instruction in the Christian Religion*, 174-175.
[712] Ritschl, *Instruction in the Christian Religion*, 179.
[713] Ritschl, *Justification and Reconciliation*, 451.
[714] Ritschl, *Justification and Reconciliation*, 31.

[715] The aim of justification and reconciliation is "lordship over the world;" justification is transcending and moving beyond the systems and stories of the world through "dominion over the world and participation in the Kingdom of God."[716] Thus, it appears as though we are the ones who justify ourselves. Though McLaren doesn't frame it in terms of justification and reconciliation—that would be too similar to a Reformed framing—he does insist we need deliverance from the world as Ritschl does. As Ritschl defines reconciliation: "[it] is not merely the ground of deliverance from the guilt of sin...it is also the ground of deliverance from the world, and the ground of spiritual and moral lordship over the world." [717] Rather than deliverance from the condition of sin, we receive deliverance from the effects of sin. This is further emphasized when Ritschl claims justification leads to eternal life now, "which is present in our experiences of freedom or lordship over the world, and in the independence of self-feeling both from the restrictions and from the impulses due to natural causes or particular sections of society." [718]

That Kingdom is the product of "love-inspired action" and "the righteous conduct in which the members of the Christian community share in the bringing in of the kingdom of God [which] has its universal law and its personal motive in love to God and to one's neighbor." [719] The Kingdom is not the eschatological reign of God per se that will restore the world

---

[715] Ritschl, *Justification and Reconciliation*, 33.
[716] Ritschl, *Justification and Reconciliation*, 609, 628.
[717] Ritschl, *Justification and Reconciliation*, 357.
[718] Ritschl, *Justification and Reconciliation*, 534-534.
[719] Ritschl, *Instruction in the Christian Religion*, 178, 174.

from the ontological consequences of sin, but rather the "moral society of nations" and ultimately "the organization of humanity through action inspired by love." [720] Salvation, then, is found by aligning one's life with the teachings and way of Jesus and participating in his own vocation as the prototype of a life of love, and liberation and elevation from the worldly motives, systems, and stories. [721] Similarly, McLaren exclusively emphasizes a salvation from the systems and stories of the world through aligning one's life with Christ and participation in the ethical, earthly Kingdom of God. Our existential problem is solved not through belief in the substitutionary sacrifice of Jesus Christ on the cross and his defeat of death through the resurrection, but instead good behavior and ethical deliverance from the world.

CONCLUSION

This historical comparative examination has sought to examine and compare elements of McLaren's theology to Ritschl along three lines of reasoning: the problem of sin, the person and work of Christ, and solution of salvation. In concluding this examination, perhaps Ritschl's theology is best summarized by his definition of Christianity:

> Christianity, then, is the monotheistic, completely spiritual and ethical religion, which, based on the life of its Author as Redeemer and Founder of the Kingdom of God, consists in the freedom of the children of God, involves the impulse to conduct from the motive of love, which aims at the moral organization of mankind,

---

[720] Ritschl, *Justification and Reconciliation*, 10, 12.
[721] Ritschl, *Justification and Reconciliation*, 469.

and grounds blessedness on the relationship of sonship
to God, as well as on the Kingdom of God. 722

According to Ritschl, the Christian religion is based on the
life of Jesus as a sort of ethical redeemer and based upon him as
the founder of the Kingdom of God. It also consists in five
things: freedom of the children of God, presumably from—as we
have already seen—the world and web of sin through an ethical
elevation and lordship; the compulsion and encouragement to
act out of love; the aim of creating ethical boundaries for moral
organization; blessedness in one's sonship and daughtership to
God by attaining the Kingdom of God through right living and
ethical practice. This definition fits within the three paths of
examination for both Ritschl and McLaren.

First, the problem with humanity is not the nature of
individuals themselves, but our bad actions. Both McLaren and
Ritschl reject the historic doctrine of original sin, rejecting the
transmission of both personal guilt and divine wrath and the
individual necessity to sin by nature. Instead, both agree that the
systems and stories of the world are to blame for the evolving
human condition. While the first parents began innocently
enough and were created with the capacity to freely choose the
highest common good, their evolution brought them to higher
planes of moral consciousness, contributing to alienating acts.
Now humans are caught: in the words of Ritschl we are caught in
a whole web of sinful actions and reactions; in the words of
McLaren we are caught in an avalanche of crises that are the
result of dysfunctional systems and destructive stories. Both

---

[722] Ritschl, *Justification and Reconciliation*, 13.

presuppose a collective "selfish bias" conscious that is the result of external bad systems and stories in the world impinging upon the individual and collective humanity. This web of systems and stories have coagulated to form a power of united sin that falls upon every person, moving us to act badly. The problem, then, is outside of us, and for that we need a better ethical system and a better story.

McLaren and Ritschl both believe the solution to our problem is found in the alternative system and story of the Kingdom of God, which represents the highest, perfect ethical common good after which all of humanity is supposed to strive. Both also believe that one human was sent and commissioned by God as a conduit for this solution: Jesus Christ. Both Ritschl and McLaren believe the inherent value in the person and work of Jesus Christ is how He lived. Because the problem of humanity is bad actions, the means by which that problem can be solved must provide a model for better actions. Thus, they envision the person of Jesus as the prototype for the best possible way to live as a human; Jesus was a master of life and lived it in such a way that teaches all the world how to live. While they do not believe Jesus was God Himself, they both maintain that His possession of the Godhead attribute is the result of His ethical service and actions; Jesus's ethics were Divine and He revealed the character of God. Thus, He was full of God because of His loving, high righteous ethics, humanity can find salvation from the bad systems and stories of the world.

There is a sort of yin-yang relationship in their theology between the person and works of Jesus: Because Jesus is full of God and sent by God to found the Kingdom, we find in His life and teachings the highest, perfect common moral good; because

He loved in the face of hatred and suffered in the face of imperial abuse, Jesus shows and reveals the character of the living God and He Himself participates in the Godhead. Jesus shares in the fellowship of the Divine because He is ethical; Jesus is ethical because He was in some real way chosen by God and possessed a strong connection to the Divine. Because of this connection and because of His higher divine consciousness He belongs to a higher order of human existence. We should note here how similar this belief is to the early church heresy known as adoptionism. Like this heresy, McLaren and Ritschl seem to believe that Jesus was "adopted" by God to be the Christ because of His higher Consciousness and obedience. Out of this connection, consciousness, and order, Jesus has enabled humanity to find salvation, primarily in attaining the Kingdom of God which He Himself founded and taught. As a chosen conduit who had a unique relationship with God and one who participated in the Divine through founding, teaching, and living the highest ethical common good of the Kingdom, he shows the way and leads the way of liberation from the bad systems and stories of the world. This display and liberation culminated at the cross, the ultimate showdown between the contrary ways of Kingdom of the World and Kingdom of God.

While the historic Christian faith has pointed to the cross as the means by which people find salvation from the problem of natural, inherited sin because of the substitutionary role of Jesus' sacrifice, Ritschl and McLaren imagine the cross plays a different role. For them, the cross is part of our salvation from the systems and stories of the world because of Jesus' moral example of vulnerability, suffering, and love. Again, because our human problem is an existential one, resulting from bad systems and stories, the ultimate solution must relate to a better way of living. At the cross, Jesus shows God's forgiving, rather than revenging, heart toward humanity. The cross is the window through which we see God rejecting the violence and dominance and oppression of the world over against the way of sacrifice and suffering of the Kingdom. In turn, Jesus' example of death beckons humanity to die to the systems and stories of the world and the selfish bias that results from the web of those systems, while rising with Him above those systems in loving, sacrificial triumph. By following after Jesus' ethical example on the cross, we find salvation from our bad actions.

In the end, Ritschl and McLaren believe our salvation is ultimately found in the teachings of Jesus on the Kingdom of God. The Kingdom offers the solution to the problem that has plagued humanity, because it provides dominion over the world and provides an alternative system and story. Ritschl explicitly says the solution to the problem that has confounded humans for millennia is found in the Kingdom of God precisely because it offers an ethical ordering, dominion and rallying point over against the web of sin and sin of society that defines the world. And those who have committed themselves to this new ethical system and story are called to bring it into existence in order to solve our ethical problem and find ethical salvation. It is when one orients his life around the loving action of the Kingdom and cooperates with God's Kingdom that one enters into communion with Him and is relieved of a guilty conscience. The salvation of the world and individuals is dependent upon humans actively bringing in the Kingdom through good deeds, which is why McLaren urges people of any faith and background to start doing good now and never give up until God's Kingdom dream is realized, until Jesus' alternative ethical system and story replaces those of the world.

Though this examination is not exhaustive, it should be clear that Brian McLaren's own theology mirrors, and perhaps borrows from, the theology of Albrecht Ritschl. In regards to the problem, McLaren follows in the footsteps of Ritschl by rejecting original, individual inherited sin in favor of the collective conscious of the world. This collective conscious has developed and grown into a web of sin and power all its own, which rests on every individual. Individuals do not sin by nature, but because of the dysfunctional systems and destructive stories of the world. McLaren agrees with Ritschl that our problem is ethical. Hence, our solution and its bearer must also be ethical. Jesus Christ is envisioned by both theologians as a superman of sorts, a divinely appointed and endowed messenger sent by God to found the Kingdom, teach its alternative system and story, and live an archetypal life of righteous ethics. McLaren agrees with Ritschl that Jesus is not Himself God, but shares in His divinity and bears the attribute of the Godhead because he lived he "highest common good." In words that mirror Ritschl, McLaren says that Jesus was the highest and deepest revelation of the character of God. It is this character that saves humanity, because it provides an alternative system and story in the teachings and life of the Kingdom. McLaren clearly shares in Ritschl's soteriology by exalting the Kingdom of God as the solution to our ethical dilemma. Though the traditional Christian faith has called us to place our faith in Christ, McLaren joins Ritschl in calling people to place their faith in the Kingdom of God, for in its ethics lies our hope for salvation.

In his new theological treatise, McLaren maintains that he is offering hope and guidance for fellow sojourners through what he has often called theological terra nova. He believes that he and others are forging a new way through new territory through Christianity by offering fresh theological perspectives for the Church. This examination reveals, however, that his new way of believing and new kind of Christianity is recycled Ritschlianism. His definition of the human problem, offered solution, and description of the solutions bearer is nothing new. Instead, it is apparent that McLaren has repackaged liberal Christian theology and is now offering it to the masses as fresh, innovative, and alternative to what Christianity has been traditionally. This is simply not the case. Roger Olson maintains that "the story of Christian theology is the story of Christian reflection on salvation." [723] This examination makes plain that the reflection on the nature of salvation offered by the emerging church and its leaders at this junction in the story is repetitive and cyclical; rehashed theological liberalism is being paraded as newfangled Christianity. It's time McLaren comes clean and acknowledge that he is a contemporary theological liberal who is refashioning contemporary Christianity in the tradition of Ritschl. Perhaps then a proper, honest dialogue can commence between him and others regarding his very old kind of Christianity and its diametrical opposition to the historic Christian faith.

---

[723] Olson, *Christian Theology*, 13.

BIBLIOGRAPHY

Livingston, James C. *Modern Christian Thought: From the Enlightenment to Vatican II.* New York: Macmillian, 1971.

McLaren, Brian. *The Story We Find Ourselves In.* San Francisco: Jossey-Bass, 2003.

_____. *The Secret Message of Jesus.* Nashville: Word, 2006.

_____. *Everything Must Change.* Nashville: Thomas Nelson Publishers, 2007.

_____. *A New Kind of Christianity.* New York: HarperOne, 2010.

Olson, Roger. *The Story of Christian Theology.* Downers Grove: IVP Academic, 1999.

Ritschl, Albrecht. *Instruction In The Christian Religion.* London: Longmans, Green, and Co., 1901.

_____. *The Christian Doctrine of Justification and Reconciliation.* Edinburgh: T & T Clark, 1902.

Swing, Albert Temple. *The Theology of Albrecht Ritschl.* London: Longmans, Green, and Co., 1901.

Afterword

When I try to describe and explain the theological quagmire modern evangelicalism is thanks to the Emergent Church movement, often I like to retell the story from 2 Kings 23 about young King Josiah and the High Priest Hilkiah.

This story from the Hebrew Scriptures about a lost book, a very important lost book, actually. This very important lost book was the foundation to Israel's life with God. And it lay missing. Forgotten, forsaken. For two generations. Like some old photo album stuffed away in Grandma's musty old attic.

While this very important lost book lay missing, a number of kings ascended the throne who introduced pagan worship practices into the life of Israel—including astrological worship, idolatry, and even child sacrifice. The people forsook their one true love—YHWH, the God of Israel—for fake gods and fake stories.

Israel lost the plot to her story as much as she lost a very important book. And it wasn't until the reign of a child king that

Israel found what she had lost. During the reign of King Josiah, Israel recovered the plot to her story. Literally.

One day our very important lost book was discovered during temple renovations by one of the priests. It wasn't until it was recovered that Israel re-discovered the plot to her story and returned to worshiping and believing in the one true God.

In many ways the same is happening in the Church. No we are not worshipping pagan gods or incorporating pagan worship practices into our Sunday worship. We are losing the plot to our own story, though, because we are forgetting and forsaking God's Story.

This forgetting and forsaking isn't anything new; we've seen this before. Unfortunately, many thinkers within the Emergent Church movement are following in the same forgetting-forsaking footsteps as plenty of other thinkers before them. As we have seen from these essays, there really is "nothing new under the sun."

Emergents such as those in these essays are reimagining the major "pieces" to the Christian faith to such an extent that they've "given up the farm," so to speak. For them, God Himself has not shown Himself, and instead our language about God is merely human conjecture; sin is not my problem because I am not the problem—my environment around me and what happens to me is the problem; Jesus is viewed as a great moral teacher on the same level with Gandhi; and, in the end, everyone wins because love wins.

Like Israel, the Church needs to recover the plot to our Story. And I hope my generation takes the lead in retracing the steps of those who've gone before us in order to rediscover what the

Church has always believed about God, creation, humanity, sin, Jesus Christ, faith, and salvation.

Leave it up to a child to lead Israel to repentance and back into rightly believing in and behaving with God. And leave it up to the next generation, my generation, to lead the Church back to the fundamentals of God's Story of Rescue by rediscovering the historic Christian faith.

The Gospel

OF

Brian McLaren

Preface

The first time I met Brian McLaren was the day I visited his church, Cedar Ridge Community Church. I was living in the Washington D.C. area and just left an area megachurch I had been part of for a few years. I left because I had entered a period of faith deconstruction and reconstruction the likes of which I had never experienced before—and this was largely thanks to Pastor Brian, or should I say Pastor Dan and his faith-deconstruction mentor Neil Oliver. While I lived nearly 40 minutes away, I felt drawn to this mini-mecca of Emergent and its good-natured prophet to experience first hand his teaching and insight into a new way of being a Christian, a new kind of Christianity.

I remember Brian greeting me as I sat pensively in an aisle seat a few rows back from the front. There he was, shaking my hand, with his infectious grin, small Buddha belly, and trademark close-cropped beard that flowed up around his balding head. He was sort of like Santa, but without that sack of toys, or long shimmery silver beard. We exchanged a few words—he asked me what I did in the city and I mentioned the organization I worked for was a ministry to politicians, which piqued his interest. Unfortunately, our conversation was cut short by the start of the service. Afterwards, I stayed for the new visitors meeting, where I got a sweet CRCC mug, which I still have somewhere in some basement box. That was my first encounter with Brian, but not my last.

A few months later, Brian helped launch a movement in the DC area, called *Worship in the Spirit of Justice*. The worship gathering event was a 5-week long series of non-violent protest worship-ins to bear prophetic witness to the atrocities committed in Sudan, particularly Darfur. Think Occupy Wall Street without all the tents and latrines. We met at strategic points around Washington—the Lincoln memorial, Capitol Building, Washington Press Club, the Sudan embassy, and White House—to worship, read Scripture (or from "sacred texts," more on that below), and pray for the genocide a continent away.

Along with his good friend Jim Wallis, several people from Sojourners, and other religious leaders in the area, Brian launched this movement after being deeply impacted by the movie *Hotel Rwanda*. As he sat in utter silence and disbelief as that movie chronicled Rwandan genocide, he vowed he would never again sit idly by while something similar was happening during his lifetime.

While at the time I appreciated Brian's gumption and valued the opportunity to lend my worship and prayers to this prophetic movement, looking back there were aspects that were, shall we say...odd. One came during the final week, which was held in a park just north of the White House. This final prophetic protest was particularly memorable because of the actors who shared the stage: along with Christian pastors and a Jewish rabbi was a Muslim imam who prayed, to Allah, and read from the Koran. It was as if we—Christian, Jew, and Muslim— were all worshiping and praying to the same God. This was the first time I realized things were a bit off, but it wouldn't be the last.

Years later, when I moved back to Grand Rapids to pursue seminary, I attended a national pastors conference in San Diego. Before the actual event started, there were several pre-conference workshops, one of which Brian led based on his newest book, *Everything Must Change.* Huddled around Brian were a handful of pastors who, like me, were interested in his sage wisdom and advice for ministering in an emerging postmodern world. And he was eager to dispense to us that wisdom. Using his handy dry-eraser board, Brian spent several hours illustrating the greatest tragedies threatening human existence, and how to solve them.

What struck me as odd during this third encounter was how Brian defined our human problem and solution: Our problem was not our personal rebellion against God (a.k.a. sin), but broad systems of injustice that oppress people from the outside and model for them a bad existence; our solution was not faith in Jesus Christ as Lord and Savior (carrying with that belief in who He is as the only one true God and what He did in life, death, and resurrection), but faith in the *way* of Jesus and His model for a better existence. In other words, I was struck by the shift in his understanding of the gospel and fundamentals of the Christian faith. I wouldn't fully understand this shift until two years later when I began to immerse myself in historical theology and when Brian fully revealed his theological hand with his magnum opus: *A New Kind of Christianity*.

This book launched February 9, 2010 with fervent cries on either side of the theological aisle. Some backslapped Brian for his theological courage. Others just slapped him for challenging historic Christian orthodoxy. Personally, I was shocked at where Brian had ended up theologically, and decided to spend several weeks reviewing the book on my blog, www.novuslumen.net. Here is what I wrote in a shorter review:

> I've struggled with how to introduce this review because of how much I've struggled with the book. Yes, I've struggled with the ideas and theology and writing itself. For me it's more than that:
>
> I don't get it.
>
> I don't understand what happened. How did Brian get from THERE <-----to-----> HERE? The Brian of ANKofXianity doesn't seem like the same guy who launched this whole Emergent journey nearly a decade ago. The man behind this book just doesn't seem like the guy I encountered in his first-ever book, The Church on the Other Side, the man who was as generous in his orthodoxy as he was genuinely appreciative toward orthodoxy itself, and the wandering, yet tethered, theo-explorer I found in his mythic characters Neo or Pastor Dan.
>
> Now don't get me wrong. I don't know Brian McLaren. I've had a few encounters and conversations with him, like at some sessions at the National Pastors Conference a year ago. But I also attended his church for half a year and was involved in a social justice

project he helped coordinate while in Washington D.C. Here's the thing: I leapt into his church and into this social activism because I trusted Brian and his voice. While wading through my own spiritual deconstruction process five years ago, I gravitated to the only person I knew who was asking the questions I was asking, but seemed tethered to the "pieces" that still mattered to the Christian faith. I respected him for his prophetic voice and when people bleated and bellowed on and on about his so-called "heresy," I defended. I went to the mat with my boss in ministry, skeptical friends, and mortified parents.

So when I ask, "what happened?" I ask the question as one who was, to some extent, personally invested. Sure I man-crushed on the guy a bit to hard, but I sought his wisdom and insight and church community to help me navigate the terra nova at the intersection of postmodernity and Christian spirituality. I saw in Brian a desire to peal away the crap the USAmerican Church attached to Jesus and the Cross, while not cashing in the farm completely.

That, however, has changed.

While I know I have shifted in my own spiritual/theological journey, it is clear Brian has progressively shifted, too. I highly doubt Brian would have guessed 28 years ago at the beginning of his pastoral Christian ministry that he would push a new kind of Christianity that scantily reflects the Holy Scriptures and subverts the historical Rule of Faith that believes Jesus Christ is exclusively Lord and Messiah. Unfortunately, this seems to be the case.

Though Brian wonders aloud "How did a mild-manner guy like me get into so much trouble" (2) and insists he "never planned to become a `controversial religious leader,'" (3) he is the one to blame. He is the one who has shifted and engaged in this current theological endeavor. This theological enterprise is not accidentally garnering unwarranted criticism because there is nothing accidental about Brian's theological endeavor: Brian's book is a bold, intentional rhetorical tour de force that strikes at the very heart of the historic Christian faith, parodying the faith that both the Communion of Saints and the Spirit of God has given the 21st Century Church; his work pushes a version of Christianity that falls far outside the witness of the Holy Scriptures to Jesus Christ as exclusive Lord and Savior.

His portrayal of conservative evangelicalism is a gross caricature and unworthy of any serious thinker. He deliberately exaggerates and distorts the theology and exegesis of those with whom he disagrees in order to create an easy rhetorical jab called a Straw Man. As you probably know, a Straw Man is a logical fallacy that intentionally misrepresents an opponents position in order to easily strike it down in order to give the illusion that said opponent is defeated. Such rhetorical devices litter this book, making it an unworthy conversational partner.

Brian makes grand, sweeping claims with skimpy-to-no scholarly support. Perhaps this is why he insists over and over and over again that he had no formal seminary training? This is one of the most frustrating aspects of a book that asks us to take it seriously. For instance, his Greco-Roman narrative claims came to him not through research and scholarly reading, but through two conversations with two separate friends. (37)

Brian's interaction with the Holy Scriptures has no exegetical methodology. Instead he simply asks the reader to take his word for it. For example, his exegesis of John 14:6 is so innovative that he could find no commentary support for it. His presupposition re: the audience of The Book of Romans is just flat out wrong; the consensus among commentators is that Paul wrote the letter to converted Gentile Christians, not Jews.

While Brian claims otherwise, the new version of Christianity he pushes bears little to no resemblance to historic Christian orthodoxy, especially Nicene Christianity. In fact, he claims the creeds were mandated by the emperor to promote unity in the church and bring about imperial control. (12) Furthermore, by shoving Christian orthodoxy into his "Christian religion" rhetorical device, he is able to transcend the Christian faith entirely with a generalized "Kingdom of God" motif.

His portrayal of the Biblical narrative is Christless, centering squarely on Abraham and the Kingdom of God (which fits nicely with his view of the Abrahamic faiths as encapsulated in the nonprofit Abrahamic Alliance, on which he sits as Board member).

His view of Jesus Christ in no way affirms that He is God. Instead Brian reduces Him to a revelation of the "character of God." Jesus is no more than a model citizen.

His view of the Holy Scripture is not divine revelation, but purely human conversations in which people simple talk about their understanding of God and progressively, courageously "trade-up' (his words not mine) their understanding of God for even better images. Brian follows Pete Rollins' suggestion that our understanding of God is not actually the knowledge of God, but simply our understanding of God. Does God present Himself to us in the Text? Is He even saying anything to us in it? Can we really possess the knowledge of God? These questions seem to have a negative answer, though it isn't clear.

He rarely uses Jesus' messianic designation (Christ), which reflects his refusal to acknowledge Jesus Christ as exclusive Lord and Messiah. (So far he uses "Jesus" 204 times, "Jesus Christ" 3 time, and "Christ" 11 times.)

He consistently preemptively belittles those who will push against his innovative, new Christianity through gross ad hominems by reducing us to "gatekeepers" (103) anxious and paranoid (212-213), "religious thought police" (85), brainwashers (48), and people who are vulnerable to repeating yesterday's atrocities in the future (including anti-Semitism, genocide, and witch burning) (85), among many others charges.

While Brian feigns theological innocence by merely offering a "new way of believing," rather than a new set of beliefs (18), make no mistake about it: Brian is absolutely, unambiguously offering new beliefs. Though he may insist he is merely offering questions to inspire new conversations in the interest of a new quest, (18) he knows exactly what he is doing. He is disingenuous when he insists he is merely offering responses to his questions, rather than answers.

In the end, Brian's McLarenism faith isn't really about Jesus Christ, but about a vanilla, generalized World-Spirit god that has visited all other religions outside the Christian faith. Like his good buddy, Samir Selmanovic, Brian believes that Jesus and the reconciliation God offers to the world is not found only in the Christian faith (or "religion" as he puts it). In Selmonvic's book (a book Brian endorsed), Samir says, "We do believe that God is best defined by the historical revelation in Jesus Christ, but to believe that God is limited to it would be an attempt to manage God. If one holds that Christ is confined to Christianity, one has chosen a god that is not sovereign." (It's Really All About God, 129) Brian agrees.

In fact, it is clear his entire theological endeavor is a concerted effort to "pluralize" reconciliation to God and His Kingdom by divorcing it from Jesus Christ entirely, rather than insisting that reconciliation to both comes through Jesus Christ alone. While Brian uses the "Christian religion" as a rhetorical device to argue against "theo-containment," the One True God described in the Holy Scriptures is exclusively revealed in the very human, very divine Jesus Christ. It's really not all about God. It's really all about Jesus Christ.

As Karl Barth reminds us, "Any deviation, any attempt to evade Jesus Christ in favor of another supposed revelation of God, or any denial of the fulness of God's presence in Him, will precipitate us into darkness and confusion."(CD II,1:319) There is little evidence Brian believes that the fulness of God's presence is exclusively in Jesus Christ, that salvation

and rescue and reconciliation is found in no other name
under heaven besides His.

    After Jesus, there is nothing left. And after Brian's
new kind of Christianity, neither is Jesus Christ.

While I had a strong sense at the time that Brian had
completely jumped ship from historic Christian orthodoxy, my
sense wasn't entirely confirmed until my Master of Theology
program in historical theology culminated with my thesis. I
chose my topic based on a growing sense of mission to interact
with Emergent theology in order to better understand the roots
from which it has grown. One of the biggest theological concepts
of the Emergent Church has been a hyper-focus on the Kingdom
of God. Furthermore, it isn't a secret that people have labeled
Emergent theology liberalism in evangelical clothing. So I set out
to prove whether Emergent understandings of the Kingdom
were similar to or different from theological liberal views of the
Kingdom. What I discovered was staggering.

Using Brian as a theological representative of Emergent
theology—an entirely appropriate representative at that—I
discovered that his theological views concerning a range of ideas
continue the theological impulse and trajectory of liberalism,
four generations deep. (This thesis project was released in 2012
as a print book and ebook under the title, *Reimagining the
Kingdom: The Generational Development of Liberal Kingdom
Grammar.*) Along with Friedrich Schleiermacher, Albrecht
Ritschl, Walter Rauschenbusch, and Paul Tillich, Brian
McLaren's view of our human problem (sin), the solution to our
problem (salvation and the Kingdom) and the bearer of our
solution (the person and work of Jesus) is nearly identical. The

only difference is that Brian's theological system revises and extends liberal Kingdom grammar for a postmodern, multi-faith world. No clearer do we see this than in his latest book, *Why Did Jesus, Moses, the Buddha, and Mohammed Cross the Road?: Christian Identity in a Multi-Faith World.*

This revision and extension is why I've released this short book. It contains the chapter on Brian's theological system from my Kingdom book and a summary and evaluation of his arguments from this new book on religious pluralism. While I trace the development of Brian's liberal theology through four generations of theological liberals beforehand, this chapter on its own in Part 1 should give you a good handle on what Brian believes, and how it is foreign to the historic Christian faith. (If you'd like the full argument, you may purchase the book from most online retailers.) Part 2 contains the summary and evaluation of Brian's arguments in his latest book in order to show how his gospel is indeed a new kind of Christianity for a multi-faith world.

In the Book of Jude, the author urges the church to "contend for the faith that was once for all entrusted to God's holy people." (Jude 3) I believe now, more than ever, we need people who are passionate about safeguarding that once-for-all entrusted faith. Part of the way we can contend for that faith is to better understand the theological roots of people like Brian McLaren. Though his influence has waned as the Emergent Church movement has fizzled, he is still a prominent voice in many corners of the American church. Such prominence and influence requires a thoughtful interaction with his gospel. And because that gospel is foreign to the historic Christian faith, a forceful response is also required. I hope this short book will provide both.

JEREMY BOUMA
GRAND RAPIDS • FEBRUARY 2013

Part 1

McLaren's *Kingdom* Grammar

1

Introduction

In recent years evangelical Christians have rediscovered the biblical emphasis on the Kingdom of God. They have written books, such as *The King Jesus Gospel*,[724] *The Secret Message of Jesus*,[725] and *The Next Christians*,[726] which remind evangelicals that the Kingdom of God lies at the heart of Jesus' mission. They lead mission trips which seek to do more than merely lead sinners to Jesus; they also want to bring the Kingdom of God to earth. In many ways this rediscovery of the Kingdom is right and beneficial, for its advent is the overarching plot line of the Bible. However, its current use often comes with problematic baggage as many of its most popular proponents uncritically borrow its grammar from unorthodox historical sources.

---

[724] Scot McKnight, *The King Jesus Gospel: The Original Good News Revisited* (Grand Rapids: Zondervan, 2011).
[725] Brian McLaren, *The Secret Message of Jesus* (Nashville: W Publishing Group, 2006).
[726] Gabe Lyons, *The Next Christians: The Good News About the End of Christian America* (New York: Doubleday, 2010).

The Kingdom of God has not always played such a prominent role in Christian theology, however. Augustine represents the typical manner in which the early church defined the Kingdom of God, equating it with the Church itself. While equating God's Kingdom-rule with the Church largely continued with medieval theological discourse, Christian princes sought to promote an imperial-political view of the Kingdom in order to control their Feudal lands. In the Reformation, Luther individualized the concept for the purpose of emphasizing the Christian's spiritual citizenship over against a citizenship of a secular kingdom. He also represented the Reformation tendency in general to view the Kingdom in entirely eschatological, even apocalyptic, terms that pointed toward heaven in the future. Eventually, the Kingdom played little role in Protestant theology, especially evangelical theology, reflecting the general trajectory of the historic Church that seems to have had little interest in Jesus' central teaching. That is until the nineteenth century.

In the late eighteenth century and early nineteenth century, historical, cultural, and intellectual forces coalesced to foster an environment that gave renewed interest in the Kingdom, giving it a place of theological prominence. The person most credited with such renewal is the German theologian Friedrich Schleiermacher. The Kingdom of God formed the basis of his teachings, governing his system of doctrine and ethics to such an extent that it rose to prominence within theology in a way it had not before. Schleiermacher's voice echoed throughout much of nineteenth century Protestant thought through the likes of Bauer, Herrmann, and Harnack, finding a strong advocate in the theology of Albrecht Ritschl. But while Ritschl praised Schleiermacher for employing the Kingdom of God as the *telos* of Christianity, he believed Schleiermacher did not go far enough in grasping its significance. Ritschl believed Schleiermacher made an important contribution to Christian theology by restoring the Kingdom to a place of importance, but he thought his *Kingdom* grammar was deficient. Building on the original work of Schleiermacher, Ritschl brought this grammar to bear on his entire theological enterprise, making *Kingdom of God* its controlling doctrine. Ritschl's Kingdom-centric theology kindled a new generation of twentieth century liberal theologians, particularly Rauschenbusch and Tillich, who envisioned the Kingdom itself as humanity's salvation.

Now, like the nineteenth century, there has been a resurgence in the use of *Kingdom* language at the start of the twenty-first century, particularly within mainstream evangelicalism. In prior generations, *Kingdom* had not been part of the normal evangelical ecclesial repertoire. Instead, evangelicalism had primarily centered upon the language of *gospel*, which translated into salvation from sins through a conversion experience, personal piety, and moral living. Rarely had *Kingdom* language been employed within evangelicalism. Even when *Kingdom* was utilized, its primary usage was usually future oriented, centering on the return of Jesus Christ and reign on earth at the expense of its present activity. This definition of *Kingdom*, however, changed with the advent of what has become known as the Emergent Church movement, originally a progressive evangelical movement that sought to re-imagine traditional Christianity in light of postmodernity. In fact, the Kingdom of God is central to the Emergent Church's protest against Traditionalism.

As Jim Belcher explains, "The emerging protest argues that the traditional church has focused too much attention on *how* an individual becomes saved and not enough on how he or she *lives* as a Christian...The critics say the good news is more than forgiveness from sins and a ticket to heaven; it is the appearance of the kingdom of God."[727] This argument, that not enough attention has been paid to Jesus' teaching on the Kingdom of God, has formed the beachhead of protest against Traditionalism, particularly mainstream evangelicalism, and is the central identifying doctrine of this movement. As two prominent Emergent researchers note, the Kingdom of God offers a "reference point for emerging churches" as they deconstruct Traditionalism and reconstruct church in a postmodern context. [728] The Kingdom-way Jesus founded through His life provides a model for emerging churches and actually is their gospel; for them, the Kingdom saves. No thinker within this movement has sought to redirect the focus of twenty-first century Christianity more than Brian McLaren, who helped found the national organization Emergent, is the author of several books that have set out to re-imagine the Christian faith,[729] and was christened as one of the top twenty-five most

---

[727] Jim Belcher, *Deep Church: A Third Way Beyond Emerging and Traditional* (Downers Grove: IVP Books, 2009), 41.

[728] Eddie Gibbs and Ryan K. Bolger. *Emerging Churches: Creating Christian Community in Postmodern Culture* (Grand Rapids: BakerAcademic, 2005), 46. This book provided one of the most exhaustive examinations of the Emerging Church movement. It especially provides an important look at the Emerging Church's *Kingdom* grammar in p. 47-64.

[729] See *A New Kind of Christian* (San Francisco: Jossey-Bass, 2001); *The Story We Find Ourselves In* (San Francisco: Jossey-Bass, 2003); *The Last Word and The Word After That* (San Francisco: Jossey-Bass, 2005); *A Generous Orthodoxy* (Grand Rapids: Zondervan, 2004); *The Secret Message of Jesus* (Nashville: W

influential evangelicals in America.[730] For some time, McLaren has been on a quest to redefine what is central to the Christian faith, a quest culminating with a new book on Christian identity in a multi-faith world.[731]

Over the past decade, McLaren has sought to reclaim what he calls the secret, essential message of Jesus, which he says has been unintentionally misunderstood and intentionally distorted, missed and disregarded.[732] According to McLaren, this message is the Kingdom of God. While many have lauded McLaren's efforts to recapture Jesus' secret Kingdom-message, others argue that his and Emergent's use and description of *Kingdom* is deficient. Belcher writes, "I worry about what is missing in the description [of the Kingdom of God]. It is curious to me that nowhere does he mention or link the kingdom of God to the doctrines of atonement, justification, union with Christ or our need to be forgiven."[733] Likewise, Scot McKnight believes what McLaren says about the Kingdom is not enough:

> [They] believe that penal substitution theories have not led to a kingdom vision. What I have been pondering and writing about for a decade now is how to construct an 'emerging' gospel that remains faithful to the fullness of the biblical texts about the Atonement, and lands squarely on the word kingdom. Girard said

Publishing Group, 2006); *Everything Must Change* (Nashville: Thomas Nelson, 2006); and *A New Kind of Christianity* (New York: HarperOne, 2010).

[730] "25 Most Influential Evangelicals In America," *Time Magazine*, February 7, 2005.

[731] Brian McLaren, *Why Did Jesus, Moses, the Buddah, and Mohammed Cross the Road? Christian Identity in a Multi-Faith World* (Jericho Books, New York, 2012)

[732] McLaren, *The Secret Message of Jesus*, 3.

[733] Belcher, *Deep Church*, 118.

> something important about the Cross; so does
> McLaren. But they aren't enough. 734

The reason contemporary articulations of *Kingdom* by Emergents like McLaren are not enough is because those articulations are simply appropriations of liberal *Kingdom* grammar.

Rather than offering the Church a new kind of Christianity that somehow recaptures a long-lost concept central to Jesus and the Church, McLaren's use of the Kingdom of God to define the Christian gospel is fully entrenched in the Protestant liberal theological tradition, a link several people have already noted. In his book, *Don't Stop Believing,* Michael Wittmer argues that a "postmodern turn toward liberalism is penetrating the evangelical church." He goes on to say that "an increasing number of postmodern Christians are practicing a liberal method: accommodating the gospel to contemporary culture and expressing greater concern for Christian ethics than its traditional doctrines,"[735] including the Kingdom of God.[736]

In reviewing one of his latest books, *A New Kind of Christianity*, McKnight notes how McLaren "has fallen for an old school of thought," rehashing the ideas of prominent classic Protestant liberals like Adolf Von Harnack and modern ones like Harvey Cox.[737] McKnight has registered such a concern in

---

[734] Scot McKnight, "McLaren Emerging," *Christianity Today Online*, September 26, 2008, www.christianitytoday.com/ct/2008/september/38.59.html.
[735] Michael E. Wittmer, *Don't Stop Believing: Why Living Like Jesus is Not Enough* (Grand Rapids: Zondervan, 2008), 18.
[736] See Wittmer, *Don't Stop* Believing, 110-115.
[737] Scot McKnight, "Review: Brian McLaren's 'A New Kind of Christianity," *Christianity Today Online*, February 26, 2010, http://www.christianitytoday.com/ct/2010/march/3.59.html.

regards to McLaren's *Kingdom* definition, as well.[738] Likewise, Belcher worries about what is missing in McLaren's description of the Kingdom, noting that his definition reduces the gospel and argues that if his gospel is nothing more than recycled theological liberalism it must be rejected.[739]

This small book, adapted from my larger book, *Reimagining the Kingdom*,[740] shows how McLaren's gospel of the Kingdom is continuous with four previous generations of Protestant liberalism, including how he defines the Kingdom of God, who is in, how one gets in, and how it solves for our human problem. The larger book traces the generational development of liberal *Kingdom* grammar from Friedrich Schleiermacher to Albrecht Ritschl, Walter Rauschenbusch, and Paul Tillich, to show how the *Kingdom* grammar of Emergent is more or less repackaged liberal grammar. By examining the most prominent Protestant liberals, I demonstrate a direct link between them and Emergent and show how they are contributing to the comeback of evangelical *Kingdom* grammar, as evidenced in McLaren's *Kingdom* grammar.

Theological liberals are remarkably similar in their definitions of our human problem, the One who bore that problem's solution, and the nature of that solution itself, the Kingdom of God. This small book features the chapter on McLaren from this larger book on the development of Kingdom grammar. In it, you will see that, while the McLaren claims to be

---

[738] McKnight, "McLaren Emerging," www.christianitytoday.com/ct/2008/september/38.59.html.
[739] Belcher, *Deep Church*, 116.
[740] Jeremy Bouma, *Reimagining the Kingdom: The Generational Development of Liberal* Kingdom *Grammar from Schleiermacher to McLaren* (Grand Rapids: THEOKLESIA, 2012)

helping Christianity rediscover an authentic Christian identity by rediscovering the Kingdom, he is merely repackaging liberalism for a new day; his gospel is the liberal gospel.

McLaren's grammar includes several features from theological liberalism: He teaches that sin is social and environmental, rather than an inherited sinful nature and guilt; Jesus is the moral, rather than metaphysical, Son of God; in founding the Kingdom of God, it was necessary that Jesus lived but he gives no compelling reason that Jesus' death was necessary; the Kingdom of God is concerned with humanity's progress; the Kingdom comes into the here-and-now through the power of loving human action; it is inclusive, in that every act counts as Kingdom acts; it is universalistic, in that everyone will be saved; the Kingdom centers on the words, deeds, and suffering of Jesus—His inspiring personality provides humanity the proper example of the universal human ideal; and ultimately, the Kingdom is concerned with bringing the universal human ideal to bear on human existence, empowering individuals and society to reach their fullest potential and live their best life right now.

McLaren's *Kingdom* grammar, and thus *gospel* grammar, is continuous with four previous generations of Protestant liberalism, including how he defines the Kingdom of God, who is in, how one gets in, and how it solves for our human problem. Like the liberal gospel, McLaren's gospel ultimately urges people to place their faith in the *way* of Jesus—i.e. the Kingdom of God—rather than the *person* and *work* of Jesus. This is a significant departure from authentic, historic Christianity.

Roger Olson has said that the story of Christian theology is the story of Christian reflection on the nature of salvation, which is why this book is important. It is imperative that evangelicals understand the contours of McLaren's gospel in order to understand how he could impact how some evangelicals reflect upon the nature of salvation, and consequently how they understand, show, and tell the gospel itself in our multi-faith world.

2

Context

How Did McLaren's Gospel Form?

In 2001 Brian McLaren, a little known pastor just north of Washington D.C., began influencing street-level theological conversations within evangelicalism with his landmark book, *A New Kind of Christian.* [741] Through the book's two protagonists—Pastor Dan and Neo—McLaren took the reader on a redefining journey through evangelical's core theological doctrines. God, creation, sin, Christ, the cross, resurrection, and judgment were all addressed and countered with alternative possibilities that formed the foundation for the Emerging Church conversation. It was also a reflection of his own spiritual journey, one that began with fundamentalism via the Plymouth

---

[741] McLaren has since retired from pastoring *Cedar Ridge Community Church* and been named one of the "25 Most Influential Evangelicals In America," *Time Magazine*, February 7, 2005.

Brethren and culminated in "a quest for honesty, for authenticity, and for a faith that made more sense to me and to others...learning that there is a kind of faith that runs deeper than mere beliefs."[742] Many in our post-9/11, recession-racked, socially-upended world who entered this church conversation found resonance with McLaren's own spiritual quest.

Those seeking to do Christianity on the other side of modernity have found solace in the questions and alternative answers offered by McLaren in response to what many perceive to be stogy, stuffy, stale theology that has outlived its lifecycle. In place of a theology he claims is beholden to modernity, McLaren insists "we need a new way of believing, not simply new answers to the same old questions, but a new set of questions. We are acknowledging that the Christianities we have created deserve to be reexamined and deconstructed...so that our religious traditions can be seen for what they are...they are evolving, embodied, situated versions of the faith." [743] Like other Emergents, McLaren has set out to construct a new, fresh, alternative Christianity in light of postmodernity, because he like others realized "something isn't working in the way we're doing Christianity any more."[744]

Of postmodernism, McLaren writes, "I see the postmodern conversation as a profoundly moral project in intension at least, a kind of corporate repentance among European intellectuals in the decades after the Holocaust."[745] In embracing the *generous*

---

[742] McLaren, *A New Kind of Christianity*, 6, 8.
[743] McLaren, *A New Kind of Christianity*, 18, 27.
[744] McLaren, *A New Kind of Christianity*, 9.
[745] Brian McLaren, "Church Emerging: Or Why I Still Use the Word *Postmodern* but with Mixed Feelings," in *An Emergent Manifesto of Hope* (Ed. Doug Pagitt and Tony Jones; Grand Rapids: BakerBooks, 2007, 144.

orthodoxy descriptor of Hans Frei, McLaren embraces a post-foundationalism posture characteristic of postmodernism to describe his flavor of Christianity.[746] Postmodernism as an intellectual movement surfaced in the late 1960s as a surrogate to the post-structuralism of France, which itself was rooted in Kantian philosophy. [747] As Carl Raschke explains, "Postmodernism in this sense was nothing more or less than a theory of language that served to demystify previous theories of language routinely utilized to undercut the language of belief,"[748] particularly the "language of belief" rooted in modernity. Stanley Grenz notes, "postmodernism signifies the quest to move beyond modernism. Specifically, it involves a rejection of the modern-mindset, but launched under the conditions of modernity."[749] Grenz goes on to describe how the modern mind is defined by the Enlightenment project, which exalted the individual rational man to the center of the universe. The goal of the human intellectual quest was "to unlock the secrets of the universe in order to master nature for human benefit and create a better world," an ethos that particularly characterized the twentieth century through technology.[750] Postmodernism, on the other hand, says there can be no objective, autonomous knower because knowledge is not mechanistic and dualistic, but historical, relational, communal, and personal; reality is relative,

---

[746] See McLaren, *A Generous Orthodoxy.*
[747] Carl Raschke, *The Next Reformation: Why Evangelicals Must Embrace Postmodernity* (Grand Rapids: Baker Academic, 2004), 35, 37.
[748] Raschke, *The Next Reformation,* 37.
[749] Stanley Grenz, *A Primer on Postmodernism* (Grand Rapids: Eerdmans Publishing, 1996), 2.
[750] Stanley Grenz, *A Primer on Postmodernism,* 3.

indeterminate, intuited and participatory.[751] Three names are almost routinely associated with the postmodern project: Jacque Derrida, Jean François Lyotard, and Michael Foucault.

Derrida is considered the father of French deconstruction, a method for rethinking long held beliefs and intellectual assumptions. One of his primary contributions to postmodern philosophy was his often repeated phrase: "there is nothing outside the text." Here, Derrida champions the postmodern sentiment that interpretation is an inescapable part of being human and experiencing the world; life is interpretation all the way down because we all bring something to the table out of our cultural, economic, and religious context. For postmoderns, no realm of pure reading exists beyond the realm of interpretation.

Lyotard is known for his "incredulity toward metanarratives," which isn't so much a rejection of grand stories, but the manner in which those stories legitimize themselves. In other words, it is not the stories themselves that are the problem, but the way they are told (and to a degree why they are told). As James K. A. Smith argues, "For Lyotard, metanarratives are a distinctly modern phenomenon: they are stories that not only tell a grand story, but claim to be able to legitimate or prove the story's claim by an appeal to universal reason." [752] Smith continues, "What characterizes the postmodern condition, then, is not a rejection of grand stories in terms of scope or in the sense of epic claims, but rather an unveiling that all knowledge is rooted in some narrative or myth. The result, however, is what

---

[751] Stanley Grenz, *A Primer on Postmodernism*, 7-8.
[752] James K. A. Smith, *Who's Afraid of Postmodernism* (Grand Rapids: Baker Academic, 2006), 65.

Lyotard describes as a 'problem of legitimation' since what we thought were universal criteria have been unveiled as just one game among many."[753] All claims to universal truth are reduced to one story among many stories. These stories are conditioned by their own sets of cultural and historical rules, a point McLaren and other Emergent Christians are quick to point out.

Finally, Foucault, the master institutional de-constructor was famous for his often quoted phrase, "power is knowledge." Foucault led the charge in cultivating a "deep hermeneutic of suspicion" that marks our postmodern culture's relationship to Institutions of Power, including and especially the institution of the Church. Like Nietzsche, Foucault traced the lineage of secret biases and powerful prejudices that lay submerged beneath institutional truth claims, especially those ideas deemed "moral" or "normal" by institutions like Christianity. According to Foucault, nothing that is "true" is innocently and purely discovered. Instead, what those institutions (State and Religious) deem normal and moral are covertly motivated by various interests of power. It is out of this historical milieu that McLaren's Kingdom grammar has been constructed.

---

[753] Smith, *Who's Afraid of Postmodernism*, 69.

3

Problem
What Does McLaren's Gospel Solve?

Like four generations preceding him, McLaren defines the problem at the root of his gospel and *Kingdom* grammar differently than the historic Christian faith's conception of the problem defined by original sin. Through his protagonist Neo in his *New Kind of Christian* trilogy, McLaren contends the Christian story has been distorted, because early Christianity imported "the Greek idea of a fall from a perfect, unchanging, ideal, complete, harmonious, fully formed world into a world of change, challenge, conflict..."[754] McLaren rejects original sin; he insists there is no event of "the Fall" or corresponding "original sin" and "total depravity" in which humanity plunged into rebellion and alienation, resulting in an inherited sinful

---

[754] McLaren, *The Story We Find Ourselves In*, 52. This is later affirmed and further developed in *A New Kind of Christianity*, 33-45.

nature.[755] Instead, the framing narrative of humanity is one of systemic progression and ascent, with corresponding descent resulting in "new depths of moral evil and social injustice."[756] Accordingly, human nature has not "fallen" but is still fundamentally good,[757] progressing from an embryonic stage to a higher stage of existence. As one can see, McLaren's understanding of human nature reflects Rauschenbusch's own strong appropriation of evolutionary doctrine. As the Earth's story is one of emergence, so too is humanity's; our story is not a fall from perfection into a state of imperfection, but "unfolds as a kind of compassionate...classic coming-of-age story." [758] McLaren does not see just one single cataclysmic crisis but "an avalanche of crises." [759] As humans "come of age" they grow beyond God, and their relationship deteriorates in progressive, fitful "experiences of alienation." McLaren equates sin with "stagnation and decay," saying, "Because of this counter-emergent virus we call sin, the stages, episodes, and levels do not always unfold as they should. There are setbacks, stagnations, false starts, premature births, retardations, impatient rebellions,

---

[755] McLaren, *A New Kind of Christianity*, 43. In an endnote McLaren asserts that these terms "frequently derive their meaning from a story that is, I believe, inherently un-Jewish and unbiblical, and so when they are read into the biblical story, they distort and pollute it." 266n.15.

[756] McLaren, *A New Kind of Christianity*, 51.

[757] McLaren, *Story We Find Ourselves*, 52. He says, "The God-given goodness in creation isn't lost...God's creative fingerprint or signature is still there, always and forever. The evil of humanity doesn't eradicate the goodness of God's creation, even though it puts all of that goodness at risk."

[758] McLaren, *A New Kind of Christianity*, 49, 51.

[759] McLaren, *The Story We Find Ourselves*, 53-54, 56. He writes, "all involve human beings gaining levels of intellectual and technological development that surpass their moral development—people becoming too smart, too powerful for their own good...Human beings leave their identity, their life, their story as creatures in God's creation...As they become more independent, they lose their connection to God, their sense of dependence...So they experience alienation from God."

emergence defects, and failed attempts at emergence."[760] Sin is anti-progress, it is the opposite of the type of human progress (i.e. emergence) the Kingdom of God promotes, and for which we will see solves our human problem. What impedes human progress are bad systems and stories.

In his re-imagined framing narrative, individuals are no longer the issue, but human systems: Rather than individuals acting out of their sinful nature and sinning, "socioeconomic and technological advances" lead to moral evil and social injustice.[761] In the words of McLaren, "it's a story about the downside of 'progress'—a story of human foolishness...the human turn toward rebellion...the human intention toward evil."[762] The problem is not that humans rebelled against God and are rebels or that humans did evil and are evil. For McLaren, the story is one where humans collectively create evil, damaging and savaging God's good world; it is a story where "humans have evil intent" instead of being evil themselves. Those evil intentions are not the result of an evil nature, but the bad systems and stories that consume humanity. McLaren believes the main dysfunctions of humanity are existential; he frames the crisis of the human condition as an existential crisis of prosperity, equity, and security.[763] These three crises form the "cogs" in what McLaren terms the *suicide machine*.[764]

The suicide machine is a metaphor for "the *systems* that drive our civilization toward un-health and un-peace."[765] McLaren

---

[760] McLaren, *A Generous Orthodoxy*, 282.
[761] McLaren, *A New Kind of Christianity*, 51.
[762] McLaren, *A New Kind of Christianity*, 54.
[763] McLaren, *Everything Must Change*, 5.
[764] McLaren, *Everything Must Change*, 53.
[765] McLaren, *Everything Must Change*, 53. (emphasis mine)

envisions the driving force behind our broken, problematic condition to reside in the systems of the world rather than in the individual person. According to him, humanity suffers from a "dysfunction of our societal machinery," which is operated not by single individuals but by humanity acting together."[766] In other words, individual sinful human nature is not the problem, but rather a universal sin of society, which of course is how four generations of liberals defined the human problem: Rauschenbusch said sin was social, Schleiermacher and Ritschl said our problem was a kingdom or systemic "web" of sin and evil.

In *A New Kind of Christianity*, McLaren illustrates this explanation of the human condition and reality of so-called "social sin." Using the story of the Israelites in Exodus, he explains that it is a story of "liberation from the external oppression of social sin," while also celebrating "liberation from the internal spiritual oppression of personal sin."[767] Because McLaren does not believe that sin is part of human nature because of an event of rebellion, he must mean something different by "internal spiritual oppression of personal sin." It seems even this internal oppression is related to the social systems of sin, because he asserts that the Israelites were freed from "the *dominating powers* of fear, greed, impatience, ingratitude, and so on."[768] The power of Fear and Ingratitude were the oppressors, which in this Exodus narrative apparently resulted from years of being "debased by generations of

---

[766] McLaren, *Everything Must Change*, 65.
[767] McLaren, *A New Kind of Christianity*, 58.
[768] McLaren, *A New Kind of Christianity*, 58. (emphasis mine.)

slavery."[769] This slave framing story, then, is what contributed to the Israelites communal and individual commitment to "fear, greed, impatience, ingratitude, and so on." The internal compulsion toward greed, for example, was an internal power that resulted from the external system of slavery and the bad framing narrative out of which Israel was liberated. Thus, our ultimate problem is bad systems and stories.

Unlike the traditional historic faith that locates the problem of the human condition in individual sinfulness and an inherited sinful nature, McLaren believes humans are in trouble because we are in bondage to the "dominant societal machinery," which entices us to keep faith in its systems of wealth, security, pleasure, and injustice.[770] This faith and bondage has led to a sort of universal consciousness that is driven by destructive, dysfunctional framing stories. The global crises of which McLaren says we must be saved are the symptoms and consequences of the dysfunction, resulting in a collection of human evil. Dysfunctional societal machinery, destructive framing narratives, and collective human evil are our problems. Rather than sinning out of an inner, natural compulsion, innately good humans are compelled to act badly because of these environmental forces; bad systems and bad stories cause us to misbehave. Thus, we need a better system and a better story to solve for our human problem. We find both in the alternative system and story of the Kingdom which came through the person and life-work of Jesus of Nazareth.

---

[769] McLaren, *A New Kind of Christianity*, 58.
[770] McLaren, *Everything Must Change*, 271.

4

Solver

Who Is McLaren's Jesus and What Did He Do?

At the heart of liberal *Kingdom* grammar and their gospel is the person of Jesus of Nazareth, whose chief work was founding the historical movement of the Kingdom of God through His loving life example. The same is true for McLaren: The man Jesus is important because of His revolutionary Kingdom movement and model of loving life. While the historic Christian faith recognizes Jesus Christ as God and in some way a penal substitutionary sacrifice for the sins of the world, McLaren recognizes neither. Instead, Jesus is merely the best teacher of a better way of living, the one who lived the best way to be human, and one who is our best picture of the character of God. In *The Story We Find Ourselves In,* McLaren describes Jesus as a

"revolutionary" who was a "master of living."[771] According to
McLaren, "Jesus really is in some mysterious and in a unique
way sent from God and full of God."[772] Notice McLaren does not
say Jesus *is* God, but merely a messenger of sorts from God. His
fellowship with God comes from His ethical way of living; Jesus
is Divine because He *acts* divinely. As with four generations of
liberals before him, McLaren seems to view Jesus as the moral
not the metaphysical Son of God.

McLaren affirms this characterization in his most recent
book, *A New Kind of Christianity*, by insisting that Jesus "brings
us to a new evolutionary level in our understanding of God...the
experience of God in Jesus requires a brand-new definition or
understanding of God," because He "gives us the highest,
deepest, and most mature view of the character of the living
God."[773] McLaren's emphasis on the "character of God" finds
substantial resonance with four generations of liberalism: "When
you see [Jesus], you are getting the best view afforded to humans
of the character of God;" "Jesus serves as the Word-made-flesh
revelation of the character of God;" and "the invisible God has
been made visible in his life. 'If you want to know what God is
like,' Jesus says, 'look at me, my life, my ways, my deeds, my
character.'"[774] Elsewhere he writes that Jesus simply identifies
Himself *with* God, telling His disciples that those who had seen
Him had in "some real way" also seen God.[775] In a "mysterious
and unique way" Jesus is full of God. He shows, images and

---

[771] McLaren, *The Story We Find Ourselves In*, 115, 121, 122.
[772] McLaren, *The Story We Find Ourselves*, 122.
[773] McLaren, *A New Kind of Christianity*, 114, 115.
[774] McLaren, *A New Kind of Christianity*, 118, 128, 222.
[775] McLaren, *The Secret Message of Jesus*, 31.

expresses God's character. This view of the person of Jesus is liberal in general and starkly Ritschlian in particular.

From McLaren's earliest writings one can detect his theological trajectory and emphasis of Jesus as "teacher" and "liver." In explaining Jesus as "Lord," McLaren argues this means Jesus "was the master of living...it would mean that no one else could take the raw materials of life...and elicit from them a beautiful song of truth and goodness. [The disciples] believed Jesus' way was higher and more brilliant, and the right way to launch a revolution of God."[776] Elsewhere he writes that Jesus' message and teachings is an "alternative framing story" that can "save the system from suicide," a message that focuses "on personal, social, and global transformation in this life."[777] Furthermore, "Jesus' life and message centered on the articulation and demonstration of a radically different framing story—one that critiques and exposes the imperial narratives as dangerous to itself and others."[778] The best teacher, way, and picture of God is the perfect solution to McLaren's problem, because as we already saw we need a better example to follow in order to live differently and avert dysfunction and destruction. Jesus' mastery over life through His higher, more brilliant way of living and alternative message provides the existential solution to our existential problem. Fundamentally, the solution Jesus provides through His work is the Kingdom of God, which is exactly how liberal *Kingdom* grammar has framed the solution for four generations.

---

[776] McLaren, *The Story We Find Ourselves In*, 121.
[777] McLaren, *Everything Must Change*, 73, 22.
[778] McLaren, *Everything Must Change*, 154-155.

Central to the work of Jesus is His vocation as the founder of the Kingdom of God, the one in whom the original way of human existence was found, taught and modeled to the world. McLaren insists that Jesus did not come to start a new religion, but to announce a new kingdom, a new way of life;[779] He was the founder of a new countermovement to all other human regimes.[780]Through His life and teachings, Jesus "inserted into human history a seed of grace, truth, and hope that can never be defeated," a seed that will "prevail over the evil and injustice of humanity and lead to the world's ongoing transformation into the world God dreams of."[781] Because the human problem is bad systems and stories, we need a new system and a new story to repair and heal us. Jesus provides humanity the solution through his teachings on the Kingdom of God and example of living out the way of that Kingdom. McLaren makes it clear that the central point of Jesus is the Kingdom of God: "[Jesus] came to launch a new Genesis, to lead a new Exodus, and to announce, embody, and inaugurate a new kingdom as the Prince of Peace. Seen in this light, Jesus and his message has everything to do with poverty, slavery, and a 'social agenda.'"[782] He insists that Jesus himself "saw these dynamics at work in his day and proposed in word and deed a new alternative. Jesus' creative and transforming framing story invited people to change the world by disbelieving old framing stories and believing a new one: a story about a loving God who calls all people to live life in a new

---

[779] McLaren, *A New Kind of Christianity*, 139.
[780] McLaren, *The Secret Message of Jesus*, 66.
[781] McLaren, *Everything Must Change*, 79-80.
[782] McLaren, *A New Kind of Christianity*, 135.

way."[783] We are called to follow Jesus in this new way by following His teachings and example of love.

McLaren believes our problem is the dysfunctional systems and destructive stories of our world. Therefore, our solution came when God called Jesus as a messenger to show us a better way of living and teach us a better story: the Kingdom system and Kingdom story. McLaren agrees with Schleiermacher, Ritschl, Rauschenbusch and Tillich before him that the work of Jesus is fundamentally rooted in founding and living the Kingdom of God. Furthermore, Jesus is the vehicle of the Divine because of the way He lived and taught. Through His vocation as founder of the Kingdom of God Jesus was filled with God— meaning He acted like God would act on earth—and ultimately revealed the character of God by what He did and with what He said. In so acting and revealing, Jesus is the vehicle for an existential solution to our existential problem. As McLaren rhetorically asks, "Is Jesus' healing and transforming framing story really powerful enough to save the world?"[784] Because McLaren believes our systems and stories are the problem, our solution is found in an alternative system and story, which we find in Jesus' message on the Kingdom of God. McLaren answers his question thusly:

> if we believe that God graciously offers us a new way, a new truth, and a new life, we can be liberated from the vicious, addictive cycles of our suicidal framing stories. That kind of faith will save us...our failure to believe [Jesus' good news] will keep us from experiencing its

---

[783] McLaren, *Everything Must Change*, 237-274.
[784] McLaren, *Everything Must Change*, 269.

> saving potential, and so we'll spin on in the vicious
> cycles of Caesar. 785

According to McLaren, Jesus' teachings on the Kingdom provides the liberation we need from the systems and stories of the world by providing an alternative new system and story, a new way, truth, and life. We find salvation when we "transfer our trust from the way of Caesar to the way of Christ."[786] Notice that McLaren calls people to transfer their trust to the *way* of Christ rather than *person* of Christ. McLaren urges us to transfer our trust from the world's systems and stories—from our bad *existence*—to the system and story of Christ's Kingdom, because the Kingdom is the actual work of Jesus. As with four generations preceding him, McLaren's *Kingdom* grammar fundamentally insists that human salvation isn't found in a *name* (i.e. Jesus Christ), but a *movement*—the Kingdom of God.

---

[785] McLaren, *Everything Must Change*, 270.
[786] McLaren, *Everything Must Change*, 271.

5

Solution

How Does McLaren's Gospel Solve Our Problem?

In one of his clearest definitions of the Kingdom, and thus the solution to our human problem, McLaren defines the Kingdom of God as "a reality into which we have been emerging through the centuries, which is bigger than whatever we generally mean by 'Christianity' but at the same time is what generously orthodox Christianity is truly about."[787] In the same section he equates the Kingdom to "the way of Jesus," which is "the way of love and the way of embrace."[788] The Way of Jesus and Kingdom of God "integrates what has gone before so that something new can emerge."[789] And toward what are we emerging? The universal human ideal, the essence of what it

---

[787] McLaren, *A Generous Orthodoxy*, 288.
[788] McLaren, *A Generous Orthodoxy*, 287.
[789] McLaren, *A Generous Orthodoxy*, 287.

means to human: McLaren writes, "Jesus invitation into the Kingdom of God was an invitation into *the original universe, as it was meant to be.*"[790] In this definition are several features consistent with liberal *Kingdom* grammar: The Kingdom is transcendent in that it is equated with an ultimate reality that supersedes any particular religion, representing the universal ideal, the essence of human existence; it is immanent in that it is most closely embodied in humanity in the life and way of Jesus and is concerned with historical transformation; it is progressivistic in that the Kingdom takes humanity from a lower level of living to a higher level of existence; it is fundamentally about love-inspired action; finally, it is universal, in that McLaren's grammar has all of humanity squarely in view.

Like the four generations preceding McLaren, his *Kingdom* grammar is inherently defined by love-inspired action: He suggests the only way for the Kingdom of God to save humanity is through "weakness and vulnerability, sacrifice and love;"[791] McLaren argues that the central governing "policy" of the Kingdom is universal love;[792] he insists the way of Christ, the way of the Kingdom, is inherently the "way of love;"[793] the mission of the Church itself is defined by the single goal of "forming Christlike people, people who live the way of love, the way of peacemaking, the way of the kingdom of God, the way of Jesus;"[794] and finally, the Kingdom of God advances, gains ground "with reconciling, forgiving love: when people love

---

[790] McLaren, *The Secret Message of Jesus*, 53. (emph. mine)
[791] McLaren, *The Secret Message of Jesus*, 69.
[792] McLaren, *A New Kind of Christianity*, 154.
[793] McLaren, *A New Kind of Christianity*, 168.
[794] McLaren, *A New Kind of Christianity*, 171.

strangers and enemies...”[795] This love activity flows from Jesus Himself who was the first Master at loving activity, which culminated at the cross. For McLaren, the cross is a stage upon which Christ renders a grand performance illustrating God's love, acceptance, and new Kingdom way of sacrifice and suffering. Jesus' life and message has been one of non-violence and triumph over enemies through peace and self-sacrifice. Like the other liberals, the cross is the culmination of those teachings as an exposé on love. Rather than joining in with the "'shock and awe' display of power as Roman crucifixions were intended to do," McLaren says Jesus gives us a "'reverence and awe' display of God's willingness to accept rejection and mistreatment...”[796] In this display of "Christ crucified," McLaren says "we see that the lowly way of Christ, the vulnerable way of love, is the only way of life."[797] And this life is Kingdom-life. This love-inspired life is what transforms and saves humanity.

Consistent with the four previous generations of liberals, McLaren's *Kingdom* grammar is inherently progressivistic vis-à-vis humanistic change. As he says, "God stands ahead of us in time, at the end of the journey...and washes over us with a ceaseless flow of new possibilities, new options, new chances...This newness, these possibilities are always 'at hand,' 'among us,' and 'coming' so we can 'enter' the larger reality and transcend the space we currently fill." He goes on to say, "We constantly *emerge from what we were* and are into *what we can become*,"[798] equating the Kingdom of God with emergence, with

---

[795] McLaren, *The Secret Message of Jesus*, 69.
[796] McLaren, *A New Kind of Christianity*, 158-159.
[797] McLaren, *A New Kind of Christianity*, 169.
[798] McLaren, *A Generous Orthodoxy*, 283, 284. (emph. mine)

humanistic progress. McLaren rhetorically asks, "What does the future hold? the answer begins, '*That depends on you and me.* God holds out to us at every moment a brighter future; the issue is whether we are willing to receive it and work with God to create it. We are participating in the creation of what the future will be.'"[799] That the future depends on you and me is patently consistent with Rauschenbusch's *social gospel.*

Along with Schleiermacher, Ritschl, and Tillich, McLaren believes that we are the makers of our best life now, we are responsible for bringing into existence the best version of ourselves, the universal human ideal; we are responsible for saving ourselves. This is the case because humanity—individuals and as a community—is the actual *medium* that contains the Kingdom of God, right here and now.[800] Furthermore, all people are called, through their own power and choice, to live in the radical new way of the Kingdom. As McLaren states, "we do indeed have the choice today and every day to seek it, enter it, receive it, live as citizens of it, invest in it, even sacrifice for it," which, depending on this choice, will create two very different worlds and futures: one hellish and one heavenly.[801] Thus, McLaren urges everyone to "start doing the next good thing now," so that the good of the Kingdom will prevail by love, peace, and endurance of suffering, while bad ethical acts like domination, violence, and torture will be overcome through our collective human effort.[802]

---

[799] McLaren, *A New Kind of Christianity*, 196. (emph. mine)
[800] McLaren, *The Secret Message of Jesus*, 101.
[801] McLaren, *The Secret Message of Jesus*, 181.
[802] McLaren, *Everything Must Change*, 146.

Ultimately, salvation is participation in the Kingdom of God, which McLaren calls participatory eschatology. While McLaren contends conventional eschatologies have cultivated resignation, fear, and aggression, participatory eschatology inspires much more:

> a passion to do good, whatever the suffering, sacrifice, and delay because of a confidence that God will win in the end; courage, because God's Spirit is at work in the world and what God begins God will surely bring to completion; a sense of urgency, because we are protagonists in a story; and humility and kindness, because we are aware of our ability to miss the point, lose our way, and play on the wrong side. 803

Furthermore, McLaren argues that the death and resurrection of Jesus are paradigms for this salvation in which we ourselves are to participate in anticipation of God's coming Kingdom: we join with Jesus in dying (metaphorically to our pride and agendas, literally in martyrdom as a witness to God's Kingdom and justice); we rise again in triumph "through the mysterious but real power of God. In this cruciform way, we participate in the ongoing work of God, and we anticipate its ultimate success."[804] For McLaren, our dying and rising with Christ are symbolic of our rejection of and triumph over the dysfunctional systems and destructive stories of our world; we are called to die to the bad ethics of the world and rise to new life by living like Jesus. Thus, salvation is entirely existential, in that His loving example is what saves us from our bad existence, an existential salvation that extends to the whole human race.

---

[803] McLaren, *A New Kind of Christianity*, 200.
[804] McLaren, *A New Kind of Christianity*, 200-201.

In this definition of humanistic progress, we find the familiar ring of universalism present in liberal *Kingdom* grammar. McLaren believes God's wish and hope is for all of humanity to grow toward Christlikeness, because we are *all* children of God.[805] In fact, McLaren believes that "a person can affiliate with Jesus in the kingdom-of-God dimension without affiliating with him in the religious kingdom of Christianity. In other words, I believe that Christianity is not the kingdom of God. The ultimate reality is the kingdom of God…"[806] Because the Christian faith is not the single container of God's reign, the Kingdom is universal; it is a universal human ideal instantiated in the person and life of Jesus whom all may join simply by emulating Him.

McLaren insists that everyone is a potential agent of the Kingdom by nature of people's loving activity, like the taxi cab driver McLaren references who treated his guests with special care and respect; Carter had within him the spirit of the Kingdom of God and was a secret agent of the Kingdom.[807] For McLaren this can be true because the Kingdom is about our daily lives, it is a daily way of life centered around Jesus' loving message and life example. He stresses the Kingdom is about so-called *purposeful inclusion*, because it "seeks to include all who want to participate in and contribute to its purpose,"[808] which of course is humanistic progress toward bringing the universal human ideal—in McLaren's words, the original universe as it was meant to be—to bear on human existence.

---

[805] McLaren, *A Generous Orthodoxy*, 283.
[806] McLaren, *A Generous Orthodoxy*, 282n.141.
[807] McLaren, *The Secret Message of Jesus*, 85-89.
[808] McLaren, *The Secret Message of Jesus*, 167.

Consequently, McLaren finds it "fascinating" to think that thousands of Muslims, Buddhists, Hindus, and even former atheists and agnostics could come from the east and west and north and south "to enjoy the feast of the kingdom in ways that those bearing the name Christian have not."[809] McLaren would believe this possible because he believes that anything that contributes to humanistic progress counts as Kingdom activity; any loving-act that subverts the prevailing systems and stories solves for our human problem and provides individual salvation.

In the end, because we are called to live in the system and story of the Kingdom by living the teachings of Jesus, McLaren says ultimate salvation at judgment will be based on behavior, not beliefs: "God will examine the story of our lives for signs of Christlikeness...These are the parts of a person's life that will be deemed worthy of being saved, remembered, rewarded, and raised to new beginnings."[810] Giving food and water to the needy, showing mercy, welcoming the stranger, and being generous like Jesus is what God cares about, what will result in salvation. Conversely, "all the unloving, unjust, non-Christlike parts of our lives...will be burned away, counted as unworthy, condemned, and forgotten forever."[811]

Notice the implicit universalism embedded in McLaren's soteriology: in the end, everyone will find salvation, because, as Tillich taught, the positive will live on while the negative will not. Ultimately, then, our salvation depends upon our *existence*, it depends upon how we live, whether we walked the path of

---

[809] McLaren, *The Secret Message of Jesus*, 217.
[810] McLaren, *A New Kind of Christianity*, 204.
[811] McLaren, *A New Kind of Christianity*, 204.

Jesus in word, deed, and suffering. Since "no good deed will be forgotten," we are urged to "start doing the next good thing now and never give up until the dream comes true," until God's Kingdom comes.[812] Therefore, in reality, salvation comes not through *Jesus'* saving act on the cross, but through every *human* act that lives out Jesus' way of life. In many ways, each person is his own savior, because every act of love counts as Kingdom acts, as saving acts that bring the universal ideal to bear on existence. In reality, the *Kingdom* saves us through humanistic progress, rather than through Jesus.

---

[812] McLaren, *Everything Must Change*, 146.

6

Conclusion

This *Kingdom* salvation of which McLaren speaks is wholly consistent with four generations of liberal *Kingdom* grammar and the liberal gospel itself. In this *grammar*, our human problem is not a sinful nature but dysfunctional systems and destructive stories. Rather than bound by sin on the inside, we are oppressed on the outside by bad social and spiritual systems and stories. Jesus is the antidote, the cure for these bad systems and stories because He provided the alternative system and story of the Kingdom through His life and teachings. For McLaren, the Kingdom of God is "A life that is radically different from the way people are living these days, a life that is full and over flowing, a higher life that is centered in an interactive relationship with God and with Jesus...an extraordinary life to the full centered on a relationship with God."[813] He contends this is what the Apostle John termed "eternal life," or "life of the

---

[813] McLaren, *The Secret Message of Jesus*, 37.

ages." Through his Kingdom message and Kingdom way of living, "Jesus is promising a life that transcends 'life in the present age'...[he] is offering a life in the new Genesis, the new creation that is 'of the age' not simply part of the current regimes, plots, kingdoms, and economies created by humans."[814]

At the heart of McLaren's gospel is a person named Jesus who came to liberate us from these old regimes (i.e. dysfunctional systems) and plots (i.e. destructive stories), to teach and show us the highest, best way found in the Kingdom. He came to end *life-as-we-know-it* and usher in *life-as-it-ought-to-be*; Jesus' life saves, rather than His death and resurrection. This essence of what it means to be human is rooted in universal brotherly love. The Kingdom represents this ultimate reality, which comes when anyone does any act of love, whether cleaning a local river, launching an adult literacy program, or returning a dropped set of keys to a stranger on a busy city sidewalk. Somehow these love-inspired acts collectively bring in the future we all long for, burning up the negative in the process and enveloping all of humanity in its arms of inclusion. And in the end, while Jesus' life provides the example and way, humanity is its own savior. That is the obvious, logical conclusion to liberal *Kingdom* grammar, which McLaren recites *in toto*.

In the end, the gospel of Brian McLaren is identical with the good news of liberalism: the Kingdom of God, the universal human ideal and essence of human existence, has come near in the life of Jesus; live your best existence now by turning from the destructive stories and dysfunctional systems of this world and

---

[814] McLaren, *A New Kind of Christianity*, 130.

turning toward everyday acts of brotherly love. We conclude this examination by considering an observation and a few implications that contemporary appropriations of liberal gospel of the Kingdom are already having within evangelicalism.

First, an observation: in tracing the generational development of liberal Kingdom grammar it is interesting to note the ways in which the focus on the Church itself shifted and waned. When Schleiermacher introduced the language of the Kingdom back into the Church's theological discourse, the Church was squarely in view: He equated the Kingdom with the Church. Ritschl maintained such a connection, yet broadened the Kingdom to include those well beyond its borders. By the time Tillich formulated his own theological enterprise, the Church had become a symbol and mostly unnecessary.

Likewise, in McLaren's theological missive arguing for a new kind of Christianity, the Church is roundly ignored in favor of the Kingdom as the ultimate religious reality. This gradual downplaying and dismissal of the Church makes sense, as the Church is simply one faith community that embodies the universal human ideal and is important only insofar as it was the original religious organization that perpetuated Jesus' teachings. Now in our postmodern multi-faith world, there is even more pressure to downplay and negate the role of the Church as the particular embodiment of Christ and agent of the Kingdom. Such maneuvers have two implications for the future of mainstream evangelicalism.

First, note how the terms *mission, evangelism,* and *gospel* seem to have shifted over the past few years in light of the resurgent use of the Kingdom of God. While perhaps the nature of Jesus and His substitutionary work on the cross is not in danger of losing their meaning and significance in such circles, one has to wonder how using the Kingdom in ways liberals have for generations will begin to affect mainstream evangelical commitment to core evangelical convictions, mainly conversionism and activism—particularly evangelistic. Popular Evangelical magazines such as *RELEVANT,* books on Christian cultural engagement such as *AND: The Gathered and Scattered Church*[815] and *For the City: Proclaiming and Living Out the Gospel,*[816] and young church leader conferences like *Catalyst* emphasize doing good by living like Jesus. Not that this emphasis is necessarily a bad thing. It seems, however, that in so emphasizing the Kingdom in ways that liberals have for years— mainly transforming human existence through mundane and supramundane acts of love—mainstream evangelicals are in danger of losing sight of what has always been central to evangelicalism, and authentic, historic Christianity.

Furthermore, evangelicals should think twice about appropriating the grammar of the Kingdom in ways liberals have because of the implications that grammar has for the Christian faith itself. How liberals like McLaren arrive at their definition of *Kingdom* depends on how they define sin, the person and work of Jesus, and other aspects of historic orthodoxy. In light of that grammar, then, what is to say mainstream evangelicals will not join progressives in transforming, say, the meaning of the cross itself? Already McLaren has accused proponents of substitutionary atonement of holding a view akin to "divine

---

[815] Hugh Halter and Matt Smay, *AND: The Gathered and Scattered Church* (Grand Rapids: Zondervan, 2010).
[816] Darin Patrick and Matt Carter, *For the City: Proclaiming and Living Out the Gospel* (Grand Rapids: Zondervan, 2010).

child abuse."[817] And while others do not go as far as this language they wonder whether we should speak of the cross in language that side-steps traditional substitutionary language altogether in favor of alternative atonement views, such as *Christus Victor.*

What is to stop mainstream evangelicals from joining McLaren in downplaying the significance of Jesus' death in favor of Jesus' significant life? Perhaps more importantly, if the deeds and teachings of Jesus are all that matter, then what would stop some evangelicals from fudging on the *person* of Jesus, including His deity? Without sounding apocalyptic, if evangelicals continue to use the language of the Kingdom in ways that liberals have for generations, they risk the potential of joining them in the other beliefs that supplied the context and definition of that grammar. So the first implication in adopting liberal *Kingdom* grammar is the danger of losing sight of the historic Christian faith.

Secondly, the Kingdom gospel of liberals and Emergent's like McLaren has massive implications for the future of missions and evangelism. A new generation is thinking differently about the nature of evangelism at home and missions abroad. For instance, in times past the typical evangelical college would take students on Spring Break trips to key beaches around the country to share the gospel with Spring Break revelers. While such methods of evangelism could be contested, it is worth noting that now it is more common for such colleges to take trips to serve the homeless in Seattle or build wells in Africa than it is to share the gospel with people in need of a Savior. Missions is now about

---

[817] McLaren, *The Story We Find Ourselves*, 102.

acts of love in the interest of serving our neighbor, rather than acts of gospel proclamation in the interest of seeing our neighbor saved. Furthermore, alongside a shift in emphasis in missions has been a shift in evangelism, the hallmark of mission work of yore. Rather than evangelism being the proclamation of the gospel, people now define evangelism using the maxim often ascribed to St. Francis of Assisi: preach the gospel at all times, if necessary use words. Words that urge repentance, belief, and confession are considered unnecessary, being abandoned in favor of actions of acceptance, service, and love.

People like McLaren now frame the gospel as the Kingdom coming to our here-and-now rather than justification by faith in Christ. While the Kingdom is part and parcel of the gospel of Jesus Christ, McLaren is pronouncing at the expense of the justification provided through Jesus' death and resurrection. Such pronouncement not only has implications for the future of mission and evangelism, but the gospel itself. Therefore, it behooves evangelicals to reconsider their *Kingdom* grammar in order to guard their *gospel* grammar. Yes, we must pray for God's Kingdom-rule to break into our existence in increasing measure. But we do so with the realization that it was God Himself through His Son's life, death, and resurrection that made it possible in the first place. It is not the *Kingdom* that saves us, but Jesus Christ alone.

Part 2

A New Kind of Christianity for a Multi-Faith World

7

Introduction

Brian McLaren reminds me a lot of Thomas Jefferson: He conveniently ignores large portions of the Holy Scripture that do not conform to His worldview.

Jefferson is known to have cobbled together a Bible that cut out the miracles of Jesus and supernatural elements of the Gospels, because they didn't conform to his modern, Enlightenment worldview. Similarly, in his newest book, *Why Did Jesus, Moses, the Buddha, and Mohammed Cross the Road?: Christian Identity in a Multi-Faith World*, McLaren has ignored entire portions of the Bible that don't conform to his postmodern, pluralism worldview.

He has ignored the Lord's command to Israel to not worship any other God but YHWH. He has ignored the anger and judgement of God over Israel's pervasive pattern of idolatry throughout the Old Testament. He has ignored the New Testament's teachings that Jesus Christ Himself is the only one true God. He has ignored Scripture's teachings on salvation by grace through faith in Jesus Christ alone.

Like Jefferson, McLaren has conveniently ignored the Bible in favor of a Christian religious identity that isn't actually Christian. Instead, it is fundamentally foreign to the Holy Scripture and historic Christian faith.

Now understand, I am not arguing McLaren *himself* is not a Christian. That's not for me to decide; God holds final judgment in that regard. What I am arguing in Part 2 of our examination of *The Gospel of Brian McLaren* is that his *ideas* are not Christian. In addition to examining his view of our human problem, the solution to our problem, and the bearer of our solution, this final section outlining McLaren's postmodern, pluralism worldview will show that his gospel is no gospel at all. His gospel is fake, because he ignores the Bible and fundamentals of the Christian faith.

McLaren's gospel hinges on his desire to develop "a healthy, sane and faithful Christian identity in a multi-faith world."[818] This is an admirable desire. Given our multi-faith reality, finding a way to get along and exist as Christians alongside people of other faiths is indeed needed. But the way McLaren goes about it is faulty, as he has no regard for the exclusivity of faith in Jesus Christ as single Lord and Savior. Instead, he wants to develop a Christian religious identity "that moves me toward people of other faiths in wholehearted love, not in spit of their non-Christian identity and not in spite or my own Christian identity, but *because of my identity as a follower of God in the way of Jesus*."[819] Notice that McLaren isn't a follower of Jesus, but

---

[818] Brian McLaren, *Why Did Jesus, Moses, the Buddha, and Mohammed Cross the Road? Christian Identity in a Multi-Faith World* (New York: Jericho Books, 2012), 9.
[819] McLaren, *Jesus, Moses, the Buddha, and Mohammed*, 11. (emph. mine)

instead a follower of God in the *way* of Jesus. This distinction is crucial, because this descriptive nuance broadens the solution to our problem well beyond Jesus Christ and into religious pluralism in ways others have argued for years. For McLaren, the point is following God—a vanilla, pan-deity that stands as the Higher Being of all religious faiths—and Jesus is merely one way among many possible ways to follow.

While the Christian gospel insists that salvation is found in no one other than Jesus Christ, McLaren's gospel insists that something good shines from the heart of all religions, which is "a saving drive toward peace, goodness, self-control, integrity, charity, beauty, duty."[820] McLaren is on mission to rethink Christian identity in a multi-faith world, and in so doing he completely redefines and reimagines the Christian faith itself.

This second part of Brian McLaren's gospel will explain how he reimagines Christian religious identity, reformulates key doctrines of the Christian faith, reconstructs important Church practices, and redefines Christian mission. While McLaren's latest enterprise is indeed sad, it shouldn't surprise anyone because it is a firm extension of the generational enterprise of theological liberalism. This iteration is the logical extension of the liberal gospel for a postmodern day.

As I read McLaren's newest book I couldn't help but think about Paul's journey to Athens recorded in Acts 17. For longtime Christians it's a well-known story in which Paul encounters a marketplace "full of idols" in Athens, much like our own multi-faith day in America. How does Paul respond? First, he follows McLaren's cues in moving toward people of other

---

[820] McLaren, *Jesus, Moses, the Buddha, and Mohammed*, 20.

faiths "in wholehearted love" by acknowledging and appreciating their religiosity. But unlike McLaren, he carries that love further, beyond mere tolerance, to confronting these religious people with the only one true God of the Holy Scriptures. After calling them "ignorant," Paul goes on to tell the Story of this God. He then boldly, courageously calls these idolaters out from their ignorance by repenting, saying that "In the past God overlooked such ignorance, but now He commands people everywhere to repent," (Acts 17:30) to repent of their false worship of false gods. In fact, God "has set a day when He will judge the world" (Acts 17:31) for the very ignorant idolatry that McLaren champions! Unlike the apology McLaren has written, what we see here in Acts 17 is the only posture the Church has ever taken toward other faiths, and it is one that's especially important for Christian identity in a multi-faith world.

So, according to McLaren, why did Jesus, Moses, the Buddha, and Mohammed cross the road? "Because they hoped we would follow them."[821] McLaren's gospel truly sketches a brand new kind of Christianity for a multi-faith world, which isn't good news for anyone.

---

[821] McLaren, *Jesus, Moses, the Buddha, and Mohammed*, 12.

8

Reimagining Christian Identity

The singular goal of McLaren's book is to rethink Christian identity in a multi-faith world. In so rethinking, McLaren insists that we (mostly conservative evangelical Christians, McLaren's favorite whipping boy) need a strong-benevolent Christian identity, a so-called "third way" Christian identity that is both strong—"vigorous, vital, durable, motivating, faithful, attractive, and defining"[822]—and kind—"something far more robust than mere tolerance, political correctness, or coexistence," and instead "benevolent, hospitable, accepting, interested, and loving...seeking to understand and appreciate their religion from their point of view."[823] He writes on this issue of Christian religious identity from his own personal experience with a problematic syndrome he calls CRIS.

---

[822] McLaren, *Jesus, Moses, the Buddha, and Mohammed*, 10.
[823] McLaren, *Jesus, Moses, the Buddha, and Mohammed*, 10-11.

McLaren insists Christians like him have a problem: They suffer from so-called "Conflicted Religious Identity Syndrome (CRIS)." This condition afflicts people like him who are "seeking a way of being Christian that makes you more hospitable, not more hostile...more loving, not more judgmental...more like Christ and less like many churchgoers you have met."[824] The word *hostile* plays an important role in McLaren's argument for reimagining Christian religious identity in a multi-faith world, as it allows him to pit hospitable Christians like him against so-called hostile Christians like conservative evangelicals.

Key to McLaren's reimagining efforts is painting conservative Christians, who care that their non-Christian neighbors place their faith in Jesus Christ, as having "a strong identity characterized by strong hostility toward non-christians."[825] He contends that such an identity, rooted in hostility and oppositionalism, "values us as inherently more human, more holy, more acceptable, more pure, or more worthy than them...Our root problem is the hostility that we often employ to make and keep our identities strong."[826] Thus, McLaren is pleading with traditional Christians to become less hostile,[827] to leave behind "an oppositional religious identity that derives strength from hostility."[828] *Religious hostility* is a potent rhetorical device that McLaren uses throughout to paint his opponents as hateful monsters. It is derived, however, from an unfair caricature of fair-minded, concerned Christians who long

---

[824] McLaren, *Jesus, Moses, the Buddha, and Mohammed*, 15.
[825] McLaren, *Jesus, Moses, the Buddha, and Mohammed*, 41.
[826] McLaren, *Jesus, Moses, the Buddha, and Mohammed*, 63.
[827] McLaren, *Jesus, Moses, the Buddha, and Mohammed*, 44.
[828] McLaren, *Jesus, Moses, the Buddha, and Mohammed*, 57.

for their friends and neighbors of other religions to find salvation through Jesus Christ, which the Bible and Church have insisted on for two millennia.

In response to the hostility of traditional Christians, McLaren argues for a different posture: He wants them to replace their hostility with *solidarity*, which he urges in the final of ten questions testing ones Christian identity:

> "My understanding of Jesus and his message leads me to see each faith tradition, including my own, as having its own history, value, strengths, and weaknesses. I seek to affirm and celebrate all that is good in each faith tradition, and I build intentional relationships of mutual sharing and respectful collaboration with people of all faith traditions, so all our faiths can keep growing and contributing to God's will being done on earth as in heaven." 829

Note several assumptions in this push for solidarity: Christianity is simply one faith option among several legitimate "faith communities;" every religious tradition is good and legitimate; Jesus Himself and His message apparently leads us to affirm and celebrate the good in other religions; every religion contributes to God's will unfolding on earth, every faith contributes to the Kingdom of God advancing. McLaren insists it is possible to accept people of other faiths "with the religion they love,"[830] because there is something good that shines in every religion.

---

[829] McLaren, *Jesus, Moses, the Buddha, and Mohammed*, 69.
[830] McLaren, *Jesus, Moses, the Buddha, and Mohammed*, 32.

Not only is McLaren's main thesis problematic from the perspective of Scripture—the Bible is clear there is only one true God, Jesus Christ, and all else are false gods[831]—it is problematic in that his starting place of *Christian identity* is a false definition of our position in the first place. We are not interested in converting people from one religious identity to our Christian identity, from another religion to Christianity, as McLaren claims.[832] The Church's mission has always been to help and provoke people to give their life and lifestyle to Jesus Christ as Lord and Rescuer, to place their faith in Him. Christianity or a Christian religious identity have never been the point. Jesus is the point. And faith in Him as Lord and Savior and everything that comes along with that faith—release from the bondage of sin, freedom from the oppression of shame and guilt, salvation from death— is the point. Again, Christianity has never been the point. Jesus Christ as the only one true God who is humanity's only hope for rescue is.

Furthermore, McLaren's assumptions regarding Christian identity also play into his broader views of religion. It seems clear that he believes every religion, or every so-called "faith tradition," is valid, legitimate, and good. Every faith has strengths and every faith has weaknesses. Thus, McLaren calls on traditional Christians to shed our hostile identity and instead walk in solidarity with our fellow brothers and sisters in faith— regardless of the particulars of that faith. But here's the problem, well several problems, actually: McLaren's optimistic, rosy-glass view of religious harmony is misguided; religion itself is a social

---

[831] See 1 Cor. 8:4-6.
[832] McLaren, *Jesus, Moses, the Buddha, and Mohammed*, 31.

construct; the whole Holy Scriptures make clear there is only one true God, and all other gods are false; and there is one way to become right with that one true God.

First, McLaren's rosy-glass view of religious harmony is misguided because every religion makes exclusive claims. I found it remarkable that McLaren seemed to downplay and even dismiss the reality that every religion makes exclusive claims, ones that tend to negate other religious claims. This is Comparative Religion 101, here. Islam declares there is only one God, Allah, and Muhammad is his messenger, implying that beliefs about all other claims to deity, like those by Christians about Jesus, are false. In fact, Muslims make the explicit claim that Jesus is merely one prophet among many, beginning with Adam, the first Muslim, and ending with Muhammed who was the last and greatest. Buddhism is complicated because of its history, but generally Buddhists have a view of God among other things, that conflicts with monotheists, or even polytheists. Though they don't deny the existence of God, or multiple gods, per se, for Buddhists whether there are gods doesn't matter because they have nothing to say about ultimate existence; only the Buddha has revealed the way beyond this existence into a higher existence. In Islam and Buddhism alone, McLaren's thesis is negated, as oppositionalism—and, we could say, *hostility*—is built into these religions by nature of their own exclusive worldview claims.

Second, religion itself is a social construct. It is a way social beings organize themselves around a particular reality defining story—and subsequent beliefs regarding that story—in response to some religious affection. The idea that multiple religions exist is true insofar as humans themselves in socially coordinated efforts have constructed belief systems in response to what theological liberals have called a "feeling of absolute dependence," or a feeling of dependence on a Higher Being. Such human affection and feeling does not validate a particular religious experience, only revelation can do that. Paul makes clear in Romans 1 that countless human societies know the only one true God, yet they've exchanged Him for "images," for socially constructed religions.

In the Bible these social constructs were known as Baal or Asherah of the Canaanites, the god Pharaoh of Egypt, or the "unknown god" of the Athenians. In our modern, multi-faith world these social constructs are known as Allah or Buddha or Krishna. The only true revelation humans have ever had regarding a "Higher Being" is the Holy Scripture, which reveals a very particular God: Jesus Christ. And that revelation insists that faith in Him is the only "religious" experience that is real, while all other experiences we define as religious are fake.

Third, as previously mentioned, the Bible makes it clear that there is only one true God. The church has always understood that one true God as Trinity—Father, Son, and Spirit. This does not mean God is three gods in one, but rather three persons with one essence. This God is not the same god worshiped by Islam, Buddhism, or even Judaism. And any attempt to blur the distinction between these fake gods and the only one true God of the Bible is nothing short of idolatry. The *Shema* of Deuteronomy makes this clear: "Hear, O Israel. The Lord our God, the Lord is One." And Paul does, too, when he address a situation in the Church of Corinth with food sacrificed to idols. He quotes the *Shema* and then amends it, saying:

> "We know that 'An idol is nothing at all in the world' and that 'There is no God but one.' For even if there are so-called gods, whether in heaven or on earth (as indeed there are many 'gods' and many 'lords'), yet for us there is but one God, the Father, from whom all things came and for whom we live; and there is but one Lord, Jesus Christ, through whom all things came and through whom we live." (1 Cor 8)

Here Paul makes clear that Jesus Christ is the only one true God. The 'gods' and 'lords' of this world are mere social constructs, created by people in place of the true God.

Finally, the only revelation we've received from God Himself makes it clear there is one way to become right with this God: Rescue by grace through faith in Jesus. There is no other name under heaven by which a person can be saved (Acts 4). No one comes to the God the Father except through God the Son (John 14). There is but one God, the Father; there is but one Lord, Jesus Christ, through whom all things came and through whom we live (1 Cor 8). Everybody is made right with God by His grace through the rescue that's come by Christ Jesus, whom God presented as a sacrifice of atonement, to be received by faith (Romans 3). To teach anything else is false teaching; to suggest the Holy Scriptures teach anything else is heresy.

It would be bad enough if McLaren stopped his enterprise here at reimagining Christian identity, but he doesn't. He takes it a step further by insisting we need to reformulate Christian doctrine itself.

9

Reformulating Christian Doctrine

In many ways McLaren's doctrine reformulation is rooted in his reformulation of two foundational doctrines of the historic Christian faith: Scripture and God. According to McLaren, the Bible isn't to be read and interpreted and applied like some do as a constitution, as if it was an absolute authority on everything in life.[833] In *A New Kind of Christianity*, McLaren couldn't (bring himself to) say that the Bible is inspired by God and is the sole textual point of God's divine self-disclosure, only that it has "a unique role in the life of the community of faith, resourcing, challenging, and guiding the community of faith in ways that no other texts can."[834] How, then, does McLaren conceive of the Bible as an authoritative document? The Bible is a community library.

---

[833] McLaren, *Jesus, Moses, the Buddha, and Mohammed*, 204.
[834] McLaren, *A New Kind of Christianity*, 83.

For him "the Bible is a library filled with diverse voices making diverse claims in an ongoing conversation."[835] As he maintained in *A New Kind of Christianity*, "This inspired library preserves, presents, and inspires an ongoing vigorous conversation with and about God, a living and vital civil argument into which we are all invited and through which God is revealed."[836] A fuller quotation from the same book illumines his view of Scripture and its authority more clearly:

> "[Revelation] happens in conversations and arguments that take place within and among communities of people who share the same essential questions across generations. Revelation accumulates in the relationships, interactions, and interplay between statements." 837

Pay attention to what he is saying here: McLaren believes revelation is about *human conversation* about God, rather than God Himself revealing Himself to humanity. This is why he can say in this recent book, "Faithful interaction with a library means siding with some of those voices and against others."[838] In fact, reimagining our Christian identity in a multi-faith world "requires us to go back and reread our Scriptures and 'flip them,' faithfully picking and choosing—subverting hostility in the strong pursuit of love."[839]

And how can McLaren suggest this? Because Paul himself faithfully picked and chose, or that's what he would lead us to

---

[835] McLaren, *Jesus, Moses, the Buddha, and Mohammed*, 204.
[836] McLaren, *A New Kind of Christianity*, 83.
[837] McLaren, *A New Kind of Christianity*, 91-92.
[838] McLaren, *Jesus, Moses, the Buddha, and Mohammed*, 204.
[839] McLaren, *Jesus, Moses, the Buddha, and Mohammed*, 203.

believe. McLaren argues that Paul edits two passages of Scripture in the Old Testament—Psalm 18:41-49 and Deuteronomy 32:43—to reimagine salvation in Romans 15:8-10. Remarkably, McLaren suggests that "Paul courageously re-articulated the meaning of salvation,"[840] which he says was inspired by Jesus himself,[841] as if both of them were simply adding their voices to an ongoing conversation about God's salvation movement. It seems clear McLaren doesn't believe God Himself is actually saying something through the Bible, merely that people are trying to say something about God. And we are called to carry forth this "picking and choosing" effort to say something more advanced and more magnanimous than other people have said, including people in Scripture. McLaren says this very thing when he writes, "It remains to be seen to what degree we Christians today will move forward with Jesus and to what degree we will dig our heels in with the less magnanimous voices in the biblical library."[842]

I'd sure be interested to know what "less magnanimous voices in the biblical library" he's referencing. And if we can simply "side with some voices and against others" because they don't conform to our current, contemporary conversations about God, how isn't this precisely "simply picking and choosing according to one's own tastes," which McLaren denies? While I acknowledge a careful, deliberate interpretive effort surrounds our interaction with the text, it seems clear that for McLaren meaning doesn't reside in the text itself, because God Himself isn't speaking. Instead, the interpreter decides by way of siding

---

[840] McLaren, *Jesus, Moses, the Buddha, and Mohammed*, 203.
[841] McLaren, *Jesus, Moses, the Buddha, and Mohammed*, 202.
[842] McLaren, *Jesus, Moses, the Buddha, and Mohammed*, 206.

and opposing what the Bible says, or perhaps more accurately, *should* say in light of our 21st century God-conversation. This makes more sense when one understands McLaren's understanding of God.

Interestingly, McLaren's understanding of God seems to mirror the view of tritheism. Tritheism is the view of God that emphasizes the three persons of the Godhead with little to no unity of essence. It denies the essential unity of the Trinity in favor of three separate Gods, which is contrary to the historic Christian faith. Brian seems to reject the way in which historic orthodoxy has understood the Trinity for centuries. In fact, McLaren actually suggests that the doctrine of the Trinity is responsible for anti-semitism,[843] the Nazi gas chambers,[844] is no more than a "sinister tool of mind and speech control,"[845] and has threatened Muslims, Hindus, Buddhists, and members of indigenous religions. [846] You may think I am unfairly representing McLaren's position here. Unfortunately, I am not for he says "Trinitarian doctrines have indeed been part of the problem."[847] While the Trinity has been central to the Christian faith from the beginning—mainly because of what it says about Jesus Christ specifically as much as it says about God generally—McLaren seems to mock its centrality and importance to the Church. [848] How, then, does McLaren conceive of God, particularly in his reimagined Trinity?

---

[843] McLaren, *Jesus, Moses, the Buddha, and Mohammed*, 126.
[844] McLaren, *Jesus, Moses, the Buddha, and Mohammed*, 126.
[845] McLaren, *Jesus, Moses, the Buddha, and Mohammed*, 128.
[846] McLaren, *Jesus, Moses, the Buddha, and Mohammed*, 126.
[847] McLaren, *Jesus, Moses, the Buddha, and Mohammed*, 127.
[848] McLaren, *Jesus, Moses, the Buddha, and Mohammed*, 127.

Of the Trinity McLaren says, "God is one and in *some sense* three; that Christ is man and in *some sense* God; that the Spirit is the Spirit of the Father and the Son but in *some sense* not reducible to the Father and the Son."[849] I'm not sure why McLaren uses the qualifier "in some sense" to describe the Trinity, especially Jesus. The historic Christian faith has always said that God is one essence *and* three persons (curiously, McLaren leaves *"essence"* out of his concept of God, which makes more sense below); that Jesus Christ is man *and* God; that the Holy Spirit is a separate Being, yet one with the Father and the Son—not merely *in some sense*, but actually so.

McLaren rejects the historical (i.e. Nicene) understanding of the Trinity in favor of so-called *Social Trinitarianism*, a view he claims is supported by church history, particularly the Cappadocian Fathers.[850] Without going into great detail here given the scope of this examination, McLaren's assumptions regarding the Cappadocian Fathers are dependent upon problematic readings of their works.[851] And because McLaren relies upon Jurgen Moltmann's trinitarian scheme—who called his own view "trinitarian panentheism"—we see an emphasis on the three persons of God at the expense of his essential unity; McLaren's view is similar to the heresy of tritheism.

Like other social trinitarians, McLaren "images God as a dynamic unity-in-community of self-giving persons-in-relationship."[852] In this view, Father, Son, and Spirit are neither

---

[849] McLaren, *Jesus, Moses, the Buddha, and Mohammed*, 127. (emph. mine)
[850] McLaren, *Jesus, Moses, the Buddha, and Mohammed*, 128.
[851] For an excellent treatment of the Trinity, especially in regards to religious pluralism, see Keith E. Johnson, *Rethinking the Trinity and Religious Pluralism: An Augustinian Assessment* (Downers Grove: IVP Academic, 2011).
[852] McLaren, *Jesus, Moses, the Buddha, and Mohammed*, 128.

three independent units bound into a larger unity, nor one independent unit with three identical parts.[853] According to McLaren, God is the relational unity in which each person of the Trinity relate.[854] Rather than God being defined as an essential unity of three persons, as historic Nicene Christianity has always defined God, McLaren's conception of the Trinity makes God out to be a *community* rather than an *essential unity*. Thus, for McLaren, the "triune God" is merely the community of divine beings, which verges on the heresy of tritheism.

While McLaren does use the Eastern Church's view of *perichoresis* (mutual indwelling) to bind Father-Son-Spirit together, like Moltmann he fails to recognize how united the East and West were in their view of the unity of the Godhead in *essence*, in nature. And instead of conceiving of this mutual indwelling as governing their essential unity as three persons, McLaren merely projects a human scheme of ideal social relatedness upon the Godhead. Theology, then, very quickly mirrors anthropology, in that humanism defines and governs theism. In the historic view of the Godhead, however, it isn't that God functions like some human community of love, where the persons of the Trinity are bound together by such love in community and thus form the Being of God. Instead, God is defined as one essential Being who knows, wills, and acts in concert as three persons, yet as one Being. This is not McLaren's understanding of God.

It is problematic that McLaren views God merely as a human community of persons without having a strong belief in their

---

[853] McLaren, *Jesus, Moses, the Buddha, and Mohammed*, 128.
[854] McLaren, *Jesus, Moses, the Buddha, and Mohammed*, 128.

essential unity of nature. It's a problem primarily because Jesus Christ is left as merely a person who exhibits the character of love. If Jesus is not united in essence with the Father as God, then He isn't God Himself. If the Holy Spirit isn't united in essence with the Father and Son, then he can act separately, particularly in other religions which McLaren affirms.[855] Because the Holy Spirit isn't bound in essential unity to the Father and Son, "we would expect the one Holy Spirit to be moving, working, 'hovering' over each religion" as McLaren argues.[856] More bizarrely, McLaren seems to suggest all people actually participate in this divine community as *interpersons* or *interpersonalities*, because we are creatures made in God's image.[857] Thus, every religious community encounters God equally, because all people share in the divine community—"we live, move, and have our being in the Spirit" and "each religion...[has] a unique, particular, and evolving perspective from which to encounter the Spirit in a unique way."[858] It is for this reasons McLaren's understanding of God is suspect and should be roundly rejected.

The danger in projecting humanistic social relatedness upon God—as merely a community of persons, while the essential unity of Father-Son-Spirit in nature is ignored—comes to the surface when one realizes religious pluralists use such a view to argue for God's different saving activities among other religious communities. We see such an advocacy when examining the rest of McLaren's gospel scheme, which includes our problem and

---

[855] McLaren, *Jesus, Moses, the Buddha, and Mohammed*, 153.
[856] McLaren, *Jesus, Moses, the Buddha, and Mohammed*, 153.
[857] McLaren, *Jesus, Moses, the Buddha, and Mohammed*, 129.
[858] McLaren, *Jesus, Moses, the Buddha, and Mohammed*, 152.

human identity; the saving solution to our problem; and the one who bore our solution, Jesus.

McLaren's gospel for a multi-faith world begins at the beginning with creation, moving from there to the doctrine of sin. I will not rehash here what I did in chapter 3 regarding our problem, except to say that it is important to realize that McLaren believes that people still exist in their original goodness. While he rightly insists that every person shares the same divine image and are created in the image of God,[859] he wrongly assumes that original good image is still intact and unaffected by original sin. As he argues, "We are trusting that original sin, for all its terrifying power, is not more powerful than the more original goodness God has written into the code of creation and of us."[860] McLaren's belief that God's original goodness is still written into the our code and creation's code reflects the 5th century heresy known as Pelagianism.

Pelagianism is named after Pelagius, a British monk who later moved to Rome and was made famous for his heated exchanges with another famous Christian thinker: Augustine. Pelagius believed that the original spark of divine goodness was still present in humanity, that we are not fundamentally cracked and broken image bearers as Augustine and other early church fathers believed. If we are still by-nature intact image bearers of God, why do we sin? Four reasons: Ignorance; bad examples, which lead to bad habits; and habits that perpetuate into continued patterns and systems of sin. Pelagius believed that people were capable of choosing, on their own, either good

---

[859] McLaren, *Jesus, Moses, the Buddha, and Mohammed*, 103.
[860] McLaren, *Jesus, Moses, the Buddha, and Mohammed*, 159.

actions or bad actions. Accordingly, nature does not compel a person to sin; ignorance, examples, habits, and systemic patterns do. Thus, because the divine image of God is still intact, and merely tainted or off-track, people can choose, on their own, to do acts of goodness that lead to salvation. Not only does Pelagianism mark McLaren's doctrine of creation, it influences his view of sin, too.

Though McLaren believes we need "a fresh understanding of original sin," how he defines it isn't at all fresh; it is recycled Pelagianism. Five concepts mark McLaren's view of sin, which he takes from Catholic theologian James Alison and philosophical theorist Rene Girard: Imitation, rivalry, anxiety, scapegoating, and ritualization. McLaren insists that "all human beings are caught in these subtle webs of destructive imitation, rivalry, anxiety, scapegoating, and ritualization."[861] Inherent to this definition is Pelagius' view of example and habit: "Humans beings are by nature imitative," says McLaren. "You start as my model for imitation" and "I may become the perpetrator of violence against those I envy;" "we imitate one another in violence" which produces patterns and systems of "social disintegration."[862] As I argued in chapter 3, McLaren believes sin isn't natural, but social; it is learned behavior from bad examples, which form bad habits, leading to bad systems and social patterns. As McLaren says, "sin is utterly derivative, utterly imitative...there is no escape from dismal, degrading cycles of mimicry apart from a return to the creative goodness

---

[861] McLaren, *Jesus, Moses, the Buddha, and Mohammed*, 110.
[862] McLaren, *Jesus, Moses, the Buddha, and Mohammed*, 109.

that is even more original than sin."[863] That "return to the creative (original) goodness" was provided by the better example and better pattern of living of Jesus.

Although I dealt extensively with McLaren's view of Jesus' person and work in chapter 4, it bears repeating his view of Jesus here, because of its implications in a multi-faith world. It seems clear that McLaren views Jesus as one religious figure among many, although perhaps a tad more special than the rest. In his introductory chapter, McLaren places Jesus among Moses, the Buddha, and Mohammed as "four of history's greatest religious leaders."[864] He believes that God was revealed to Jesus in the same way God was revealed to Adam, Noah, Abraham, Moses, and Mohammed, going so far as to say God spoke "to humanity through these great men and that each ones teaching and example should be trusted and followed" along with Jesus'.[865] He even thinks it ridiculous to pit Jesus as a rival against other prophets or gods or saviors, suggesting that Jesus himself would not condemn or counter other religious figures.[866] So it seems clear that for McLaren, Jesus is one valid religious figure among many legitimate figures. But who is Jesus and what did he do?

In a remarkable reinterpretation of the Colossian hymn that the historic Christian faith has taken as a pivotal text teaching Jesus' deity and exclusivity, McLaren says that Jesus is "the true image of God," he is "the true embodiment of the fulness of God."[867] As I pointed out earlier, notice that McLaren doesn't

---

[863] McLaren, *Jesus, Moses, the Buddha, and Mohammed*, 112.
[864] McLaren, *Jesus, Moses, the Buddha, and Mohammed*, 2.
[865] McLaren, *Jesus, Moses, the Buddha, and Mohammed*, 90.
[866] McLaren, *Jesus, Moses, the Buddha, and Mohammed*, 136.
[867] McLaren, *Jesus, Moses, the Buddha, and Mohammed*, 136-137.

say Jesus *is* God, rather he is the *image* of God or *resembles* and is *like* God; Jesus embodies and models God in how He lives. McLaren goes on to say that Philippians—another crucial passage of Scripture the historic Christian faith has used to teach Jesus' deity—makes the point that Jesus is "a true image bearer of God," he "reveals the true nature of God." Again, McLaren isn't saying Jesus is God, merely that He *lived* like God; Jesus is the moral Son of God, not the metaphysical Son of God.

In another remarkable turn away from historic Christianity, McLaren counters the traditional meaning of the deity of Christ—"God = Jesus; Jesus = God" [868]—by cleverly reframing Christology to mean "What is true of Christ is true of God" and "God is like Christ." Rather than Jesus being God himself, He is merely a model of God, He merely images God. Thus, the incarnation is transformed from God becoming man to "Jesus embodies the divine creativity that makes impossibilities possible and that makes new possibilities spring forth into actuality." It's as if for McLaren God is merely an idea that Jesus embodies, like Paul Tillich's (a theological liberal) view of God as the symbol of the universal human ideal. Again, rather than the actual Being of God becoming a human being, Jesus is a man who embodies "the deepest meaning" of life. As McLaren argues, "in [Jesus'] story we see the syntax of history, the plot-line of evolution, the deep meaning of the surface events, the unified field of theory that explains all data." Later, he makes this obtuse statement more clear when he says that "the true logic of the universe—the true meaning or syntax or plot-line of history—

---

[868] McLaren, *Jesus, Moses, the Buddha, and Mohammed*, 139.

has been enfleshed in Jesus and dwelt among us..."[869] As I argued in chapter 4, for McLaren Jesus' life embodies the universal human ideal, which is love. That's what makes Him divine, not that He Himself is actually God.

So if this is who McLaren's Jesus is, what did He do? Again, I've outlined much of Jesus' works above in chapters 4 and 5, but it bears some repeating here. Because McLaren's problem hinges on the Pelagian view that the human problem is bad habits formed by bad examples and ignorance, we need a better example to form better habits in order to form better patterns and systems of living. Thus, what Jesus did was to give us a better, truer example and model to live. This work of Christ, then, is something that any person of faith can follow and accept, all the while never leaving their own religious identity.

This is why McLaren could write approvingly of his Muslim friend, who believed that Jesus was a great prophet through whom God was speaking to all humanity, and that Jesus' word and example must be followed and that God would evaluate people against the measure of Jesus' life and teaching.[870] In a multi-faith world, all that matters is Jesus' loving life and example, and His words and teachings that urge humanity to pursue the universal human ideal of love.

Of course for McLaren, this call to pursue love was the crux of Jesus' greatest contribution and life work: His "community organization movement." "What did the movement do?" McLaren asks. They spread their message, looked for "people of peace" and networked them together, they fed the hungry and

---

[869] McLaren, *Jesus, Moses, the Buddha, and Mohammed*, 143.
[870] McLaren, *Jesus, Moses, the Buddha, and Mohammed*, 135.

healed the sick, they offered hope to the depressed and promised freedom, they confronted oppressors and conversed with their critics.[871] In other words, they spread the universal human ideal of love. According to McLaren this was the saving message proclaimed by Jesus and then carried along by His followers. The saving significance of Jesus, then, was "the light of Jesus and his example." And this true light was His attitude of loving descension "into common humanity, down into servanthood, down into suffering, down into death," which in turn revealed the true nature of God.[872] As we saw in chapter 5, this loving example actually *is* our salvation, because Jesus' loving life presents an alternative system to the destructive ones of this world.

More specifically, what is the salvation that's inherent in McLaren's gospel, in the new kind of Christianity tailor-made for a multi-faith world? From both this book and *A New Kind of Christianity*, it seems clear McLaren's good news is the offer of the "life of Christ." And by *life of Christ* I don't meant the born-again life of the historic Christian faith, where the sinner is freed from the wages of sin, delivered from death, and literally re-created a new. I mean the model and example of Christ, the *life* of Christ.

To understand this style of salvation, it's important to understand what McLaren means by the wrath of God. Rather than God's wrath being directed toward sinners, as the Church and Scripture have taught, McLaren believes God's wrath is against "evil things." As McLaren argues, "If we speak of an

---

[871] McLaren, *Jesus, Moses, the Buddha, and Mohammed*, 233.
[872] McLaren, *Jesus, Moses, the Buddha, and Mohammed*, 137.

angry God at all, we will speak of God angry at indifference, angry at apathy, angry at racism and violence, angry at inhumanity, angry at waste, angry at destruction, angry at injustice, angry at hostile religious clannishness."[873] McLaren makes clear God's anger is never against us, it is against "what is against us," which are the dysfunctional systems and stories of chapter 3, and things they produce.[874] In other words, "the greed, pride, fear, craving, and hostility that infect humanity" are the objects of God's wrath, not people who are greedy or prideful. And here is where salvation comes in: "and they are what God loves to save us from."

For McLaren our salvation isn't from a sinful nature, but sinful systems; we don't need salvation from death, but from life, or perhaps the bad things in life that affect us. Thus, he proclaims the salvation of his gospel is exclusive, inclusive, and universal:

> our saving message is indeed exclusive in the sense that it excludes hostility, injustice, apathy, and violence. And it is inclusive in the sense that everyone is welcome to participate, regardless of religious label. And it is universalist in the sense that it will not rest until everyone who wants to can and does experience the abundant life of shalom, humility, kindness, and justice that God desires for all. 875

For McLaren's gospel, this last part is fundamental: He wants to share "the treasures of Christ" universally with everyone, which

---

[873] McLaren, *Jesus, Moses, the Buddha, and Mohammed*, 259-260.
[874] McLaren, *Jesus, Moses, the Buddha, and Mohammed*, 260.
[875] McLaren, *Jesus, Moses, the Buddha, and Mohammed*, 261.

is Jesus' example and model of abundant life. It is in following Christ's example that we are saved, that we are liberated from the dysfunctional systems and stories of this world. Remarkably, he even claims Paul and Silas proclaimed this while in jail in Acts 16.

In this episode of Paul's missionary journeys, Paul and Silas are brought before the Roman authorities for their proselytizing activities and put in jail, where an earthquake later frees these two missionary prisoners. (It should be noted that McLaren interprets this event symbolically, arguing that the story "symbolized the earthshaking radicality of the liberating message Paul's team proclaims...") Afterwards the jailer rushes in to find that his two prisoners didn't run away but stayed put. The jailer is dumbfounded and, according to McLaren, cries out "What must I do to be liberated?" Here is McLaren's interpretive paraphrase: "Paul and Silas said something like this: 'You live in the fear-based system of the Lord Caesar. Stop having confidence in him and his system of domination, hostility, and oppression. Instead, have confidence in the Lord Jesus. If you do, you and all those in your household will experience liberation."[876]

Notice McLaren doesn't say the jailer is living in rebellion to God, but living in response to the system of Caesar. Salvation, then, comes by putting confidence in Jesus' life-system, instead of Caesar's life-system. It isn't that the jailer would experience salvation from the wages of sin, which is death, but rather liberation from a bad life-system. Of course this life-system of Jesus is the Kingdom of God, which "confronts Caesar's empire

---

[876] McLaren, *Jesus, Moses, the Buddha, and Mohammed*, 235.

of fear and death" with "liberation and reconciliation."[877] And what McLaren insists this world needs are "teams of unlikely people," Christian or not, who come together and proclaim "the way of Jesus," which is "the way of liberation;" Jesus' way, example, model of love, humility, and servanthood liberate us—save us—from the dysfunctional, destructive ways and patterns of this world. This way of Jesus is salvation, and proclaiming this way is the heart of McLaren's redefinition of Christian practices and mission.

---

[877] McLaren, *Jesus, Moses, the Buddha, and Mohammed*, 236.

10

Reconstructing Christian Practices

This reformulation of doctrine has an inevitable sister act: the reconstruction of the Church's liturgical practices. Because the core doctrines of the Christian faith can no longer be conceived in ways exclusive to the Church, now the liturgy isn't even the Church's; now it's for the world. Which makes sense because the Church holds zero place in McLaren's religious enterprise. How could it? If the Church is the exclusive membership of those who've placed their faith in Jesus Christ, as the New Testament says it is, then how could such an exclusive group have any mention in such an overtly inclusive enterprise? Likewise, how could the exclusive liturgical practices of the Church remain so in such an inclusive religious reidentification exercise. They can't, beginning with Christmas Day.

Yes, you read that correctly. Now Christmas isn't even the Church's day, but humanity's day: "On Christmas Day, we would celebrate the birth of the man who repudiated the violent path of obsessive taking and blaze a new path of generous self-giving...And the celebration of Christ's birth could become a birthday party, not just for Jesus but *also for the new humanity* that transcends and includes all previous identities."[878] Now Christmas is a celebration of the new humanity, not for Jesus the Messiah.

Not only is the birth of Jesus the Messiah reformulated with a decidedly humanistic bent, other major Church holidays are, too, including Lent, Holy Week, and even Easter. For McLaren, Lent should simply be considered an annual season devoted to the life and teaching of Jesus.[879] For Palm Sunday, McLaren calls on people to join Jesus in "weeping over Jerusalem for its ignorance of the ways of peace,"[880] rather than of their ignorance and rejection of Him as their Messiah. Maundy Thursday is merely a celebration of Jesus' command to love one another.[881] Good Friday isn't the glorious day when the Son of God went to the cross as an atoning sacrifice for human rebellion. Instead, it "becomes the great celebration of God's empathy with all human suffering and pain."[882]

And what of Easter? After defining miracles as something that convey "an unexpected meaning or message," McLaren goes on to say there was a scandalous meaning conveyed in the resurrection of Jesus.[883] What's important isn't that Jesus actually, physically, bodily rose from the dead. What's important

---

[878] McLaren, *Jesus, Moses, the Buddha, and Mohammed*, 171.
[879] McLaren, *Jesus, Moses, the Buddha, and Mohammed*, 172.
[880] McLaren, *Jesus, Moses, the Buddha, and Mohammed*, 173.
[881] McLaren, *Jesus, Moses, the Buddha, and Mohammed*, 173.
[882] McLaren, *Jesus, Moses, the Buddha, and Mohammed*, 173.
[883] McLaren, *Jesus, Moses, the Buddha, and Mohammed*, 174.

is the *meaning of the story* of the risen Christ. Similarly, the meaning of the ascension is far more important than the fact of the ascension.[884] While some might be surprised by this characterization of the most important events in the church, the resurrection and the ascension, it makes sense considering McLaren's liberal roots.

For generations theological liberals have meant something very different than what the Christian faith means by the resurrection. For liberals, Jesus resurrected spiritually or existentially. Spiritually, Jesus lived on in the memory of the disciples. Existentially, Jesus lived on in the example or lives of the disciples. Similarly, for McLaren what's important isn't what happened at the tomb, but what the story of the empty tomb means, particularly for all humanity. Because according to McLaren, Easter means something "more" than "the resurrection of a single corpse—it means the ongoing resurrection of all humanity from violence to peace, from fear to faith, from hostility to love, from a culture of consumption to a culture of stewardship and generosity...and in all these ways and more, from death to life."[885] So the resurrection stands as a symbol for the movement of all of humanity from that which brings death to that which brings life.

As the previous section revealed, this part carries with it an explicit universalism, in that everybody is "in" regardless of their commitment to Jesus Christ as exclusive Lord and Savior. And along with the universalism is an obvious religious pluralism, because the Christian faith and Church of Jesus Christ is not the

---

[884] McLaren, *Jesus, Moses, the Buddha, and Mohammed*, 176.
[885] McLaren, *Jesus, Moses, the Buddha, and Mohammed*, 175.

exclusive vessel through which Christ-centered belief and practice are encountered. That universalism and pluralism is carried to its full logical conclusion in the final chapter where McLaren completely redefines Christian mission by writing the Church out of it.

11

Redefining
Christian Mission

The heart of McLaren's redefinition of Christian mission for a multi-faith world lies in completely writing out the Church in favor of "teams of unlikely people—Christians, Jews, Muslims, Hindus, Buddhists, people from a whole range of indigenous religions, together with agnostics and atheists—coming together, not in the name of the Christian religion, but seeking to walk in the way of Jesus, learning, proclaiming, and demonstrating 'the way of liberation.'"[886] Mission for McLaren has nothing to do with the *Great Commission*, but everything to do with so-called *Great Commandment* of love: Mission is spreading and sowing the universal human ideal of love—which everyone can do, whether they believe in anything at all.

---

[886] McLaren, *Jesus, Moses, the Buddha, and Mohammed*, 236.

The point of mission, then, is making people "a little more Christ-like," which has nothing to do with the Holy Spirit transforming people into Christ, but our shared commitment to love somehow magically influencing our behavior to reflect Jesus' loving example. After listing several people he knows who he thinks model well or fight for the universal human ideal, McLaren goes on to say "What [they] and so many other people are doing is a lot like what Jesus did: bringing together unlikely people to serve and heal together, to liberate the oppressed and their oppressors together, and to model, in their collaboration, the kind of harmony and human-kindness the world desperately needs."[887] Again, for McLaren, mission isn't about the Great Commission, but the Great Commandment.

Now, to be sure, the historic Christian faith has also been about the Great Commandment to love God and neighbor. History is riddled with examples of Christians who love the world because Christ first loved them by giving up His life, even to death on a cross. So, yes, the Christian faith is about doing acts of love, but those acts can never replace or compete with the greatest act of love we could ever give: Making disciples, baptizing them into the Church, and teaching what Jesus commanded. This is the Great Commission that Jesus gave exclusively to the Church, which involves influencing people to give their life and lifestyle to Jesus as the one and only Savior and Lord; initiating people who have been saved from death to life into the Church; and teaching them how to live out the teachings of Christ through the power of the Holy Spirit. This Commission

---

[887] McLaren, *Jesus, Moses, the Buddha, and Mohammed*, 247.

is fundamentally absent from McLaren's gospel, because the Church itself is fundamentally absent.

Stretching back to *A New Kind of Christianity* and even to *Everything Must Change*, one can see the curious absence of the Church in McLaren's religious enterprise. Instead, what's important are "religious communities...organizing for the common good."[888] Remarkably, McLaren seems to believe that any religion can solve our human problem. McLaren doesn't seem to have any issue with people of other faiths cherishing and maintaining their "distinctive religious identity." In fact, he encourages it.[889] So instead of challenging other religions to convert to faith in Jesus, we are called to band together to work toward solving our dysfunctional, destructive systems and stories by working for the common good, the commonwealth or Kingdom of God.

Because every religious identity is valid and each religion has a "unique, particular, and evolving perspective from which to encounter the Spirit in a unique way,"[890] McLaren considers the old language of saving souls is meaningless.[891] Instead, he says our collective "sacred mission of salvation" is saving people, human societies, and this planet from "the dehumanizing effects of hostility to God and other."[892] This collective saving mission calls every individual to make a saving decision: "the choice to live not for our own selfish interests alone, and not for the groupish interests of our clan or caste or civilization alone, but

---

[888] McLaren, *Jesus, Moses, the Buddha, and Mohammed*, 250.
[889] McLaren, *Jesus, Moses, the Buddha, and Mohammed*, 256-257.
[890] McLaren, *Jesus, Moses, the Buddha, and Mohammed*, 152.
[891] McLaren, *Jesus, Moses, the Buddha, and Mohammed*, 258.
[892] McLaren, *Jesus, Moses, the Buddha, and Mohammed*, 258.

for the common God, the good of all creation."[893] Since our problem is a bad way of living and our solution is the ideal way of living born by an ideal liver (Jesus), our collective human mission is to get people to live better in relationship with themselves, the Other, and the planet. And the way we do this is to issue what McLaren calls an *alter call.*

Not an *altar* call—which long-time Christians will recognize as a come-forward call to confess Jesus as Lord and Savior—but an *alter* call, a call to "consider turning around and choosing a new path," an alternate path of understanding and living. McLaren invites people to confess these things: Where they stand; who they are becoming; where they are going; how they believe; and why they believe.[894] Of course, there isn't anything particular about this confession. And frankly, it is rather humanistic, in that the confession isn't rooted in God, but in the one confessing and even in humanity, in our collective power to change the world through love.

Rather than calling people to believe on the name of Jesus Christ, as the Gospels reiterate countless times, Brian seems to transform Christian missions into a humanistic call to loving action. Which makes sense because what is minimally necessary for so-called "salvation" in Brian's gospel isn't faith in Jesus, but rather faith in the universal human ideal, the idea of love, the common good. By neglecting the Church, the gospel of Jesus isn't at all unique to the Christian faith and is radically transformed from salvation from sin and death through Jesus' life, death, and resurrection. Instead, it is merely a way that

---

[893] McLaren, *Jesus, Moses, the Buddha, and Mohammed*, 258.
[894] McLaren, *Jesus, Moses, the Buddha, and Mohammed*, 263.

liberates people from bad living, a liberation that's accessible to every person regardless of their creedal beliefs. In the end, the mission of Brian's gospel is transformed from calling people to have faith in Jesus Christ into a belief in humanity. As with every aspect of Brian's gospel, humanity is squarely at the center.

12

Conclusion

There's a fun song that's often sung in Sunday School, called "Father Abraham." Perhaps you've sung this song yourself. It goes like this:

> Father Abraham had many sons.
> Many sons had father Abraham.
> And I am one of them.
> And so are you.
> So let's all serve the Lord.
> Right arm, left arm, right foot, left foot...

The song is repeated several times, looking sillier and sillier as people move their right arm, left arm, right foot, and left foot all around. I think by the end even peoples' tongues are sticking out, which adds to the silliness as one tries to sing the words of the song! The song, of course, speaks of the reality that the Church is made of a diverse group of people who are called to serve the Lord together, as right feet and left feet, right hand and left hand, and yes even tongues. Paul reminds us that those who are in Christ, whether Jew or Gentile, are sons of Abraham who make up the Body of Christ, called to serve the world as Jesus' hands and feet.

In more theologically liberal circles, though, I've heard this song sung a different way. They sing it like so:

Father Abraham had many sons.
Many sons had father Abraham.
And I am one of them.
And so are you.
So let's just get along.
Right arm, left arm, right foot, left foot...

Did you catch the changed phrase? Rather than serving the Lord together as *one Church*, we are beckoned to "just get along" as *one humanity*. For them, every person on the planet is a son (or daughter) of father Abraham, which means we're all also sons and daughters of the *God* of Abraham—so let's just get along. This thinking reflects what J. Gresham Machen calls "the universal fatherhood of God and the universal brotherhood of man."[895] These "doctrines," as Machen called them, form the foundation to theological liberalism. They insist what McLaren insists in this newest book: that "God" is the God of everybody universally, regardless of how He is approached, worshipped, and named; that people are one in some universal religious community, regardless of their sinful condition and regardless of their beliefs or practices.

Machen makes it clear, however, that "The modern doctrine of the universal fatherhood of God is not to be found in the

---

[895] J. Gresham Machen, *Christianity and Liberalism* (Grand Rapids: Eerdmans Publishing, 1923), 18.

teaching of Jesus."[896] Furthermore, "the really distinctive New Testament teaching about the fatherhood of God concerns only those who have been brought into the household of faith."[897] In other words, while the New Testament describes God as Father, and His children relate to Him as such, those who are His children in the first place are only those who have come to the Father through Jesus Christ.[898]

Not Moses. Not the Buddha. Not Mohammed.

Jesus Christ is the only one true God through whom we are rescued and re-created. And it's unfortunate that McLaren seems to have given up on this basic, foundational belief of the Christian faith. You cannot be a "follower of God in the way of Jesus"[899] without insisting that Jesus is God Himself, and consequently that every other so-called "god" and "lord"— Buddha, Mohammed, Krishna, and all others—are not.

This was the apostle Paul's very own confession in a letter to the Church of Corinth:

> So then, about eating food sacrificed to idols: We know that "An idol is nothing at all in the world" and that "There is no God but one." For even if there are so-called gods, whether in heaven or on earth (as indeed there are many "gods" and many "lords"), yet for us there is but one God, the Father, from whom all things came and for whom we live; and there is but one Lord, Jesus Christ, through whom all things came and through whom we live. 900

---

[896] Machen, *Christianity and Liberalism*, 60.
[897] Machen, *Christianity and Liberalism*, 60.
[898] John 14:6.
[899] McLaren, *Jesus, Moses, the Buddha, and Mohammed*, 11.
[900] 1 Corinthians 8:4-6.

Paul makes it clear that at least for Christians, there is one God, the Father; one Lord, Jesus Christ. Here Paul is quoting a portion of the cornerstone to the Jewish faith, the *Shema*—Hear, O Israel, the Lord, the Lord is one[901]—and redefining it to refer to Jesus Christ. In other words, the one God who created all things is Jesus Christ. Those "so-called gods" and "so-called lords" are neither of the two. They are fake. Jesus and Jesus alone is the only real God and Lord.

This would have been as radical in Paul's day as it is in ours to suggest there is no God or Lord but Jesus Christ. In Paul's day you couldn't travel anywhere in the Roman empire without being confronted by the multi-faith and multi-god nature of the world. Every city had its own god. Every part of creation itself—from the seas to war to agriculture—had its own god. Yet, at every turn in Paul's ministry he insists that Jesus and Jesus alone is the only one true God.

So why wouldn't we do the same in our day? Is ours really all that different than Paul's?

One day while Paul was on one of his missionary journeys, he stopped in Athens to wait for Silas and Timothy to join him. As he impatiently wandered the streets "he was greatly distressed to see that the city was full of idols." A Roman nobleman, Pliny the Elder, estimated the Greek city of Rhodes had 73,000 statues of multiple gods and insisted that Athens had no fewer. So it's understandable why Paul was so distraught and distressed!

And how did he respond? Did he claim that "something good still shines from the heart" of those religious shrines and

---

[901] Deuteronomy 6:4.

artifacts, as McLaren would insist?[902] While Paul did commend the Athenians for their religiosity, he also called them "ignorant"—twice![903] And he insisted that, while God in the past had overlooked such ignorant religious living and worship, now He was calling people to repent from their idolatry, "For he has set a day when he will judge the world with justice by the man he has appointed. He has given proof of this to everyone by raising him from the dead."[904] Of course "the man" is Jesus. It is by Jesus that people from every false religion on the planet will be judged, whether in Him or not in Him. And Paul called on them to believe in Jesus.

I wish that McLaren would make the same call to his friends from other religions. For we know from Scripture that rescue from sin and death is found in no one else but Jesus Christ— "there is no other name under heaven given to mankind by which we must be saved."[905]

Not Moses'. Not the Buddha's. And not Mohammed's.

---

[902] McLaren, *Jesus, Moses, the Buddha, and Mohammed*, 20.
[903] Acts 17:23, 30.
[904] Acts 17:31.
[905] Acts 4:12.

Afterword

If I have learned anything over the years in my academic pursuits it's this: theology matters. Getting the "pieces" of theology right, as much as we can in our finiteness, matters because when we get one of those pieces "wrong," the rest fall in lockstep.

How one defines our human problem has great bearing on how one defines our human solution. How one defines our human solution has great bearing on how one defines the One who bore that solution. This book has demonstrated as much in its overview of the generational development of Protestant liberal theology. When you define our human problem environmentally, then our solution must do something with our environment; when you define our human problem as having to do with bad examples, then our solution must provide a better example; when you define our human problem as narratively driven, then our solution must provide a better narrative to live and lean into.

Perhaps more significantly, our definition of the One who bore our solution, Jesus of Nazareth, is reduced to a prophet-like character who came simply to provide us a better example and better story to live; He came to change our environment in order to change us. So what's important about Jesus becomes His life and way of living. This means He doesn't have to be God and doesn't have to actually be alive.

If I have learned anything in the last few years, it's that theology matters, and when you get the pieces of theology wrong you ultimately get the gospel wrong. Of late, my generation is all a flutter with reimagining the Christian faith—reimagining the pieces of the Christian faith. I understand this pull toward reimagining the Christian faith, because I have been there myself. But what I have learned as I have journeyed into, through, and beyond the Emergent Church and gospel of Brian McLaren is that what my generation needs is not to reimagine the Christian faith, but rediscover it. We need to rediscover what and how the Church of Jesus Christ has always believed about our problem, solution, and the One who bore that solution. We need to rediscover the gospel.

To be frank, that rediscovery effort is not going to come through the Emergent Church generally and Brian McLaren specifically. It is clear their reimagination enterprise is simply one iteration in a long line of Protestant liberal leavers— Emergents have left the historic Christian faith in the same way liberals have every generation since Schleiermacher, yet in a way that's palatable for our postmodern, post-Christian day. Which, for this post-Emergent who had high hopes of a genuine third way that cuts through the malaise of contemporary liberal-conservative theological discourse, is sad indeed.

This book on McLaren's gospel is deeply personal. It's personal because I myself was involved with and hoodwinked by the Emergent Church. And it's personal because I myself still long for a third way. I realize this term is over used, yet as I survey our current evangelical landscape that is split between progressive Emergent evangelicals on the one side and traditional Young Calvinist evangelicals on the other, I'm left wanting. I—and my gut tells me plenty more people—want an alternative that cuts through the current evangelical malaise and recaptures the gospel in all of its grandeur and majesty and revolutionary character—a gospel that includes the Kingdom in all of its already-not-yet glory in order to provide new life right now and is still exclusively tied to the only one true God, Jesus Christ.

Now more than ever the Church is in need of passionate ambassadors of Christ who take seriously their calling as ministers of reconciliation, in the fullest sense of that Kingdom calling. Yet, I hope that a new generation of Christians will rediscover what the Church has always believed regarding God's magical, revolutionary Story of Rescue in order to bring the type of right-now transformation for which our world longs— without reimagining the Kingdom for, and consequently the gospel, along the way. What the Church—and even the world— does not need now is a new kind of Christianity for our multi-faith world. What the Church needs is the old, old gospel Story of Jesus and His radical, furious love.

WHAT'S NEXT?

Thank you for reading my work. I sincerely hope that it encouraged and informed your spiritual journey and faith in Jesus Christ!

If you found this book helpful and have a moment to spare I would really appreciate a short review by following this link: http://bouma.us/uet. Your help in spreading the word is gratefully received.

I would also love to hear from you if you have feedback. You can contact me directly at http://bouma.us/hello or tweet me @bouma.

Finally, if you'd like to receive curated content on faith, life, and everything in between delivered straight to your in box, or if you'd like to stay up on my latest work join my newsletter at http://bouma.us/list.

grace.peace

Jeremy

www.jeremybouma.com

www.facebook.com/bouma

www.twitter.com/bouma

9780985470302